WINNING
AT ALL COSTS

Paul Gogarty and Ian Williamson

WINNING
AT ALL COSTS
SPORTING GODS
AND THEIR DEMONS

JR
BOOKS

For Susanna and Emilia

First published in Great Britain in 2009 by
JR Books, 10 Greenland Street, London NW1 0ND
www.jrbooks.com

A catalogue record for this book is available from the British Library.

ISBN 978-1-906779-18-4

10 9 8 7 6 5 4 3 2 1

Printed in Great Britain by Clays Ltd, St Ives plc

Contents

*'The heart has its reasons that reason
knows nothing of.'*

Blaise Pascal

ACKNOWLEDGEMENTS

First and foremost, huge thanks to Susanna Abse for all her insights, criticisms and ideas throughout the project – we owe a huge debt of gratitude. Thanks, too, to Emilia Duarte Williamson for her objective reading and support as the project unfolded; fledgling sports journos Rahul Ambasna and Paul Goatman provided valuable research; and Olympic gold medallist Jonathan Edwards and psychoanalyst Andrew Balfour both gave up their time and wisdom in interviews. Thanks to our agent Laura Susijn, our publisher Jeremy Robson, editor Lesley Wilson, publicist Catherine Bailey and Jon Davies at JR Books. Thanks to *Observer* sports editor Kevin Mitchell for chewing over the fat over a couple of pints and to Nigel Richardson, Dannie Abse and Guido Casale who read chapters and offered constructive criticism. Our biggest thanks, of course, must go to the sporting legends who continue to hold us in awe and who inspired this book.

ABOUT THE AUTHORS

Paul Gogarty is a journalist, television presenter and award-winning author of *The Water Road* and *The Coast Road*. His personal sporting past is typical of an Everyman – a reasonable footballer, squash player, hurdler and swimmer, lacking the necessary psychological profile to rise above his ordinariness.

Ian Williamson is a practising Harley Street child and adolescent analyst. For 15 years, he played rugby for and captained Blackheath and was on the fringes of the England national team. He is also a former Cambridge Blue and general sporting all-rounder and obsessive.

For 30 years, the pair have been close friends, participating in, watching, talking and arguing sports. The book is a result of those ongoing discussions.

Note: Ian Williamson is a practising child analyst. In order to protect the confidentiality of the children he sees, those cases referred to in the book are not factual accounts of specific cases but are composites of a variety of different individuals and their experiences. The intention is to offer an insight into the issues and dilemmas that relate to the topics raised in this book.

INTRODUCTION

O ne lazy lunchtime beside the Thames, the two of us were engaged in a typical pub discussion concerning a disclosure by Steve Redgrave that he'd trained 4 times a day, 49 weeks a year throughout his career. We reasoned that to become the greatest all-time Olympian, pocketing gold medals at five different Olympic Games, Steve must have minimally served the equivalent of 20 years' hard labour. The mental arithmetic – 20 x 4 x 7 x 49 – required to discover the total number of sessions took us just about as long as one of Redgrave's training sets but we finally got there: 27,440!

We next moved on to discussing whether, forced to choose, we'd prefer to endure Redgrave's life sentence, or spend three or four years in jail. What swung the decision was the insight fellow Olympian Matthew Pinsent provided on those training sessions in which he admitted to regularly reaching the point of being physically sick before pushing himself further. All this for five Olympic finals lasting no more than seven minutes each? No contest we decided – we'd take the jail sentence.

Without the nine gold medals they share, Redgrave and

Pinsent's punishing regime might well be considered pathologically masochistic. Instead, they're lionised and recruited as role models for health campaigns.

For the pantheon of sporting greats in this book, there would seem to be no areas of grey between success and failure. Being first is the altar on which they're willing to sacrifice anything and anyone because victory is psychologically a matter of life and death.

Seeking psychological triggers in our iconic line-up of sporting superstars, we discovered that for Redgrave and his ilk, 40 days and 40 nights in the desert of the training camp was not the real starting line on the journey to greatness. Instead, the psychological dawn of their single-minded obsessions appeared to lie considerably further back in childhood experience. The more we read, the more we became convinced that it was the motivational imperative to outrun the ghosts of the past that lifted them above their peers and propelled them to singular success.

In researching the book, we uncovered states of mind that were as dramatic and extraordinary as the athletes' achievements themselves. As Lance Armstrong comments in his autobiography, *It's Not About the Bike*, 'Athletes don't have much use for poking around in their childhoods, because introspection doesn't get you anywhere in a race ... But that said, it's all stoked down in there, fuel for the fire.'[1]

Like the Romanian orphan banging his head against a cot to silence his emotional nightmare with recurring physical pain, there would seem to be a similar suppression going on in our sporting giants. Instead of using the hard end of a bed to manage otherwise unmanageable feelings, however, the athletes set themselves punitive training schedules and persecutory goals. The defence against deep emotional suffering often denies both the need for others and indeed others' needs. The magnitude of the achievement, however, effectively compensates for the enormous cost to family, friends and to the sports stars themselves.

Greatness needs ruthlessness, blinkers and a single track to run down in the stadium of the mind. Inside that athlete, however, there's often a Doubting Thomas, racked by anxiety, who is only momentarily silenced by success before demanding fresh, ever-greater victories. Invincibility, like immortality in the sporting arena, is, of course, a fantasy, for each champion one day must lose, each match end, and each hero one day retire.

It is when the hero returns to the earth's atmosphere that the Doubting Thomas really goes to work and wreaks his revenge. Tom House, an American former Major League baseball player and pitching coach, claims 'recent statistics indicate that the rate of divorce and separation among newly retired athletes is close to 80 per cent'.[2] He also found almost 50 per cent of marriages involving baseball stars end within the first 18 months of retirement. It would seem that sporting success can only temporarily lock up the ghosts from childhood and, when that sporting endeavour comes to an end then the phantoms really get to flex their own muscles.

Sporting literature of a psychological persuasion tends to favour a cognitive, developmental approach, focussing on the role played in refining and fine-tuning the conscious mind in the pursuit of success. Such books tend to reduce all achievement to a matter of willpower and grit. What we are examining in this book, however, are the defensive mechanisms that provided that extra grit and may have had even more influence on success than the simple cognitive mantra 'who works hardest wins'. While hard work and repetitive practice may be at the heart of exceptional success – whether in virtuoso musical accomplishment or sport – the really interesting question remains: what drives the really exceptional athlete to practise harder and longer than others?

It's difficult to imagine that our heroes were once small children who cried, missed their mothers and wet their beds just like the rest of us. In *Winning At All Costs*, we look at how the childhood dramas of these athletes may have provided the psychological electricity that powered their victories and, in some cases, eventually destroyed them. We also attempt to illuminate the psychological processes that transformed that electricity into unimaginable endurance or transcendent moments of sporting heroism and magic.

Even evangelical psychoanalytic sceptics would probably concede that there is an unconscious that influences our thoughts, feelings and actions. Over the past 100 years, since Sigmund Freud disturbed the sleep of the world for ever, psychoanalysis has irrefutably shown that we do repress that which we find painful and intolerable and we create elaborate defensive systems specifically designed to aid that repression. The truth is that the way we live our lives as adults is largely shaped by our experiences in childhood.

At no point in this book do we claim our interpretations as truths, for only the athletes themselves can know this. Adam Phillips in his illuminating book, *Side Effects*, refers to the work of psychoanalysis as attending to 'what falls out of his [the patient's] pockets once he starts speaking'.[3] Adams notes that often the real meaning and feeling of who we are is found in what is revealed accidentally aside from the matter in hand – the 'Freudian slip' being the most obvious example of this.

Why did Zinedine Zidane, on a balmy night that was to be both the pinnacle of his career as well as his swan song, suddenly implode, head-butting an opponent in the final of the 2006 World Cup? Why did Michael Schumacher, already established as the greatest motor racing champion of all time, get himself involved in a controversial crash towards the end of the qualifying circuits for the 2006 Monaco Grand Prix?

In this book, we try to build a picture from what falls out of these great athletes' pockets. The contents can often be disconcerting because the unconscious (the desires of childhood) is fundamentally made up of thoughts and feelings that are hidden to both others and ourselves. Most of us are aware of perverse repetitive behaviour at work in our lives that returns us again and again into damaging places or relationships. If the picture we paint fleshes out more of our athletes than before, we will have provided an illumination that behavioural and cognitive approaches can never get close to. What we are seeking, in essence, is the psychological core of our sporting giants' being.

Just as we attempt to steer towards truth rather than fact, similarly our views should not be construed as morally judge-mental or critical. The dentist is not attacking the patient when drilling out decay. Like everyone else, we are fans, and stand in awe of the achievements of our sporting colossi.

In the theatre of the athlete's body, all the dramas are enacted in a physical sense – damaged metatarsals, coping with exhaustion, getting the body to peak at the right time. These are dramas, however, that contain coded messages. The real question for the England rugby stand-off Jonny Wilkinson is: why so many injuries? The question for endurance athlete Dean Karnazes is: why, having successfully completed 50 marathons in 50 states in 50 days, does he head off immediately on a seemingly meaningless 1,300-mile run? For the troubled former footballer, Paul Gascoigne: why so many pranks that lead to disaster?

We also focus on the parallel mental landscape where the past informs the present and the future. The story of the athletic contest is also the story of the battle within the athlete himself, a battle that has its genesis in the dramas of childhood. Golfer Sergio Garcia once said he would rather never win a major tournament than spend several years of unhappiness pursuing a crown. This is probably the reason, up until now, he's never won one.

The Achilles heel can be responsible for both greatness and profound psychological suffering in sporting greats. The layman, sceptical of 'psychobabble', may think his heroes to be simply endowed with exceptional genetic gifts, strolling like Clint Eastwood through a Sergio Leone movie. But athletes know better than anyone that winning is all in the mind. What many don't realise, however, is that winning often has as much to do with suffering, vulnerability and the defence against these feelings as it does toughness and mental resolve. The clock is ticking. It is time to join some of the world's greatest sportsmen and women on their respective roads to hell and high water.

1

THE ACHILLES HEEL

The flawed football genius and the crisis of faith

'Show me a hero and I will write you a tragedy.'

F. Scott Fitzgerald

The first half of the 1986 World Cup quarter-final had been a tight, dour affair with the Argentinian defence easily containing England's primitive long-ball game. Five minutes into the second half, the diminutive Diego Maradona rose to challenge the English 'keeper Peter Shilton. Following the inevitable clash of bodies, inexplicably the ball appeared in the net. We all blinked and rubbed our eyes.

The second of two iconic Maradona images engraved on the consciousness of even those who loathe the people's ballet occurred four minutes later. Again, we stared in disbelief as the same number 10, having slalomed his way through the English defence, scored a goal of such breathtaking audacity that we knew we had either just witnessed a second mugging or a second coming.

One of the founders of psychoanalysis, Carl Gustav Jung,

claimed that the crucial moment of Christian faith for believers takes place when the priest turns his back on the congregation symbolically to transform simple bread and water into the flesh and blood of Christ. That is what it felt like that day. If those goals really did happen, then it had to be down to sleight of hand, mass hypnosis or we'd just witnessed a god coming down to earth. History – in the form of constant replays – taught us that Maradona had, in fact, scored one goal with the Hand of God and another with the fleet feet of a god. The two goals came to symbolise the man: footballing genius and street pickpocket; Madonna and whore.

Maradona neatly sidestepped accusations that he had blatantly handled the ball for the first goal by claiming he was merely God's conduit. Such an explanation might be considered simply being economical with the truth – the kind of comment a manager passes on an executioner's tackle that he simply never saw – but in Maradona's case it may have had deeper significance, reflecting a messianic delusion that he was indeed God's football representative on earth and, as such, was accountable to no earthly being. To suggest he cheated was tantamount to accusing God of cheating. Perhaps he was in his own mind (and in many others') already an immortal.

Fast forward 18 years of self-abuse to April 2004. A grotesquely overweight Maradona is admitted to an intensive care unit in the private Swiss clinic in Buenos Aires Hospital having collapsed with arterial hypertension. The immortal, like Achilles, clearly had a very human weak spot. True, he had the feet of a god but the heel was that of a mere mortal and it had brought him down – just like Achilles – from behind. News filtered through of his critical condition and, when rumours were fanned that he might need a heart transplant, the hospital switchboard was inundated with offers of donations. Maradona survived, as he has a knack of doing. Argentina had never been in doubt. His deification was already assured in a country ruled by a Roman Catholic hagiology of saints-from-sinners that comfortably encompasses everyone from Saint Paul to Eva Peron.

The notion of a football genius with a predisposition for serial self-destruction and resurrection is a seductive psychological proposition. Once every generation, a player with extraordinary skill, pace, strength, balance and vision explodes into the football consciousness and attains folkloric status. Such one-offs have an aura about them, an otherness that uniquely excites and enthrals on the pitch and pulls at our heart strings off it with the pathos of the drama they act out. Such gods play on the edge, able to see and do things that others can only imagine but their genius is often undermined by a frail psyche beneath which one senses demons playing their own games. The fragile interplay makes compelling, if occasionally macabre, viewing. Such is the energy and intensity, we instinctively feel it cannot be sustained too long and that there can only be one winner.

The traditional football view is that the Maradonas, Garrinchas, Bests and Gascoignes of the world possess some inherent genetic flaw that – despite their God-given footballing gifts – inevitably leads them to self-destruct. This basically Darwinian explanation is about as complex as football psychology gets. In an age where many businesses and organisations use psychometric testing and depth psychology as a matter of course, football remains locked in the Dark Ages jealously watched over by superstitious priest-managers.

The romantic view is certainly seductive – that these complex and beguiling personalities are merely victims of their genetic make-up. In reality, there are more complex processes at work and the psychological trigger to the wreckage strewn across their private lives may well be the very thing that also enables them to achieve greatness in their chosen sport. The Achilles heel may be the human weak spot, but it's also the name of the incredibly strong tendon that connects the calf muscles to the heel bone.

Although very different in many ways, Gascoigne, Best and Garrincha follow the same blueprint in coming from poverty and having close, complex relationships with their mothers, and fathers who are somewhat peripheral figures.

Garrincha was the Brazilian genius of the 1950s of whom Pelé wrote, 'Without Garrincha I would never have been a three-time world champion.'[1] The 'Little Bird', as Garrincha was known, was a freak of nature on and off the pitch. His legs were so deformed that it looked as if he could barely walk; and his astonishing capacity for both drink and sex (he fathered at least 14 children) led him to an early death at 49. Ray Castro's hopelessly romantic biography of Garrincha describes his childhood as time spent in 'Shangri-la'. The reality was far from it. Garrincha's father was a philandering alcoholic and it was left to his doting mother to raise her nine children single-handedly. She died when he was in his early teens and the 'Little Bird' effectively became a feral child.

In George Best's case, very little has been written about his early life and its impact. In his autobiography, *Blessed*, he refutes any notion that his mother's alcoholism and subsequent early death were in any way connected with his fame, fortune and problems. What is clear is that she was the rock of the family, providing the love as well as the discipline. His father worked long shifts at a shipyard and seems a rather peripheral figure. What is interesting is Best's choice of opening chapter, 'The "Other Woman"'. He is, of course, referring to alcohol. Implicit in this is the notion that alcohol became a maternal substitute, one he could have complete control over and to whom he was ever faithful.

Paul Gascoigne's father had seizures, migraines that could last 14 days and fits that rendered him unable to speak. On one occasion, he was hospitalised for eight months following a brain haemorrhage. At other times 'he wouldn't know who he was or the names of his children.'[2] When Paul witnessed a seizure alone with him, he confesses, 'I was afraid he would die in front of me and it would be my fault for not rescuing him.'[3]

The greatest of them all in our opinion, Diego Maradona, was born in October 1960 in Avellaneda, a poverty-stricken shanty town in the suburbs of Buenos Aires that he shared with hired assassins, petty thieves and pimps. His desperately poor parents – a mix of indigenous Indian and poor Italian immigrants – lived in a hut built by his father, Chitoro, out of scrap metal, loose bricks and cardboard.

Every tabloid agony aunt knows that poverty leaves more than the memory of an empty stomach, and has a profound impact on family dynamics. Maradona's subsequent trials and tribulations are rooted in the psycho-dynamics of poverty. While his father worked all day in a bone-crushing factory, Maradona's care was left to his mother, grandmother and sisters. In his autobiography, Maradona tellingly describes how his father simply smacked him as he didn't have time for talk. Such strategies are a commonplace recourse when the father is dissatisfied, poor and harried.

As the only male child, Maradona was fêted and indulged by the women who looked after him and he seems never to have really moved on from this early model of family life. Wherever his football travels took him – Barcelona, Napoli, Seville – he recreated a circle of hangers-on and devotees united in their unquestioning acceptance of his iconic status and who imposed no boundaries upon him. He, in return, unconsciously allowed them to exploit him.

Outside his protective coterie, however, there were endless fights with managers, coaches and club presidents – with any authority figure, in fact, who attempted to curb his impulses and behaviour. It would appear that he never really found and accepted a resilient father figure until Fidel Castro – 'father' to the Cuban people – took him under his wing, providing the medical care and sanctuary Maradona desperately needed to survive.

The romance implicit in this classic football background – namely the poor boy honing his skills day and night in the streets of Avellaneda or Toxteth – glosses over the absence of the most basic requirements of childcare – education, structure, guidance and boundaries. Any analysis of such football geniuses has traditionally begun and ended with the notion of innate ability, sharpened by poverty and transformed into obsession by a lack of any formal education that could provide an alternative escape route.

Certainly there may be some contributory truth in the romantic view, although it is only part of the picture and certainly doesn't explain why Garrincha, Best, Maradona and Gascoigne possess a unique footballing vision, nor why such talents have a tendency to self-immolate.

A starting point in trying to understand their extraordinary capacity to see things that others can't is by thinking about the relationship between mental and physical space. The psychoanalyst and paediatrician Donald Winnicott coined the phrase 'good enough' parenting to describe the minimum quality of parenting needed to create emotionally healthy children. In order for the infant to grow into a child who can make sense of the world and feel safe in it, the parents have to be available and emotionally engaged so that fragments of experience – what Wilfred Bion called 'Beta Elements' – can be transformed into mental contents with meaning, which he termed 'Alpha Elements'. What both Winnicott and Bion confirmed was the common-sense view that, with loving parental guidance, the child will internalise a relatively ordered and benign view of a safe and predictable world, one that will provide his or her psychological map for life.

Conversely, if the process goes wrong because the parent is unavailable either emotionally or physically, the child may be left with fragments of experience; thoughts and feelings that, without someone to make sense of them, spiral into overwhelming anxieties. The mental map in this instance becomes chaotic, unregulated and dangerous.

What elevates this band of iconic footballers above their journeymen team-mates is to be found in the very different psychological map they're using on the playing field. Lacking proper parental boundaries and a feeling of psychological safety, Maradona, Best and Gascoigne survive by becoming psychologically hyper-vigilant in a world that is felt to be internally threatening. They learn to be fleet of foot and fleet of mind. Because of the anxiety created in the face of both the real world of their childhoods and their subsequent inner fears, they compensate by over-developing physical skills in much the same way that a blind person might sharpen and heighten a sense of hearing. Through endless, repetitive practice, they learn to control and tame a seemingly uncontrollable ball as well as the space round them and this provides the illusion of mastering the bigger ball – the world itself. The threatening emotions they feel trapped by are thus transcended and their weakness is transformed into their strength.

At the age of six – while his parents were alleged to have been regularly fighting at home prior to their estrangement – Paul Gascoigne confesses to having been overwhelmed at the prospect of dying one night on his way back from playing football in the park. The game was over and now his demons were back taunting him. What this 'death' or obliteration was all about, one can only hazard a guess, but more likely than not a fear of not being contained, separation worries and an anxiety about his own destructive aggression produced a frightening psychological cocktail of worries that were experienced as death-like and which could only be alleviated by the warmth and security of his parents. Terrified, he screamed and cried his way home but, having crawled into his mum and dad's bed, tellingly, he could not vocalise (process) his fears.

We shall return to the marital bed later, but let us for the present stick to the map that allowed our heroes to express themselves so bewitchingly on the field and provided them with a containment akin to parental boundaries. Football, with its simple rules and physical boundary, became a kind of containing parent for Gascoigne and for Maradona. Here they found clarity between off- and on-side, they also found a clear role in the extended family of the team and, with their massively over-developed compensatory physical skills, also discovered they could express themselves ('talk') like nowhere else. Because their internalised emotional map is hard-wired to see danger every-where, their hyper-vigilance allowed them to see things coming before others could and their sublime skill allowed them to find ways of overcoming those threats. Other lesser mortals were tied to the limit of what was possible; our heroes, meanwhile, saw no limit to what they imagined.

Whilst the playing field, with its simple rules, provides a parental container, the crowd, too, provides vocal parental approval and support and, in this symbolic parenting environ-ment, the football genius feels free to weave his magic. The chaos and lawlessness of the inner world are momentarily transformed as sublime skill and kinaesthetic intuition come together to produce transcendent moments of bewildering beauty. For a period of time, such footballing gods can triumph over their demons in the most dramatic way. For Paul – like Garrincha, Best, Maradona, Eric Cantona, Ronaldinho and Cristiano Ronaldo – the game is a series of endless possibilities rather than problems. Off the field, however, the chaos of the internal world saw to it that he regularly dropped off the edge.

In a Channel 4 fly-on-the-wall documentary, *Surviving Gazza*, broadcast on 5 January 2009, Gascoigne admitted he wasn't eating properly because he felt fat. Along with his food disorder, he confessed to mood swings, anxiety and getting bored with life. When the interviewer asked what he did with these feelings, he paused before replying "Sit here and get pissed."

Unfortunately for Gazza and Maradona, every game and career had an ending. Like other wayward geniuses, once the latest match was over, they once again felt abandoned and uncontained. From Gazza's autobiography with Hunter Davies, it would seem that he was in as much psychological distress as an adult as he was as a child, and this is a sad indictment of the primitive levels of care offered in professional football.

Gazza talks of being constantly overwhelmed in life. A telling example occurred during his Tottenham days under Terry Venables. As the clock ticked down to kick off, Venables remembers Gascoigne being in a particularly agitated state, obsessively preoccupied with a plumber who should have repaired a leak in his bathroom that morning. Venables knew Gazza would be useless to him in the game unless the matter was dealt with, allowing him to re-focus. Venables phoned the plumber, got him to the house Gazza was sharing with his fiancée and then passed the receiver to Gazza for reassurance that the problem was resolved. The feelings that were flooding Paul vanished. Using the plumbing analogy, the blockage was cleared. Gazza went out and played a blinder. Venables' intervention alleviated Gazza's internal distress and, as always, what follows was a temporary euphoric state, a kind of orgasmic release. Gazza's relief resulted in him playing 'out of his skin'.

In his brutally honest autobiography with Hunter Davies, it would appear that Gazza finds it difficult to deal effectively with his feelings and that they overwhelm him. He confesses to Davies that throughout his very first flight in 1986, he had to hold the hand of the England Under-21 doctor as he was convinced the plane would crash and he would die. He also admits that, in his early life, he staved off panic attacks with food binges and, as a podgy rooky pro at Newcastle, later became bulimic without even knowing what it was.

Compulsive, manic and addictive behaviour may be just part of the package. Conquests (sexual or otherwise), drugs and alcohol provide the rocket fuel for manic excitement that gives a temporary and illusory sense of triumph and respite until the fuel runs out and depression, anxiety and phobias return. The triumph may be illusory and fleeting but it is nevertheless a relief and addictive. Yet another rocket ride to the sun is sought as a means of regaining the heady sense of being on top again and suppresses feelings of inadequacy and despair. The process may be as doomed as believing a football match can last for ever but nevertheless the cycle is repeated with ever-increasing manic intensity and desperation.

What is it about those seminal family dynamics that proves so urgently creative on the one hand and yet so destructive on the other? In an ideal scenario, the father's active presence leads the child out of the dependent and mutually gratifying world of the mother/child Garden of Eden to a more complex social world of sharing and conflict. It is the father generally who provides the structure and authority, both internal and external, and acts as a moral and behavioural compass for the child. An overly close relationship with the mother, allied to an absent or weak father can leave the child trapped in a maternal complex.

Psychoanalysis shows us that when the Oedipal Complex (those childhood desires and fantasies to usurp the father) remains unresolved there is a persistent and sometimes addictive need for instant gratification allied to persistent destructive battles with authority. The father's (or authority's) attempts to 'break in' are unconsciously seen as threats to the mother–son idyll (this will be discussed later in more detail in chapter 6).

The absence of an internal authority creates difficulties in maintaining the discipline needed for a mature life. 'Outlaws' like Gazza, Maradona, Garrincha and Best invariably seem to have fragile, volatile temperaments capable of switching from states of consummate self-belief to raging omnipotence in seconds. Because of this, the flawed genius walks a fine line both off and on the field.

The lack of boundaries and a coherent emotional map, allied to the adoration of the fans who replace the adoring mother, have led certain gifted footballers into uncharted territory and sublime genius, but it has also steered them off the edge of the world when they leave the stadium of shared dreams.

Gascoigne is known as much for the pathos of his life and his 'pranks' as he is for mesmerising defenders. His sense of loyalty, humour, kindness, generosity and fun endeared him to fans and everyone who met him. Indeed, his playing the fool off the field –

Bobby Robson, the England manager, memorably called him 'daft as a brush' – only seems to have further heightened his achievements on it. Robson's affectionate description, however, is a gross simplification of Gazza's difficulties as his life became a catalogue of dangerous self-inflicted accidents covering up desperate pleas for help.

His miscellany of 'pranks' is legendary and include tricking his best friend Jimmy 'Five Bellies' into eating a mince pie whose filling he had replaced with excrement; burping loudly when a comment was requested during an Italian television interview; and offering 'Fuck off, Norway' live on national Norwegian television when asked if he had a message for the host country prior to a World Cup qualifier.

Humour and tragedy are opposite ends of the same spectrum as the lives of many comedians show. Freud had a great deal to say about jokes and their relation to the unconscious. They are, as Adam Phillips describes in his book *Side Effects*, 'The black market of pleasure.'[4] Put simply, we are able, by use of a joke, to say and express feelings and thoughts that are forbidden or unacceptable to both ourselves and others. They circumvent that which is forbidden and disarm possible criticism and censorship. As Phillips says (quoting Freud), jokes are, in fact, bribes that soften cruelty by adding the coda 'It's only a joke' or 'I'm only joking'. The reality, however, is that we are, in fact, indulging deeply held transgressive desires and attitudes. Rather like Sacha Baron Cohen, the Jewish comedian, making jokes about killing Jews through his alter ego from Kazakhstan, Borat.

Gazza's prankish jokes bribe us into laughing at the often cruel behaviour that masks his own unbearable feelings of inadequacy, humiliation and guilt. Stripped of the veneer of humour, Gazza's 'pranks' reveal a great deal about the difficulties he was grappling with and his damaging state of mind. The 'pranks' were there as far back as Gazza remembers, as were the litany of self-inflicted accidents that resulted when the pranks regularly went wrong. Hunter Davies records that, as soon as he was old enough to drive, Gazza 'borrowed' his girlfriend's dad's car without permission and ran someone down in the street (he fled the scene and tried to get his friend, Jimmy, to take the blame when the police arrived at his house). And when Gazza requisitioned the Middlesbrough team bus after seeing the keys in the ignition, his outing ended up costing him £14,000. This latter crash followed hot on the heels of Gazza driving a Middlesbrough courtesy car through a hedge.

Gazza's unfolding story is that of a person who burns up each time he re-enters the earth's atmosphere. From a very early age, he conceals his loneliness and unhappiness in a series of high-energy, dangerous 'pranks' for, like Maradona, Gazza loved excitement. The adrenalin-fuelled rushes are the junkie's fix, creating an illusory sense of wellbeing and drowning out the pain of life without a game.

Gazza admits to stealing regularly as a young boy. But the buzz he says it brought was probably really just the excitement of having momentarily triumphed over his feelings of deprivation. In one act of theft, he was no longer the deprived but the depriver. Later, this thirst for excitement off the pitch transformed itself into booze binges that led to even more erratic behaviour. Like all artificial adrenalin highs, alcohol provides only temporary respite and eventually can nosedive into alcoholism and/or drug addiction. Instead of providing a buzz, it becomes a sedative, indispensable for calming nerves and dampening anxieties. George Best described alcohol as the one woman he could rely on. Gazza, lacking care in so many other parts of his life, basically became self-medicating by regulating his inevitable 'down' after the match.

Gazza refers to his prodigious catalogue of injuries as simply the result of 'the daredevil in me'. This is a telling phrase because it literally implies 'daring the devil'. Gazza's so-called 'accidents' were barely-disguised attempts to overcome the anxieties about death and destruction that plagued his life. By surviving these self-inflicted, dangerous accidents he was able to create an illusion of having triumphed over them. His first hospital visit and introduction to stitches was at the age of three when he was hit on the head with a brick. By seven, he'd already had 56 stitches in his legs. Diagnosed hyperactive and unable to concentrate at school, he saw a psychiatrist for the first time at the age of 10 but – with his father's blessing – never returned. That same year he took his friend's brother to a sweet shop where he often stole. While Gazza was busy in the shop, his young friend ran out into the street and was run over and killed. Gazza blamed himself and could not sleep at night (he has remained an insomniac all his life).

Intriguingly, Gazza confides to Davies that he only failed his CSE Maths because his desk collapsed and he spent the rest of the session trying to reassemble it. The fact that the reason it collapsed was that he was nervously playing with the screws in the first place is largely overlooked. It is perhaps the most revealing metaphor of all for Gazza's unconscious attacks on himself. Throughout his life, Gazza has been unscrewing his desk.

At the age of six he was thrown out of school and claims to have had his first morbid premonition of death (at a time when his parents were constantly fighting at home). Twelve months later, his nervous preoccupation with death resulted in a number of nervous twitches. Perhaps the twitches – like the phobias he admits to and the inordinate number of sweets he ate – felt like they were all that separated him from chaos and disaster. Perhaps his ritualistic behaviour and tics were all that protected him from 'death'.

Gazza's private life may have been a walking disaster but on the pitch he was elevated to a heavenly plain that mere 'water-carriers' (Eric Cantona's memorable phrase for lesser footballing mortals) could never approach. As Gazza himself said, 'I didn't have twitches or worry about death when I was playing football.'[5] Football was at the core of his being, the one place where the vagaries of his emotional life could be transcended, the one place self-doubt left him.

The one thing Paul hated, he confessed in his wonderful collaboration with Hunter Davies, was being on his own as solitude always seemed to make his problems worse. Sometimes, Venables would provide the company, sometimes the team doctor, but more often than not it was Jimmy 'Five Bellies' Gardner, his closest and most enduring friend. Gardner, like the wife Gazza never managed to keep, travelled with him on all his transfers – to London, Italy and even to China. Jimmy was Gazza's unquestioning, devoted family, no less than the excessive entourage and hangers-on that Maradona surrounded himself with.

Gazza tellingly confessed in an interview following yet another hospitalisation in January 2005 that he liked hospitals. He said he liked 'being cared for'. Current psychological advances in attachment theory are particularly pertinent here. The fear of being alone stems from what is known as an 'insecure attachment'. People can be divided into those who are reasonably securely attached and those insecurely attached. Those belonging to the latter category can be further sub-divided into what are known as 'precoccupied insecure' or 'dismissive insecure'. The latter are the types characterised as having a 'stiff upper lip' and defend themselves against need by steering clear of relationships. Gazza falls into the second 'preoccupied' category, constantly clinging to people in a manner that makes his relationships an emotional roller-coaster of lows and highs, hate and love. Such characters tend to be scared of being alone and perhaps this explains why Gazza would rather be hospitalised than in a room alone. Whatever we think of Jimmy 'Five Bellies' Gardner, and whatever his own motivation, he has been the one constant throughout Gazza's career.

The latest research in Attachment Theory by Professor Peter Fonagy at University College London has confirmed that early experiences in relation to our primary carers are what largely decides our predominant adult attachment patterns. What more controversially is also being suggested after studying children's brain scans, however, is that these early experiences also fundamentally effect our neuro-biological psychology. Just as poverty starves physical development, it is now being suggested that emotional starvation also affects the brain's functioning.

Gazza's penchant for hospitals is also echoed in his preference for hotels over private homes. In a hotel, you never have to be alone. At the semi-final defeat to Germany in the Italia World Cup, when Gazza's tears were beamed across the world, perhaps he was agonising not only because England had lost but also because his ultimate dream of round-the-clock company would be terminated again. The hotel would be left and depression would inevitably follow.

The counterpoint to the tears – and perhaps the second most enduring image of Gascoigne's own career – was the frenzy into which he merged when he took to the pitch for the 1991 FA Cup Final against Nottingham Forest. The portents were not good when a horrendous tackle caught Forest's Gary Parker in the chest. Worse was to follow as Gascoigne made an even more horrific challenge on Gary Charles which resulted in the rupture of his own cruciate ligaments. He missed the cup final, the injury took 16 months to heal, and some pundits believe Gascoigne was never the same force again. When the ticking stops and the bomb goes off, the result may be a six-match ban and/or a career-threatening injury for the victim or the perpetrator.

Destructiveness and chaos often seem inextricably bound up with instinctual genius. The balletic, anarchic displays of Garrincha, Gascoigne, Best and Maradona are windows of beauty on an internal maelstrom from which they have no defence. Those who live instinctually have a tendency to spiral out of control when they lose their balance. Football appears to be the one place where energy and aggression can be garnered for a purpose; where others can be legitimately attacked, where a beautiful and creative path can be carved through any defence.

But the internal world of Gascoigne and Maradona is not the whole story. There is another more subtle, insidious and potentially dangerous process at work between the fan and these players. The relationship starts benignly enough with the realisation that we are watching a football genius emerge. For a while, we are in awe of the magic. But soon the wonderment becomes incorporated into our own hopes and dreams. That which we are watching becomes ours: Maradona, Best, Gascoigne and Wayne Rooney embody our own desires for success and recognition, and provide us with bragging rights over rival supporters.

Unfortunately, it is often not enough simply to bear witness. Hero hunger is insatiable. Fans want more. What starts as transfixed awe through time transmutes into a demand, an expectation, a right even. Macabre though it sounds, at the heart of this relationship is a destructive greed, a kind of psychological cannibalism, with fans frenziedly feeding on the banquets the stars serve up. For Gazza and Maradona, the intoxicating adulation and celebrity status needs constant feeding. The daily demand for miracles on the scale of Jesus' loaves and fishes creates an unsustainable pressure that blurs the boundaries between fantasy and reality. This is the world that Maradona, Gascoigne, Best and now Ronaldo and Rooney inhabit and the more they deliver the goods, the more fantastical become both the demands and their own reality.

Ian Williamson's casebook: Jack

Jack was 16 when his parents, 'at the end of their tether', referred their once amiable but indulged son for treatment to me when he morphed into a tyrannical and confrontational adolescent. No rule for Jack was deemed too petty to challenge. At school, the talented musician had become a nightmare, constantly arguing with teachers. At home, he was a law unto himself: rude and abusive to his mother, contemptuous of his father and unwilling to abide by any of the boundaries that his parents attempted to set.

When the boy stole the father's car following a row over a mobile phone, the parents decided it was time to seek help. The police finally caught up with Jack – following a chase in which he refused to pull over – when he lost control of the car outside Exeter and crashed on to a roundabout. A furious row developed with the arresting officers, Jack insisting that it was their fault that he had crashed and that he would have been fine if they hadn't chased him. He was duly handcuffed and charged.

Jack's mother doted on him. His father, although essentially loving, was a rather distant figure who travelled a great deal for work. At his first session, Jack was adamant there wasn't a problem. 'The legal age for driving is ridiculous,' he claimed, 'I've known how to drive for years.' Later in his therapy, however, he divulged the fact that throughout his younger years he had slept in his mother's bed whenever his father was away. The mother was complicit in the secret, welcoming his company at night to stave off loneliness. This all stopped when Jack was 13. And that's when the trouble started. Although it was not possible to clarify exactly why his mother stopped the night-time liaisons, it's likely that the onset of Jack's sexual life aroused uncomfortable incestuous feelings and she banned him from the bed. For Jack, this banishment was experienced internally as a rejection and ushered in a 'bloody' battle with authority both real and symbolic, for the right to possess his mother.

The therapy was a turbulent experience dominated by Jack's abusive and contemptuous outbursts towards anyone who ventured an alternative viewpoint. Curiously, in the light of the rages that exploded in the consulting room, he never missed a session. Some part of him seemed to know that he was locked in a dangerous place full of destructive, incestuous desires, a place that might, if left unchecked, ruin his life. He seemed almost relieved to have found someone who might evict him once and for all from his mother's bed. It took a long time for things to calm down both in and out of the therapy and it coincided with him finding a girlfriend to whom he became devoted.

The frustration of working with adolescents is that the work often ends before it is completed. A holiday, a few missed sessions can lead to treatment breaking down. When Jack found that our meetings sometimes interfered with his now burgeoning social life, I knew the end was near. An hour before I was due to see him one day, I received an SMS message from him: 'Kant cum 2 busy. Will cal 4 appt. Thx.' And that was how it ended. I didn't hear from Jack or his parents again so I assume he kept out of trouble. But the real challenges for Jack lie later in life.

If we are going to have a three-dimensional understanding of the flawed footballing genius, we need to start by redefining how we see such heroes and how we think about what they do. To reduce the complexity of their lives to 'Well, they're on £130,000 a week – where's the pressure there? Try working in a mine for a week', does not get us far. To the fan, a sportsman's personality is largely an amalgam of form, fantasy and folklore. This distorted creation of fact and fantasy remains hermetically sealed off from the real issues and struggles in the hero's life: children; marriage; injury; death; divorce. At best, the real life issues occupy a place in the footnotes of their personal football history.

These players become conduits through which our vicarious football dreams and fantasies can be lived. The passionate affair, of course, eventually wanes as age and excess take its toll and we then rage at the dying of the light by growing increasingly weary at their unpredictability and excesses. We watch bemused as they slip ever further into the abyss. Such characters on the football stage only have one aspect: they are the living embodiment of the maxim, 'I am what I do'.

In many other walks of life, this distorted psychological truth continues undisturbed by the march of time, but in sport, psychological death comes quickly and brutally leaving an unimaginable emptiness. When I am not doing what I do, then who am I? This issue of identity lies at the very heart of any analysis of the football genius. Needless to say, the lethal combination of myth, fantasy and reality can have a dangerously destabilising effect on the personality. Understandably, such gods, revered for their daily miracles, often develop a distorted psychological sense of entitlement which sees society's boundaries only applicable to mere humans.

Maradona's story is the epitome of the flawed football genius – a Shakespearean tragedy that follows every triumph with hubris. Eric Cantona claimed that in the course of time, it will be said that Maradona was to football what Rimbaud was to poetry and Mozart was to music. (Cantona came pretty close himself, excelling equally at football, kung-fu and poetic whimsy.)

His impossible heroics on the pitch for Boca Juniors, Argentina and Napoli are well documented. Three decades after he led Argentina to World Cup glory, he is still prayed to in Buenos Aires churches – indeed, there's even a Church of Maradona. When he was banned from the 1994 World Cup after failing a drugs test, several hundred people in Bangladesh attempted a mass suicide. It is easy to see how messianic delusion can be fanned by such adoration.

But grandiose and delusional beliefs exact a heavy price on the psyche and Maradona paid in full. Flip over a messianic delusion and you'll find doubt, insecurity and often self-loathing. Maradona has talked about the unsettling impact of falling literally into a ditch of human shit as a young boy. He never lost the smell in his nostrils, he never forgot what he rose up out of.

And perhaps too a small corner of him never escaped the feeling of being 'shit'.

His greatness, like Gazza's, was regularly derailed by injury, chaotic self-destructive behaviour and huge mood swings – what Maradona calls in his autobiography, *El Diego*, 'a daily toboggan into hell'.[6] Despite the chaos of his private life, his claim to greatness lay not only with his consummate skill and his capacity to deliver the goods under the most intense pressure but also in making an adoring public mythologise him.

Behind the sensational headlines of wonder goals, drugs, drink and women lies a complex story of a desperate and painful struggle to separate the myth and madness that assailed him from inside and out. There is some evidence that Maradona was aware of the dilemma he faced – he complained repeatedly of feeling trapped by the expectations of family, friends, team-mates and, ultimately, himself. But he never really grasped how these expectations would blur the boundary between myth and reality and the impact that such distortions and delusions would have on his personality. Sport being sport, no one was inclined to tell him. While he was producing the goods and turning the turnstiles, he remained iconic and untouchable. Everything else, however disturbing, was deemed manageable.

Maradona's parents were the first to realise their financial future – the family's escape from poverty – lay with their son's God-given football skills. Jimmy Burns' illuminating biography – *Hand of God, the Life of Diego Maradona* – has become a footballing classic, uncovering many of the mysteries surrounding Maradona's fall from grace and resurrection in Napoli. Burns records that, by the age of eight, Maradona's identity was already becoming subsumed and distorted by the dreams and wishes of others as he was regularly fed a cocktail of dubious drugs and vitamins to build his physique. It was a process that would culminate in his shouldering the hopes of a nation in the 1986 World Cup.

By the age of 15, when he signed his first professional contract, he received the keys to an apartment big enough for the whole family. From this moment on, his destiny was sealed. The favoured son had moved up the food chain to head the family but crucially lacked the experience and maturity needed for the job. Inside, he was still a small boy, anxious for his mother's attention and approval. Lacking education, he believed he had been singled out, chosen from the bottom of the ditch to be God's footballing ambassador.

Emotional indulgence was the payback for being everybody's meal ticket from an early age. The adulation was a double-edged sword, however, and meant he was never able to build up any sense of a real self away from football and was singularly ill-equipped to deal with the 'nothing' off the football field. There was no fall-back position. There was no Maradona the man, only Maradona the footballer. Jorge Valdano, a team-mate in the 1986 World Cup-winning Argentinian side wrote, 'Poor Diego, for so many years we have told him repeatedly, you're a God, you're a star, you're our salvation . . . that we forgot to tell him the most important thing: you're a man.'[7]

By adulthood, the distortions, confusions and deprivations of childhood – allied to the mythical status accorded him as a footballer – meant that Maradona's identity was always likely to exist on a knife edge. While the pressure built up around him off the field, further problems began to emerge on it – his undoubted ability to perform was being compromised by his susceptibility to injury. Burns, in his biography of Maradona, suggests that this may have been a consequence of the way in which his body's development was accelerated when he was a child. And once injured, he became rudderless as his purpose dissolved.

Maradona was still only 21 when he flew into Barcelona to sign one of the biggest transfer deals in football history. Burns suggests that it should have been a match made in heaven: arguably the best player in the world joining one of its greatest clubs. The reality turned out to be very different for his time at Barcelona was a disaster professionally and psychologically. Although there were flashes of genius, illness and injury meant he was never able to sustain the kind of form needed to weave his particular magic over the fans.

Maradona's failure was perhaps all too predictable. Barcelona was not only a huge football club but also a corporation, with a structure and organisation that made Maradona's other clubs – Argentinos Juniors and Boca Juniors – seem like Sunday afternoon park sides. Although he was a god in Argentina, psychologically he was fragile and behaviourally a law unto himself. Allied to his need for unconditional adoration, Maradona demanded that he be allowed to do whatever he wanted, whenever he wanted. It was a foregone conclusion that in a club that already had a tough authoritarian coach, Utto Ladek, an autocratic president, Jose Nunez, and two superstars – the German Bernd Schuster and the Danish international, Allan Simonsen – he was doomed to fail. There was nothing in Maradona's history, either professional or personal, to suggest that he could settle and thrive in such an environment. He needed a team built around him and an organisation that catered for his every whim.

Burns describes how a month into the season Maradona pulled out of the team, complaining of a pulled muscle. He refused to allow himself to be treated by the club doctors and insisted on flying in Dr Oliva from Milan as his personal physician. On the recommendation of his girlfriend, Claudia, he also hired Fernando Signorini as his personal trainer. They both shared a common view that Maradona was special and, as such, needed special treatment. As long as they continued to hold that view, they would continue to enjoy his patronage. This was the unwritten rule for entry to what would become 'Clan Maradona' – a veritable army of friends, employees and hangers-on, united in their deification of Maradona.

The Clan was Maradona's attempt to replicate the kind of family dynamics he had enjoyed in Argentina as a young child, where he was both favoured son and king. In reality, the Clan was a psychological hall of mirrors, a narcissistic enclave where all he would see was his own reflection. But it also served another dangerous purpose – the creation of a rival fiefdom with him as head of state.

Freud made a clear distinction between what he called Primary Narcissism – a healthy love of oneself that developmentally precedes love of another – and Secondary Narcissism which is a state whereby the whole world and everything in it is understood only in relation to the self. In other words, events and 'things-in-the-world' are only seen and thought of as relevant to a 'me' state of mind. This, of course, makes it impossible to see others' needs or the world with any degree of objectivity. A sense of disconnectedness and messianic delusion are often part of this package. It was this secondary narcissistic state that would appear to have made life so difficult for Maradona.

Scarcely a month later, Burns recounts that Maradona was involved in a revealing confrontation with the club hierarchy following a rejection of his request to be rested against the French champions, Paris Saint-Germain. Barcelona won comfortably and, that evening, Maradona persuaded half the team to celebrate the victory by spending the whole night in Parisian nightclubs. When news filtered through to president Nunez, he was incandescent. Maradona, meanwhile, was equally outraged that his right to do whatever he wanted was questioned. The row was never likely to be resolved for the only authority to which Maradona deemed himself accountable was God.

The two men – stags locking horns in a struggle for dominance – refused to back down. There is a fine line between authoritative behaviour and omnipotence. The former is healthy, implying strength and substance, while the latter is delusional, and involves posturing and little substance. In challenging Maradona's messianic delusion, Nunez removed the carapace of bravado, revealing the 'nothing' that was behind it. With the posturing gone, there just remained the small boy shivering, still covered in shit.

Back in Barcelona, there were more rumours of all-night parties with pornographic videos, prostitutes and drugs – all manifestations of the omnipotent behaviour of someone out of control. One is reminded of soul singer Marvin Gaye's similarly disturbed psychic state on tour when backstage he reputedly kept a preacher in one room and his coke dealer in another. Like Maradona, Marvin Gaye said he only found peace performing in front of an audience.

On the field, given centre stage and the adulation of the crowd, Maradona's life was given meaning and sanctified, but his football skills were the only tools he possessed for silencing both his own demons and his critics. His first six months at Barcelona were nothing short of a disaster; he managed only six goals, was involved in several disputes with the management and contracted viral hepatitis which necessitated 12 weeks' rest. Deprived of doing what defined him as a person, he seemed to spiral into depression. When he did return, respite was brief: he was hacked down by the Bilbao defender, Goikoetxea (subsequently infamously nicknamed the 'Butcher of Bilbao'). It was potentially a career-ending tackle, and bad enough for Goikoetxea to be banned for 10 matches. The injury to Maradona's ankle tendons was so severe that he was unable to play for three months. By the end of the season, following his return to the team, there was no league title or European Cup to celebrate. This was unacceptable for a club of Barcelona's stature and Maradona, for his part, had hardly covered himself in glory during the campaign.

When Terry Venables took over as manager, he immediately realised the scale of the problem. 'Like most people, I'd heard the rumours about his big entourage. But until I got to Barcelona and made my own enquiries, I didn't realise the hopelessness of the position. There were hundreds of bills all over town all signed in the name of Maradona. Most, of course, had been signed not by him but by his family, friends and assorted hangers-on. He'd been practically bled dry and the only solution was for him to secure the kind of money that a transfer would bring.'[8]

Venables knew the only way out for Maradona and the club was a big-money transfer.

Maradona duly signed for Napoli, an unsuccessful and unfashionable club that had never won an Italian championship. On the surface, this seemed an unlikely setting for one of the world's great footballers to display his skills. But the move proved an inspired decision from a football point of view. His arrival in the city was greeted with near hysteria by the football-mad Neapolitans. Seventy thousand crowded into the stadium to welcome Maradona and, over the next two seasons, they all bore witness to his resurrection.

During his time at Napoli, despite chaos and mayhem in his private life, Maradona played his most sublime football. Napoli won their first two league championships and Argentina the 1986 World Cup. The wonder, and also the paradox, of the Napoli experience is that the chaos of his personal life was also reaching a climax. If the Barcelona experience could be thought of as a frontal assault on his narcissistic/messianic states of mind, the Napoli experience was the exact opposite: the psychological equivalent of letting the patient run the asylum.

The love affair with Maradona extended beyond the football club and embraced the whole city. The Maradona Clan, frowned upon in Barcelona, now took centre stage and Maradona himself moved around Naples like a Roman Emperor, unchallenged by authority or media, surrounded only by people willing to satisfy his every whim.

Myth and reality coalesced, his omnipotence and grandiosity fuelled at every turn. His relationship with his long-time girl-friend Claudia deteriorated, made more difficult by Maradona's controlling mother Tota. He sacked his long-time business manager and childhood friend Jorge Cyterszpiler as his behaviour became increasingly more unstable.

About this time he became romantically involved with a 20-year old Neapolitan called Cristiana Sinagra. Burns writes that it seemed that the relationship had the potential to transform his life; Maradona changed his lifestyle, stopped going out and devoted his free time to Cristiana. He genuinely seemed to have found love and talked about the possibility of marriage. Cristiana even received the blessing of the Madonna herself, Tota. This, however, all changed when it became apparent that Cristiana was pregnant. Maradona, under the influence of his family and friends, effectively ended the relationship. Even Maradona's mother was said to be encouraging her son to turn away from the relationship.

The fallout from this affair damaged Maradona's relationship with the fans in a city where family ties provide the social fabric. Although it was clear that Maradona was the father, he stead-fastly refused to publicly acknowledge that 'Diegito' was his. An acrimonious five-year legal battle ensued before Maradona was required to accept his responsibility. Interestingly, his autobiog-raphy makes no mention of it nor of his son but the fall-out from the affair damaged Maradona's relationship with the fans.

This affair goes right to the heart of Maradona's psyche, for becoming a father would destabilise and threaten his status of favourite male child and threaten the narcissistic base of his personality. His own son would become his rival. To protect his position, it would seem Maradona simply pushed the imposter out of the nest. After initially giving her blessing to the relation-ship with Cristiana, Maradona's mother changed her mind when she heard that Cristiana was pregnant. If an Oedipus Complex had not existed pre Maradona, then we might now be talking about a Madonna-Maradona Complex.

Despite his off-field problems, Maradona emerged from the 1986 World Cup in Mexico as indisputably the world's best player, scoring the goal of all goals against England as well as the goal-that-was-not. Both goals in their different ways rejected boundaries, limits or jurisdiction. Following the World Cup victory, he returned to Italy to perform more miracles leading lowly Napoli to their first championship in 100 years. The euphoria surrounding Maradona's elevation to sit at the right hand of God (Pelé was now relegated to the left side) following his successes at the World Cup and Napoli was again short-lived for the football fan can only momentarily be satiated. As the public demanded more miracles daily, Maradona's demons were also gorging.

The break-up of his relationship with Cristiana Sinagra, allied to the chaos of his life, took a heavy toll on Diego's psyche as he reputedly became overwhelmed with depressive anxieties. It is interesting to reflect on whether he had any inkling that the end was in sight or whether that indispensable quality for sporting success – denial – obscured what was evident to others. His relationship with Napoli predictably deteriorated following repeated squabbles with the management. He frequently missed training sessions as a result of his night life and his always fragile body was increasingly and irreversibly breaking down.

The rest of Maradona's career was mired in controversy and scandal, punctuated by brief glimpses of his former genius. He won another league title with Napoli but the 1990 World Cup in Italy ended with the greatest footballer on earth being ignominiously jeered and whistled from the field. The rest is a sorry catalogue of failed drugs tests, bans, rants and paranoid conspiracy theories culminating in the ultimate humiliation of failing a drugs test at the 1994 World Cup in America.

For many fans, Maradona's moments of greatness provided some of the most climactic moments in their own lives. The miracle that happened on the field was the transubstantiation not of bread and wine but instead anxiety and neuroses into something exquisitely beautiful.

Understanding why Maradona, Gascoigne, Best and Garrincha were who they were is only of real worth if we can learn from it. Does the cost of transcendental football have to be self-destructive personal lives? Are the two inextricably linked as we have suggested? If they are, then who wouldn't sign the contract to sell their soul to the devil as blues legend Robert Johnson reputedly did down at the crossroads when he made a pact to burn in hell in return for guitar mastery?

The answer to this question depends on whose perspective we

are viewing it from and how much we understand the predica-
ment each faced. The bottom line is that, despite their fortune
and celebrity, such footballing gods are ruthlessly exploited and
their emotional difficulties often ignored. In a *Daily Mail* feature,
psychiatrist Dr Raj Persaud asked the obvious question about
Gazza, one that so long had been ignored: 'Some people cry
through pain but I don't think that's the case. I think Gascoigne
was crying because he was in despair with himself. Many of his
problems and his injuries have been self-induced. Gascoigne has
cried regularly for years. That tells you something: that nobody
in football has done anything about it. If a snooker player or
golfer cried during a game, I think people in sport may realise
there was a problem. Gascoigne could have been helped a long
time ago.'[9]

The problem of what to do about these flawed geniuses is
compounded both by their temperament and the instinctual and
two-dimensional nature of what they do. While they are capable
of creating beautiful, magical moments, these are 'happenings',
not classic works of art. Their creations are magical moments of
transformation. They are instinctual and impulsive. On the
football field, it may work, but off it, the qualities that produce
such works need careful management and containment.

Tony Adams' Sporting Chance clinic is a start in helping
sportsmen with some of the symptoms of their narcissism –
alcoholism, gambling and drug addiction. But as the clinic itself
admits, there is no real substitute for education. Certain managers
have a reputation for being good handlers of precocious talent
and fragile temperaments because they provide strong discipline.
However, their own livelihood depends on producing winning
teams, not developing balanced individuals. If strong discipline
amounts to no more than a dose of the legendary hair drier
treatment from old-school football managers, what happens away
from the field when no hair drier is handy? The only real
discipline and control is internal. When Freud was first
developing fledgling psychoanalysis, it was referred to as 'the

talking cure'. It's a good name for what is required. However, by the time the next flawed genius explodes on to the scene, Robert Johnson's deal with the Devil may well already have been struck.

Of the present crop of candidates, Wayne Rooney is currently believed to hold pole position. When we watch him performing miracles, do we imagine him having a brilliant career, winning trophies – and, who knows, maybe even a World Cup – and then retiring gracefully in his mid-30s to take up a place as a pundit on *Match of the Day*? Unlikely. The touchpaper seems to have already been lit and we are standing back both fearing, and perhaps secretly hoping, we have another Gascoigne, Best or Maradona about to flash like a comet through our atmosphere. Rooney is indisputably a colossal talent but is capable of Jekyll and Hyde transformations.

The metaphor that most often appears in the sports columns alongside adjectives such as 'majestic', 'balletic' and 'sublime' is 'ticking time bomb'. At the June 2006 German World Cup, it was a frustrated Rooney who casually back-heeled into Carvalho's groin, auguring his dismissal and England's exit once more. Two months later, before the 2006/07 season had even got under way in earnest, Rooney had already been sent off in another 'friendly' and claims had been made (but later dropped) that he had hit someone in a nightclub. The response of his manager, Sir Alex Ferguson, was to send him for anger management – the psychological equivalent of putting a plaster on a severed artery.

In the longer term, would it not be better to address the deeper question: what is he angry about? Where has he 'gone' in these 'moments of madness'? From his behaviour on the field, it would appear that there are three things Rooney, like our other flawed geniuses, cannot bear. The first concerns 'losing', for loss is a taboo emotional experience. Embracing it opens the internal door to all the unprocessed losses and humiliations of childhood. The second concerns injustice, which he experiences as a brake being applied to his creative acts (or acting out) on the field but, in reality, is a psychological battle for the supremacy of the narcissistic mindset. And the third is an intolerance of incompetence either in himself or others. The fact that Ferguson has followed the traditional line and argued that 'the boy's edge' (unprocessed rage) is what makes him the player he is, sounds worryingly familiar.

Rooney was easily the best England player on show in the World Cup qualifier against the Ukraine in March 2009. For one footballing pundit, Teddy Sheringham, however, Rooney's reckless two-footed studs-up challenge on the Ukrainian player Aliyev brought to mind Paul Gascoigne's near career-ending lunge at Gary Charles in the 1991 FA Cup Final. Sheringham cautioned that unless Rooney managed to control himself, his career may well end prematurely with serious injury.

In our view, an even more likely candidate for burn out in the star-struck firmament is Cristiano Ronaldo. By finally making his £80 million dream move to Real Madrid, Cristiano finally severed ties to his surrogate father Alex Ferguson. His own father, by all accounts, followed the seemingly ineffectual blueprint of Maradona, Garrincha, Gascoigne and Best – an alcoholic, he was dead by the age of 52. When the news of the transfer broke, Cristiano was playing the playboy in LA and Las Vegas with his coterie of friends. Will his stay in Madrid follow the Barcelona Maradona pattern of hangers on and partying? We believe that Cristiano – who had to sacrifice adolescence by moving to Portugal at 11 to prepare for stardom – will find the distractions just as compelling. Since Alex Ferguson took him under his tutelage, the familial boundaries of the team were clear but now that he has broken the shackles, we believe the chance of a downward rather than upward trajectory is hugely increased. His much publicised petulance and strutting, the fact he has generously brought the family into his business (his sister now runs his clothing chain), and the fact that he may see the team as bit players to the Ronaldo show, would all suggest his marriage to Real Madrid will be eventful – and not necessarily for the right reasons. Hopefully someone like Sir Alex will be there to puncture the sycophancy and prevent him from buying into his own myth.

And what now of Gazza, Maradona and Best? In January 2005, Gascoigne was hospitalised with pneumonia and, in 2007, underwent emergency surgery for a perforated stomach ulcer when taken ill celebrating his 40th birthday. In 2006, he was appointed manager of Conference North club Kettering but only lasted six matches, Kettering chairman Imraan Ladak claiming that he was 'under the influence of alcohol before, during and after several first-team games and training sessions'.[10] In 2007, Gazza split with his agent Jane Morgan Management and was reputedly trying to make a career as an actor under the pseudonym G8.

On 20 February 2008, the police were called to the Hilton in Gateshead because of worrying behaviour following trouble at the Malmaison hotel earlier. Paul Gascoigne was detained under the Mental Health Act. In lurid detail, the *Sun* announced on its front page: 'Coke-crazed ace Paul Gascoigne stunned hotel staff before being sent to a psychiatric unit by answering his door in the buff – with "MAD" scrawled on his forehead.' The *Daily Mail* was meanwhile claiming Gascoigne had grabbed a night porter by the throat while carrying a steak knife. Paul was released in early March.

In April that year, Mike Tyson publicly offered Gazza counselling. On 5 May, the BBC announced he was back in hospital following another incident at a hotel, this time in West London after earlier being seen staggering across four lanes of traffic in Kensington. On 10 May, the *Daily Mirror* announced, a little wearily on page 19, that Paul had been admitted to the Priory clinic in Roehampton after an apparent suicide attempt. In the clinic, Paul was said to be refusing to eat and chain-smoking 60 cigarettes a day. This was, the *Mirror* claimed, the seventh time Gazza had 'sought help after being treated at a mental health unit this year for a £2,500-a-day drink and drugs habit.' His step-daughter Bianca, 21, was reported to have said that his family are 'powerless to help him'.[11] By August, there had been a reunion with his former wife Sheryl and even talk of a second marriage before Gazza went

AWOL once more with his old pal Jimmy 'Five Bellies'. In the Channel 4 documentary mentioned earlier, screened in January 2009, Sheryl announced she was finally calling time and wouldn't allow Paul back in her life.

Maradona, meanwhile, had been transformed from the bloated, grotesque caricature of his former self, supported by two minders and restored courtesy of father Castro's doctors in 2005. Lazarus-like, Diego had risen again and gone from heavyweight-in-every-way cocaine addict with a failing heart to the slimline star (thanks to stapling his stomach) of the most popular South American chat show. In March 2007, it was time for the roller-coaster to plummet again as he returned to a Buenos Aires hospital to be treated for hepatitis and alcohol abuse. He was released on 11 April and readmitted two days later. After transferring to a psychiatric clinic specialising in alcohol-related problems, he was discharged on 7 May. Eleven months later, while Gazza was being sectioned, tennis star Potito Starace was threatening to 'bash a racket in Maradona's teeth'[12] after being subjected to a torrent of Maradona abuse during his match with Argentinian David Nalbandian at the Buenos Aires Open. The Maradona roller-coaster climbed again when he was appointed in 2008 manager of the Argentina national team. It remains to be seen how this fragile soul manages his life in the pressure cooker of international football management and one can't help feeling that it will end in tears.

And Best? On 25 November 2005, George Best died in a west London hospital aged 59. Republic of Ireland and Leeds mid-fielder Johnny Giles described Best as 'the most naturally gifted player I have ever seen. He had the lot – balance, pace, two good feet, he was brave, strong and a good header of the ball.' It wasn't enough. Bravely, Bobby Charlton reflected, 'We at Manchester United have learned from our experience with Eric Cantona . . . we had to treat him differently, make allowances. If, instead of being hostile to George, which I was, we had leaned a bit his way and tried to help him, who knows?'[13]

2

THE PAIN GAME

The suicide of self –
sado-masochism and endurance sports

*'Pain is something to carry, like a radio. You
feel your strength in the experience of pain.'*

Jim Morrison of *The Doors*

On the night of his 30th birthday, Dean Karnazes was
celebrating with friends at Paragon, a plush nightclub in
San Francisco, when he experienced something of an
epiphany. As the night was wearing drunkenly on and Dean
already feeling the worse for wear, an attractive woman began
flirting with him. It provided a moment of blinding illumination:
the life he'd bought into was not the one he wanted. Finding
himself in the guise of a successful corporate executive, hitting 30
and being encouraged to cheat on his wife, he realised that
something fundamental needed changing. Karnazes excused
himself, slipped out the back door and started running.

It was hard at first as he hadn't run for over 15 years but
something inside him knew it was a pivotal moment and it was

important to keep going. Around 4.00am he found himself in Daly, a residential neighbourhood, some 15 miles south. Despite the apparent absurdity of his situation, dressed in boxers and still mildly drunk, he made a decision to continue.

When the sun eventually came up, he'd reached Half Moon Bay on the San Mateo coast. He had run for seven hours, covered around 30 miles and was in a state of delirium. He rang his wife and asked her to pick him up. When Julie arrived, she found him in a semi-catatonic state. On the car journey home he passed out.

Karnazes describes this battering experience as akin to religious conversion in his autobiography *Ultramarathon Man: Confessions of an All-Night Runner*. Despite the fact it took him several weeks to recover, it was the moment he believes he was reborn.

The epiphany occurred in August 1992 and, over the next 15 years, Dean Karnazes went on to complete almost every known endurance run from winning the Badwater Ultramarathon – a 135-mile battle through 120-degree temperatures in Death Valley – to running in -40°C to the South Pole. In between these bookends, he completed 128¾ miles in 24 hours on a treadmill, ran 350 miles in 80 hours and 44 minutes without stopping, and completed the 1,000 mile/10-Day Western States Endurance Run. When Karnazes wasn't involved in extreme marathons, the 'hobbies' he took up were no longer exactly leisure breaks either – swimming across San Francisco Bay, mountain biking non-stop for 24 hours, climbing the Half Dome in Yosemite, and surfing the world's biggest waves off Hawaii.

The mantra for Karnazes, like all great endurance athletes, would seem to be if it doesn't hurt like hell, you're not going at it hard enough. The climax to Karnazes' career in pain came at the age of 44 when, between 17 September and 5 November 2006, he completed the North Face Endurance 50, AKA the 50/50/50 – 50 marathons in 50 States on 50 consecutive days.

With 49 of the 50 marathons successfully completed, in interviews prior to the final New York event, Karnazes said he couldn't wait to get home to spend time with his family. By the time he'd completed the course, however, he'd had a radical change of heart and announced that instead of taking a break, he'd carry on running. For some reason known only to Karnazes, he then ran back to St Louis, Missouri, where he'd started the first of the 50 marathons nearly two months earlier. In doing so, he clocked up a further 1,300 miles. We can only speculate on the reason. Perhaps he wasn't happy with the irritating 37 seconds that took his New York time over the three-hour mark. Maybe he was irked because rookie marathon runner Lance Armstrong (who had supposedly retired from endurance sports) came in ahead of him. Whatever, 50 marathons in 50 States in 50 days wasn't enough. So he kept on keep running.

The question on everyone's mind – if not Karnazes' – is why? What scared him about stopping? And why did each success feel like a failure that needed further cathartic penitence pounding the lonely road? What kind of rebirth is it that leaves someone constantly seeking punishment? And what, ultimately, would be enough for someone whose sense of worth, like the early Christian saints, relied on such suffering?

In the health column of the *Observer* magazine on 2 December 2007, a number of experts in different fields attempted to answer a young woman's concern about what she perceived as her exercise addiction. Each expert recommended she seek psychological help of some kind but one went a little further in saying that sometimes over-exercising is an attempt to gain control over other stressful events in life that simply appear too daunting. This chapter will examine those avoidance psychological processes and structures that drive athletes willingly and serially to the pain of endurance sports.

If Karnazes' endurance feats belong at the far end of the masochistic spectrum, those of a group of ascetic Japanese monks belong to an altogether different realm. The Kaihōgyō Buddhist monks live on Mount Hiei, overlooking the ancient capital of Kyoto, and are given just one week to prepare for the 'circling the mountains' challenge. The rather fey title given to the task may suggest something of a gentle meditative stroll but, in reality, it is an assault on the body and mind that even the toughest endurance athlete would deem impossible.

At the end of the preparatory week, instead of the latest Nike trainers, each monk is given a pair of straw sandals and a pure white outfit. A rope is then tied around the waist holding a sheathed knife. Both rope and knife are there to remind the monks of tougher days when it was expected of anyone failing the test to either hang or disembowel himself. For the successful, reward does not come in the form of tangible fame and fortune but, instead, the invisible prize of a heightened spiritual enlightenment arrived at by severing all attachment to what is considered the illusory physical world.

In *The Marathon Monks of Mount Hiei*, author John Stevens describes the 1,000-year old running style as a critical part of the ritual. The posture – straight back and eyes focused ahead – must be rigorously maintained while simultaneously carrying devotional books detailing mantras that must be chanted while running. The Kaihōgyō then begin their first nightly 40km run over uneven and poorly marked mountain paths at midnight; en route, during their ordeal, they are permitted to sit and rest just once. This routine is repeated every night for 100 consecutive days. At some point during this period, an additional 54km run must be shoehorned in and no allowances on any occasion is made for inclement weather, illness or injury. Once the 100-day challenge is successfully completed, the monk is given the opportunity to volunteer for a 1,000-day marathon programme.

The initial 300 days of this ultimate challenge is considered basic training. After the 700th day, the monk must survive seven days without food, water, sleep or rest while continuing nightly runs. This is the most demanding time of all and is known as *doiri*. The first day usually goes reasonably smoothly but on the second and third, the monk often experiences nausea. By the fourth day, the hunger pangs disappear but the monk becomes so dehydrated that there is no saliva in his mouth and he begins to taste blood. By the fifth day he breathes ever more deeply to absorb moisture from the mountain air. However, a far greater difficulty than thirst or hunger, according to those who have experienced it, is keeping awake and maintaining the correct posture.

The *doiri* is a period of intense sensory illumination in which the monk is said to be able to hear the ashes of incense hitting the floor and smell food being cooked miles away. Its purpose is to bring the Kaihōgyō as close as possible to the physical sensation of death. Physiologists who have examined monks at the end of the seven-day period found that many even take on the appearance of cadavers.

Following the fast, the daily run over the final 200 days is upped to first 60km and then 84km. During this period, monks speak of experiencing all notions of good and bad slipping from their minds, replaced by a crystal clarity. On completion, the monks are celebrated as Saintly Masters of the Highest Practice. Unsurprisingly, since 1885, only 46 have completed this challenge and the course is littered with the unmarked graves of those who failed.

Karnazes would seem to share with the Saintly Masters a similar attitude to his running: that each race should involve such intense endurance that everything is shed but pain. He claims the satisfaction for the endurance runner does not come from winning but instead 'crossing the finishing line after 50 hours as close to death as you're likely to get.'[1]

In his autobiography, Karnazes powerfully evokes the privation endured by ultra-marathon runners when describing an early 50-miler he had to complete in under nine hours in order to qualify for the Western States 100-mile Endurance Run. The first half of the race was fairly routine – Karnazes had trained hard and was well able to run a marathon distance. In the second stage, his limbs started rebelling and, by the 38th mile, the race had become a battle of mind over matter. He confesses to running the final 10 miles on autopilot, alternating numbness with intense, excruciating pain. Eventually, he staggered over the finishing line in 8 hours 27 minutes.

After receiving his medal, Karnazes got into his car to drive home. It was then that his body launched into a traumatic spasm, his torso swinging violently and uncontrollably from side to side as if in the grip of an epileptic fit. His legs and feet locked and he screamed in agony but the seals in the car were so effective that no one outside could hear. It was as if his body was so outraged at its abuse that it was now wreaking its own revenge. Feeling on the verge of blowing apart, Dean Karnazes vomited violently over the steering wheel and his body cramped so badly that all he could move were his eyeballs.

Eventually, some semblance of control returned. He managed to drive himself home and told his wife Julie that it was the hardest thing he had ever done and that he loved every minute.

While the Kaihōgyō monks push the limits of human endurance in the search for a higher spiritual plane, many endurance athletes instead appear to seek excruciating pain for personal and private reasons. Rather than psychic change or spiritual renewal, such athletes seem to be engaged in a perverse process of enduring endless punishment in an attempt to suppress mental anguish. Shorn of the spiritual element, the challenge becomes a straightforward masochistic attack on the body.

There is something magical about watching sublime moments of sporting genius: a Roger Federer forehand, a dazzling run by Cristiano Ronaldo or a try by South African ace Bryan Habana. One experiences something entirely different, however, watching endurance athletes. To witness Paula Radcliffe's anorexic-looking frame pounding the tarmac in the final few miles of a marathon – her face etched in agony, head bobbing from side to side, arms flailing – is to be gripped by a peculiar mixture of awe, incomprehension and unease. If the masochism took a different form, it would be labelled 'self-harming', but in the sporting context, the applause is rapturous. We are witnessing someone inflicting enormous pain on themselves, someone on the point of collapse and yet still going on. It seems impossible they will ever make the finishing line but somehow they do. And we rightly applaud their enormous bravery and achievement.

The will to transcend the limits of existence through acts of self-denial has a long and complex history. At the healthier end of the spectrum, it is a part of normal development: being a good parent requires a great deal of self-sacrifice; being a healthy child involves disappointment, pain and adaptation. At the more extreme end, however, we are required to explore both the issue of spirituality and more primitive and pathological states of mind.

The struggle to renounce one's egocentric existence is at the very heart of a rigorous religious life as well as that of the extreme endurance athlete: self-denial, self-sacrifice and suffering is the energy behind Karnazes' 'success' as well as the self-flagellating transcendental experiences of holy men. In order to understand the nature of this self-sacrifice, we need first to understand that, in essence, it is not really about loss but rather about gain. Both athlete and spiritual penitent in some way have accepted the notion that they are incomplete, sinners, lazy or quite simply 'bad' and both want to avoid this painful experience to feel 'good'. The route they take is the expurgation of guilt through suffering. The spiritual motive behind this self-sacrifice and self-denial is the need to relinquish all that is felt to be shallow or worthless in themselves so as to be able to connect with that which is felt to be meaningful, respected and pure. In the case of the monks, it is to unhitch themselves from the physical world to inhabit a spiritual Zen plane; in the case of Karnazes, it is giving up a meaningless job and the temptations of the flesh to become a pure endurance athlete. To become a human bomb is the fastest route to paradise for a spiritual terrorist. What all three share is a willingness to suffer to feel good about themselves.

When Karnazes reflected on his Road to Damascus moment, he made clear that before he discovered endurance athletics, his life felt empty and essentially meaningless. What is less clear is exactly what meaning endurance running brought to his life. It's a question he frequently asks but admits never really to answering. 'Some seek the comfort of the therapist's office, others head for the corner pub and dive into a pint, but I choose running as my therapy . . . What drug could compete?'[2]

Karnazes' obsession wonderfully illuminates the mindset of endurance athletes from Sir Steve Redgrave to Lance Armstrong. What they share, among other qualities, is their ability to endure more suffering than their rivals for longer, and then addictively do it again and again. It is the repetitive aspect of the endeavour that separates the spiritual penitent from the endurance athlete. After completing the seven-year marathon, the Hiei monks have no desire to run again, so what compels competitive endurance athletes like Redgrave, Armstrong and Karnazes to keep repeating the cycle? Why so many gold medals? Why so many Tour de France victories? Why longer, tougher, more punishing?

Endurance athletics is essentially a compulsive, neurotic activity and one of the paradoxes of the accompanying state of mind is that there is always something to be gained psychologically from what is apparently endlessly sacrificed. What the neurotic gains – through suffering – is the right to remain unchanged. Without a psychological component – the illumination of the desires, anxieties and conflicts that lie behind the sacrifice – the deeper meaning of the challenge remains hidden and no transformation or emotional growth takes place. Without the illumination of unconscious drives, the athlete remains locked in a repetitive cycle on a road that has no room for demons. The psychological rut the athlete inhabits is fed by the dramatic opiate of the next challenge. And these, like the junkie's fix, need constantly to get larger to maintain equilibrium.

It is one of psychoanalysis' seminal insights that neuroses, especially obsessive compulsions, are essentially private religions. Dean Karnazes is a devotee of the religion of endurance running. Although Karnazes graphically details the pain and suffering of his feats, he is aware that he has to provide some explanation as to why he feels compelled to keep pushing his body beyond the limits of endurance. He struggles for an answer because he finds it impossible to reconcile how it's possible to get so much pleasure from putting himself through so much pain without appearing to be some kind of freak. He rarely gets further than the mantra that suffering is the essence of a meaningful life or that he wants to discover the limits of his endurance. However, he has a sense that it is linked to something unresolved inside him. He muses at one point, 'Whether my affliction was clinical is anyone's guess; I never did submit to testing . . .'[3] and at another point; 'Plenty of people are discontent with their lives, but not many come to the conclusion that running for 24 hours straight will solve the problem'.[4]

When reading his autobiography, there is an inescapable feeling that guilt somehow lies at the heart of Karnazes' real pain. He constantly refers to the 'tremendous punishment' being dealt to his body and his capacity to 'endure unfathomable amounts of pain'.[5] At another point he admits, 'Maybe I like pain.'[6] The question that we all would like to ask him when reading this litany of self-abuse is what crime, real or imagined, has he committed to deserve being flogged virtually to death?

It was not until his 30th birthday that the cocktail of tantalizingly illicit sex and drink triggered an extreme panic that launched him on that 30-mile all-night run. Karnazes uses the language of a born-again Christian to describe his epiphany: 'In the course of a single night, I had been transformed from a drunken yuppie fool into reborn athlete. During a period of great emptiness in my life, I turned to running for strength. I heard the calling, and I went to the light . . . Every devout runner has an awakening. We know the place, the time and the reason we accept running into our life . . . Most runners are able to keep a rational perspective on the devotion, and practice responsibly. I couldn't – I became a fanatic.'[7]

The 'light' Karnazes found in the dark that night was an effective mechanism for keeping his inner turmoil at bay. Put simply, he discovered he could run his demons into the ground. What perhaps became liberating for him was his new-found way to exert control over that psychological turmoil. His weekly training schedule – which involved getting up at 4.00am after four hours' sleep, and starting the day with a three-hour run – would be considered purgatory by most of us, rather than liberation. As Karnazes says, 'The average obsessive-compulsive takes seven years to get help. The average runner covers 10,920 miles in that time.'[8] Some retreat from the world into darkness, others use it to achieve greatness.

Karnazes recounts that at the height of his 'fitness', he was comfortably able to run all night then play all day with his young children without experiencing any fatigue. Alongside confessing he didn't sleep much, he also admitted that over the previous 10 years, the longest he'd managed to go without running was three days. During that period, he describes becoming irritable and depressed and openly admits 'relaxing to me is really stressful'.[9] By the fourth day, he could stand it no more and put on his trainers despite having had 'flu and a 103°F fever. One is reminded of the photographs of Paula Radcliffe after she won the 2007 New York marathon, one arm holding the Union Jack and the other cradling her 10-month-old child. The media championed her return to pounding the lonely road so soon after childbirth but there were also many dissenting voices questioning the compulsion literally to run away from her baby so soon.

What could possibly be stressful about relaxing for Karnazes? Perhaps unbearable accusations swim across from the unconscious into consciousness when he is inactive. But what exactly is it that is so persecutory and thick with guilt?

Of course, it is impossible to know definitively but the lessons of psychoanalytic theory would suggest it likely that real or imagined transgressions – sexual or otherwise – stemmed from Karnazes' fears of both death and his own aggression and it was these two ingredients in his 30th birthday cocktail that really set him off running.

By the time Karnazes was an adolescent, he was already a successful runner. In 1976, he ran his first marathon and was named Most Inspirational Member of his high school cross-country team. That same year he met Julie, who a few years later would become his wife and the mother of his two children. For the time being, however, she had to content herself with sitting at Dean's left hand as his younger sister and best friend, Pary, already occupied the right.

Karnazes' life seemed to be pretty perfect. Then, seemingly out of nowhere, he gave up running after an angry clash with his athletics coach. In his autobiography, *Ultramarathon Man: Confessions of an All-Night Runner,* Karnazes admits tensions had been building between the two over what was essentially a philosophical difference. The coach wanted to monitor his times with a stopwatch and Karnazes thought this unnecessary as he liked to run with his 'heart'. Karnazes was ridiculed for this comment and, being a proud Greek-American, didn't take it well. He quit and didn't run again for 15 years until the night of his 30th birthday. It was a curious bust-up; ostensibly, it seems to have been a clash between two stubborn personalities with Karnazes wanting to do it his way and the coach wanting it done by his rules.

This seemingly innocuous event seems to have been the trigger for a period of delinquent acting out through his remaining school years and into college. He was expelled from two schools for being drunk and had major battles with his brother Kraig. It was as if, without the containment and structure of running, a more destructive side broke loose. What augured an end to this delinquent stage was a knock at his apartment door after a particularly wild evening.

Waiting on the other side of the door that night was a priest bringing the news that Pary, aged 18, had lost control of her car the night before and been killed in a crash. The sister he speaks adoringly of was dead. This tragic accident devastated the family and in, Karnazes' words, left an unbearable void in his life. A few years later, he married Julie. Much of what Dean Karnazes subsequently achieved and the punishment he inflicted on himself in that achievement, perhaps was an attempt to prove himself worthy of Pary.

Around the same time as Dean and Julie married, Dean's father entered the Los Angeles Marathon. According to the Greek origins of this gruelling sport, in 490BC, after the Persian Army had been defeated at Marathon, the Athenian messenger Pheidippides ran over 20 miles to Athens to bring news of the victory. What was the message of victory that Dean's Greek father was relaying? Perhaps that salvation and victory were to be found by pounding in penance a road with no end? Pary had lost control of her vehicle. At the age of 30, Dean decided he would never risk losing control of his life again. At the front of his autobiography we read: 'This book is dedicated to my sister, Pary, who always encouraged me to follow my heart.' She is a constant, often invisible, presence throughout his book and would appear central in the matrix of Karnazes' inner life.

The psychological complexity of Karnazes' personality becomes most visible when he fails to complete the Badwater Ultramarathon, the ultimate endurance challenge (later he will return not only to complete the race but win it). It is essentially a 135-mile race through Death Valley in the middle of summer, where the temperature on the road can reach over 200°f. He passes out before the finish and describes a feeling of 'incomprehensible devastation' and wanting to die rather than have to endure this feeling of failure. It was a failure both to defeat the pain ('I was nothing more than a loathsome creature undeserving of the least bit of sympathy ...'[10]) and perhaps, more importantly, measure up to some perceived duty towards his sister ('I had failed my sister'[11]).

Karnazes claims that 'pain is the body's way of ridding itself of weakness'[12] and his inability to suffer sufficient pain is in itself the most unbearable thing of all. It would appear he feels that he has to bear willingly any suffering thrown at him to defeat feelings of guilt.

Freud's view was that masochistic activities and accompanying fantasies represent a cover up and flight from intense, dreaded and forbidden desires. In Karnazes' case, it was the offer of an extra-marital liaison at his 30th birthday bash that panicked him into an all-night run. And as he ran through the night, according to his autobiography, thoughts and feelings about his sister flooded him. 'So I ran, and became filled with emotions and memories. I thought about my sister, Pary, and how much I missed her every day, even now, almost a decade after her passing.'[13] Perhaps residual feelings of guilt at not being able to protect his sister resurfaced when a woman flirted with him at his birthday party, threatening collateral damage to his wife, Julie. His extreme solution was the 'punishment' of endurance sports.

In every family there are secrets and guilt from a very young age. It is possible that Dean's guilty feelings about somehow having some responsibility for his sister's death (even though this is clearly not the case), as well as the fact he couldn't change the course of that event, stirred up familiar, unbearable persecutory feelings from early childhood. In sibling battles in every household, frustrated calls of 'I hate you and wish you'd die' ring out, followed by a parent scolding, 'That's a wicked thing to say.'

When Karnazes fails to finish the Badwater Ultramarathon, he is left feeling broken, worthless and undeserving of sympathy or respect. Paradoxically, finishing – surviving the unfathomable amounts of self-inflicted pain – creates a sense of triumph; a sense that he has rendered the torturing part of himself helpless and impotent. But where did he get the idea that he had somehow failed his sister or even that she would want him to endure such pain in her name? This was, after all, the same Pary who never judged him 'however badly I screwed up'.[14] Dean knows deep down surely that all Pary would really want is to cuddle and love him; she certainly wouldn't want him to suffer in her name. The truth is, feelings of dreadful guilt and the need to be punished often have very little to do with reality.

Psychoanalysis teaches us that our feelings and attitudes to psychological experiences of loss are derived from our earliest experience of the loss of, or separation from, the mother. It's therefore possible that Karnazes' feelings about the loss of his sister are also mixed up with his other experiences of loss, perhaps the separation from his mother as a young child, perhaps the birth of his younger brother Kraig. The birth of a sibling raises a seminal dilemma for the displaced child – 'If you love me so much, why do you want another child?' The child's answer to this question is nearly always the same: 'Because I wasn't good enough or loveable enough.' Juliet Mitchell discusses this problem in depth in *Siblings, Sex and Violence*, and suggests that, for some, the experience of having a sibling is a real trauma. Karnazes' endurance running may have helped overcome two critical psychological dilemmas. By the performance of such heroic feats, he was in some measure able to prove to his mother/sister that he was worthy and, secondly, by self-harming, he was able to protect his sister from his anger about her loss.

For a deeper understanding of these dynamics we need to dip into the complex psychoanalytic theory of masochism, a concept that sheds light on lives where rituals of pain are prevalent. The term 'masochism' – and that of 'sadism' – comes from the autobiographical writings and fiction of Sacher-Masoch and the Count de Sade but its roots predate Sacher-Masoch's writings. Solomon in old age had himself pricked by women to excite his failing virility. There are images, too, of the philosopher Aristotle on all fours, carrying his wife Phyllis on his back armed with a whip. In fact, it was only in the 19th century that masochism came to be described as a sexual perversion.

Masochism is described as a neurotic state characterised by the search for suffering. Since the masochist's behaviour is an attempt to relieve himself of guilt, we can more easily understand the role played by pain – the architect of relief from guilt – in such lives. The masochist considers suffering as having value because it ennobles and purifies. And the suffering is almost invariably physical.

The active seeking out of suffering at the extreme end of the spectrum reveals a tendency towards self-destructiveness and the biological universality of this tendency led Freud to consider it an independent drive, called by him 'the death instinct' (or Thanatos). We will return to this seminal drive later when discussing the endurance feats of Sir Ranulph Fiennes. Freud's view was that masochism results from a transformation of sadism through feelings of guilt or shame. The question, however, is guilt or shame about what? To answer this, we have to go back to the child and how he or she manages aggression.

According to Freud, the child completes the transformation of sadism into masochism by not only identifying with the perceived aggressor but by turning aggressive feelings on him/herself. The child is now able to control two different roles and experience two distinctly separate feelings as he/she becomes simultaneously both perpetrator and victim. He/she can now experience both the pleasure of inflicting pain and the suffering of being on the receiving end without feeling guilt or damaging an external relationship.

As we can now see, the relational dynamic inside the mind of the masochist is much more complex than just a search for suffering. In endurance athletics, it manifests itself in a split between the body and the mind. The mind inflicts the pain on the body and ignores the body's cries to stop. The endurance athlete decides on the severity of the challenge and the amount of pain he will have to go through; the more severe the challenge, the greater the pain he will have to endure. Thus it is the victim that gets to decide how much pain the perpetrator, in the guise of the challenge, will inflict. The real challenge the victim is thus setting is to survive the pain and, by doing so, render the perpetrator defeated. Karnazes' failure to finish his first Badwater Ultramarathon leaves him feeling devastated and broken. He wants always to be the 'King of Pain'[15], but he failed (as victim) to survive the challenge. However, as perpetrator he had, of course, succeeded and, as the perpetrator of that pain, 'I'd loved every second of it.' [16]

Ian Williamson's casebook – Jessica

Jessica was 19 when she first sought help because she was in an emotionally abusive relationship with an older man and was angry and frustrated at not having the strength to leave it. In the course of the work, a complex and traumatic picture emerged. Jessica had been neglected as a child and had attached herself to a family living down the street. The mother was felt by Jessica to be kind and attentive, almost a surrogate mother. However, there was a dark side to this family; from time to time, the husband would touch Jessica inappropriately. In time, this escalated to full-blown sexual abuse, which went on for several years and only stopped when the family left the area.

Jessica admitted that, during the abuse, she had coped by trying to 'exit' her body whenever the man touched her. Sometimes this worked, allowing her to dissociate herself from the experience but, at others, it failed and her body responded. When the latter occurred, the shame and guilt Jessica felt led her to think mistakenly that she was somehow complicit in the abuse. It was during this period, she said, she developed a deep disgust for her body as a result of the experience. During adolescence, Jessica started self-harming by cutting herself and also became anorexic. Her anorexia could be understood as an attempt to punish her body for responding by starving it of food. But she was also angry with herself for her inability to 'exit' and the cutting was her self-inflicted punishment for this failure. The intensity of the pain from the cutting and the bleeding gave her a momentary sense that she had atoned in some way for these imagined past sins.

Dramatic though Jessica's story is, it illuminates the part that guilt and shame play in the dynamic of self-abuse.

Today, we know much more about the effect of trauma through neurological research into brain mapping. Writing in 1991, American psychiatrist Lenore Terr explained that 'children old enough to remember their traumas may defend themselves from prolonged or repeated trauma by putting their traumas out of their mind, deliberately suppressing or unconsciously repressing them. Traumatised children may also dissociate, teaching themselves to self-hypnotise and enter planes of consciousness in which they fail to take in or register full memories of their trauma. They may displace, concentrating deliberately on something similar but less emotionally connected to the trauma, thus making their memories slip away.'[17] Fortunately for Jessica in the casebook above, it was the gradual illumination of the meaning and purpose of her self-destructive behaviour that allowed her to recover and change her life.

At first glance, we would seem to have found a link between the mindsets of the great endurance athletes and the Zen masters. Both survive the pain by 'exiting' or dissociating. But if we look more closely at the purpose and meaning of their respective suffering, we can see a fundamental difference. While the Marathon Monks suffer intense physical pain to 'exit' the material/physical world in order to attain another plane of consciousness in search of spiritual enlightenment, the endurance athlete 'exits' to overcome more effectively the challenge and defend themselves.

But there is another aspect to the notion of dissociation in connection with suffering that links Karnazes and Jessica's experience and that is the idea of being abandoned. At the moment of the abuse, Jessica is no longer safe; she is no longer being protected. She has effectively been abandoned to her fate. In order to survive the experience, she abandons her body. Karnazes would seem to do something similar. He inflicts extraordinary suffering on his body and, in the process, abandons it, leaving perpetrator and victim to fight it out alone. The dynamic suggests that in some way Karnazes may have been enacting a painful experience of loss and/or abandonment from childhood (quite possibly coinciding with the birth of his brother) and that its echo in Pary's death provided a convulsion that prompted an equally extreme reaction in dealing with it.

Jessica's case is certainly at the extreme end of this spectrum but the trauma need not be so severe or explicit to be a defining experience for an individual. The idea for this book, as mentioned in the introduction, started after listening to a speech by Britain's greatest Olympian, Sir Steve Redgrave, during which he casually mentioned the fact that he'd pushed himself through 20 years' worth of training sessions, which we have already established must have totalled around 28,000. Lest us mere mortals delude ourselves into thinking that this involved nothing more strenuous than a gentle scull in the sunshine at Henley; Redgrave describes it thus in his autobiography, *A Golden Age*: 'Training was never really enjoyable. It had to be done. Indeed, perhaps there was an element of masochism about it . . . that it was no good unless it hurt.'[18]

British cyclist David Millar gets to the heart of the endurance athlete's state of mind when he branded the Tour de France's gruelling mountain stages as sado-masochism on a major scale. Lance Armstrong, the undisputed king of the mountains, answered in typically blunt fashion a question about what pleasure he took in riding for so long – he said that he didn't do it for the pleasure but rather for pain. If Millar and Armstrong consider 8½ hours on a bike sado-masochism on a major scale, where might they locate a Karnazes 80-hour+, 350-mile run?

Sir Steve Redgrave's autobiography is standard sports fare, high on narrative and low on insight into what drove him to become one of the greatest of all Olympians, or to question why each gold medal was never enough. In a relatively normal childhood, his much publicised dyslexia stands out. He describes how it was discovered around the age of 10 but the condition was never formally diagnosed and so he didn't receive specialist help. Although he claims he wasn't taunted by his peers (his size probably helped), he acknowledges that he knew he couldn't compete academically and that he would fail the 11+. In secondary school, he sank to bottom of his class in English, was never good enough academically to take an O-level, and had to content himself with a Grade 1 pass in CSE woodwork.

The effects of learning difficulties on the personality of the child are well documented and include depression, high stress levels, frustration and, unsurprisingly, low self-esteem. The discovery of dyslexia at the age of 10 is relatively late. By 10, much of the child's personality has already been shaped. One can only guess at what it must have felt like for a 10-year-old to be unable to read or write properly and not know why. The reality is that often by the time children are diagnosed as dyslexic, they're already saddled with a low opinion of themselves. More often than not, they feel simultaneously stupid and angry – stupid at not being able to read or write properly; angry at themselves for their ineptitude and difference from other children.

Before they can begin to tackle the problem effectively, such children generally have to go through a process of grieving for the child they thought they might have been. Redgrave's sporting prowess at school seems to have been the antidote that kept him afloat but it is intriguing to note in his autobiography that he dates the first real stirrings of athletic ambition when watching the 1972 Munich Olympic Games and thinking he would like to win a gold medal at something. It happened at the age of 10, the same age that his dyslexia was discovered. One might speculate that he intuitively saw an escape from the constraints that dyslexia imposed. Winning a gold medal would mean he was the best at something, rather than the worst.

Psychoanalysis is not a tidy science. It offers only possible insights that may help a person to the understanding of their own truth. Redgrave was the youngest child by some distance, his sisters being nine and five years his senior. Too distanced from them to experience sibling rivalry, his classmates and rowing competitors probably took on this role. Redgrave admits to being fiercely competitive and adds revealingly that the River Thames was the mistress in his life – 'the other woman' whose charms he found irresistible. In his autobiography, he claims to know her secrets, her moods, her idiosyncrasies better than anyone. The Oedipal/maternal symbolism of this is obvious – Redgrave devoted 20+ years of his life to competing and beating all his sibling/rivals for the accolade of being the best on the river – in other words, being his mother's favourite son.

Having famously declared post-Atlanta, 'If anybody sees me near a boat again, they have my permission to shoot me,' he cannot resist her charms and, returning to the river after a break, admitted to feeling 'like a baby being returned to its mother'.[19] The need endlessly to return to this 'mother' that protected him and allowed him to achieve and feel special was perhaps what lay behind his drive to compete for so long.

Because of the enormity of the mental and physical challenges involved in endurance sports, 'goal setting' is an important component of the challenge. A fascinating paper by Schofield, Dickson, Mummery and Street in the *Journal of Sports Psychology* suggests some individuals set abstract high-order goals – such as happiness – conditionally upon the achievement of lower-order goals like completing an ultra-distance triathlon. This process is known as 'linking'. Linking theory proposes that some individuals are vulnerable to depression because they utilise inappropriate strategies to pursue life goals. In a nutshell, such linkers may believe they can only attain the 'goal' of happiness if they achieve the goal of winning an Olympic gold medal.

This type of connection can lead to a number of difficulties. The individual may experience disengagement problems due to the importance of the goal – single-mindedness or selfishness in common parlance. If the athlete does achieve the goal, he or she may experience a brief period of elation but will quickly need to set a new goal to restore the link to 'happiness'. This sort of linking is also usually accompanied by a low level of depression because the goal pursuit is accompanied by the belief that the individual is not yet happy or content in the present.

Redgrave does not dwell on past glories. He loves the satisfaction that comes from winning but once the fleeting euphoria of triumph dissolves, he instantly moves on to the next challenge. Schofield, Dickson, Mummery and Street's paper also claims 'linkers' suffer from high levels of pre-competition anxiety. In his autobiography, Redgrave talks about his stress levels before the Atlanta Olympics. He describes the internal battle to stop himself being overwhelmed by feelings of doubt and anxiety about both the meaning of what he is doing and his ability to perform. Later, he is diagnosed with colitis, a serious medical condition in which the intestine gets red raw and loses its capacity to hold anything. He admits to worrying about the longer-term implications of having such a condition and is taken aback when some of the experts suggest that it could be a stress-related condition. Initially, he claims his life is not unduly stressful but later concedes it indeed must be stressful being in a must-win situation every time he goes out to race.

If trauma, real or imagined, is the unconscious driving force behind many endurance athletes, might it also be possible that the intensity and nature of the endurance activity is directly linked to the severity of the perceived experience of early trauma?

At the extreme end of the endurance scale – and, by implication, the extreme end of the trauma scale – the extraordinary endurance feats of the world's greatest living explorer, Sir Ranulph Fiennes, seem to combine exceptional bravery with a recklessness bordering on the suicidal. In 2002 alone, Fiennes managed a 125-mile canoe race, a 40-mile night marathon, a 78km Alpine marathon, the London Marathon, Grizzly Marathon, a 7-mile Mud Race and the New Zealand Southern Traverse. The following year, on 7 June 2003, Fiennes suffered a massive heart-attack and fell into a coma. Four months after his triple bypass operation, he ran seven marathons on seven consecutive days on seven continents.

In the winter of 2007, at the age of 62, suffering from severe vertigo and a heart condition, Fiennes attempted to climb the notoriously difficult north face of the Eiger to raise funds for his chosen Marie Curie Cancer Care charity (to date, his career has raised more than £10 million for charities). An additional handicap was the fact that he effectively only had one hand to climb with, having earlier carried out a DIY fretsaw amputation of the frostbitten fingers of the other in his garden shed (the legacy of a solo polar journey in 2001).

Prior to the Eiger climb, in a *Times* interview with fellow explorer Stephen Venables on 27 August 2007, he admitted, 'I enjoy completing the climb but not the actual climb itself; it's not easy to enjoy something you're frightened of.' This succinct comment encapsulates the psychological essence of endurance feats, for it is not the 'doing' but rather the 'triumphing over' that is crucial.

As with Karnazes, Fiennes dedicates his autobiography *Mad, Bad & Dangerous to Know* to his sister. But in his case, he tellingly adds the word 'surviving'. Does 'To my surviving sister Gill' simply record the fact that the rest of his family are dead – mostly to cancer – or is he anticipating his own death?

In 1982, psychoanalyst Betty Joseph published what was to become a seminal paper. In it, she tried to shed light on a particular group of patients whose lives were inextricably bound up with activities that seemed destined to destroy them physically and mentally. She felt that the pull towards death and despair was not a longing for peace or respite from torment but involved an unusual form of masochism. For these patients, just to die was not enough, they needed to have the satisfaction of seeing themselves being destroyed. She called this state an 'addiction to near-death'.[20] Joseph suggested that such patients are involved in a kind of physical brinkmanship in which seeing themselves in perilous situations, unable to be helped, is a critical part of the dynamic. She believed that in reaching such points in their lives, they had withdrawn from a connectedness with others into a secret world of aggression against themselves. Joseph identified a perverted relationship in this secret world in which one part of the self had turned against and attacked another part – an example of such a state might be head-banging, cutting oneself or pulling one's own hair.

The essential question Joseph attempts to address is why this kind of behaviour should be so addictive and so hard to give up. She believes that the pain of psychological trauma experienced by the adult has been so great and so impossible to alleviate that a fundamental connectedness and trust in others has broken down. The unalleviated pain is then turned into torment; the individuals take control of the dynamic by identifying with the tormentor and inflicting extreme physical pain on themselves. Perverse though this behaviour is, for such individuals it is an escape from the far riskier option of relatedness to others.

Fiennes' triumphs are on the epic scale and so are the losses he has endured. His father died stepping on a German mine in Italy before he was born and, in adulthood, he has lost his first wife, his mother and two sisters to cancer. The complexities of Fiennes' mindset were tellingly illuminated in a conversation with cameraman and climbing mentor, Ian Parnell, in ITV news coverage broadcast live in March 2007 from the Eiger. Asked whether now that he'd remarried and had a new daughter he had contemplated the fact that Elizabeth might grow up without him, Fiennes replied, 'I would just judge it in a way which possibly no one else would judge it, which is that when I was born, my father had been killed a couple of months before, and I was brought up just by my mother, and I never missed having a father at all. My mother was a very good mother and Elizabeth's mother is an extremely good mother, too. So I wouldn't feel there would be a big gap.'

This is an extraordinarily paradoxical and sad comment. On the one hand, Fiennes willingly and regularly risks his life to raise money for charity (and perhaps to defeat fleetingly his unconscious terror of loss and death?); on the other hand, he cannot imagine his loved ones being hit too hard by the trauma of losing him. Perhaps despite his extraordinary qualities, at heart he may have such a low opinion of himself that he cannot imagine that he is really needed or will be missed.

At one point in his autobiography, with a boy's unbridled innocence, Fiennes brags of how his father heroically captured three Germans 'at the point of his Briar pipe'.[21] Fiennes' father – another Ranulph – commanded the Royal Scots Greys at Solerno and provided a military blueprint for a heroic life and death. It was an impossible model to live up to but Ranulph could never be accused of not trying. Despite having what he claims to be a poor academic record, he, too, rose to become Colonel of the Royal Scots Greys and then peppered his life with extraordinary feats that would make any military father proud.

Fiennes' autobiography is a litany of self-deprecation that borders on self-loathing. At prep school he commends his head-master who 'beat me from time to time for good reason.'[22] At Eton, he bemoans his prettiness that leads to him being labelled 'a tart': 'My tormenters were unremitting. I seriously considered throwing myself off the bridge over the River Thames.'[23] Despite this, extraordinarily, he confesses that if he had a son he would unhesitatingly send him to Eton. Fiennes' own survival solution, despite suffering vertigo, was to turn to stegophily, climbing the school buildings by night.

On the Eiger climb, Fiennes confesses, 'I feared my own inadequacies, of being revealed as a coward or, at best, a wimp.'[24] He speaks of being constantly vigilant not to let his companions and climbing mentors – who perhaps can be seen as father figures – see his fear. His major concern, he confesses, is if he falls, will he scream? Fiennes speaks of attacking an obstacle at a rush providing 'no tiny chink into which sheer terror could claw, then spread incubus-like and render me a gibbering fool, an embar-rassment to myself and to others.'[25] Tellingly, he also says, 'With fear, you must prevent, not cure. Fear must not be let in in the first place.'[26] And at the end of the climb, he confesses, 'I suspected that nothing had really changed. There had been no actual confrontation within myself. No fearful struggle I had bravely and finally won.'[27] Although he is speaking of his vertigo, it could well apply to the broader fears that he has perhaps always challenged but not overcome. Faced by the fragility of life that Fiennes has experienced at close range, what do you do? You close it out or 'exit' by challenging the fear rather than understanding it. You climb up the school building or mountains, or cross a frozen wilderness. Fear is the foundation of each achievement and sadly, unprocessed, each victory over it is fleeting.

Fiennes' romance with death (Thanatos) might be understood as an attempt to wrest control of extremely traumatic experiences of loss and terror and bring them into an arena where he can create the momentary illusion of having conquered them. It is often the case that a child unconsciously feels guilt for a sibling or parent's death, however illogical that guilt is. In the face of random terrible events, it is also common for people to act out guilty feelings by putting themselves in danger and thus feel they have some control and not be impotent in the face of random fate. Now in his sixties, time is running out for this most remarkable of endurance explorers. Despite the scope and scale of his achievements, they never seem to quench his thirst. One fears that without an understanding of the internal nature of the challenge, it may all end in disaster. This is why endurance feats are often referred to as a 'mug's game'. We, the public, can see the masochism. The truth is that although the suffering the masochist inflicts on himself is real enough, the deeper dangers he is struggling to overcome are often so embedded in the unconscious that they cannot be resolved physically.

Speaking to Mark Mackenzie of the *Independent* in November 2006 after he had finished his 50 marathons in 50 days in 50 States, Karnazes stated, 'Last Sunday was the first day in 50 that I hadn't run a marathon and, to be honest, it didn't feel very good.' His solution was to go out and, like Forrest Gump, simply keep running. Between completion of this chapter and it going to press,

Fiennes carried out several more endurance feats 'just to keep my feet out of the grave as long as possible'.[28] These included two attempts at cracking the highest peak on earth. He finally summitted Everest in late May 2009.

3

THE FASTEST ON EARTH?

Cheating – the athlete's perverse resistance to health

'The most important thing in the Olympic Games is not to win but to take part, just as the important thing in life is not the triumph but the struggle.'

Baron Pierre de Coubertin (1896)

When Usain Bolt made it to the final of the Olympic 100m in Beijing, there were plenty of sage sceptics dismissing his chances. How could anyone become the fastest on the planet having only seriously taken up the distance four months earlier? Then there was the matter of his unnaturally long legs which surely wouldn't have time to properly unravel and gobble up the track like they did in the 200m. Doubt was what Usain Bolt should have been feeling, especially now that his lunchtime double helping of chicken nuggets had set like concrete in his stomach. But as Bolt prepared to launch himself into the 2008 final, a strange detachment and calm settled on him. As he was introduced to the crowd, he even felt sufficiently relaxed to mime firing off his trademark lightning bolt into the sky. Starter's orders . . . Usain stretched, then packed his 6ft 5in frame into his blocks like he was ramming an overcoat into a matchbox. A mere 8 seconds and 80m later, he thrust his arms into the air triumphantly and started his customary showboating. This was too easy. These other guys were supposed to include three of the fastest to have ever run the earth and they were still the length of a London bus behind.

On Saturday 16 August 2008, Usain Bolt crossed the 100m finishing line in Beijing's Bird's Nest stadium in 9.69 seconds with one lace undone. Having smashed both the Olympic and world records, he raised his invisible bow again and sent the crowd wild; he was Superbolt, a superhero, a celestial archer . . . a bolt out of the blue. He'd beaten the rest of the Olympic field by the biggest margin for 40 years and, if he'd been inclined, it could have been even greater. But Usain liked to preen, entertain the crowd and enjoy himself. For mere mortals, athletics may be a punishing mistress but, for Bolt, it was fun and he'd still annihilated the field and burned up the record books. As another legendary 200m world record holder, Michael Johnson, said while covering the event on television, 'We have seen the greatest display of 100m sprinting in history.' A couple of days later, Usain again obliterated the field – and Johnson's own world record – in the 200m before going on to strike gold in the 100m relay.

Bolt had achieved beyond his or anyone else's dreams and still hadn't yet turned 22. So why did we all have such rueful expressions as we applauded? Though enjoying the celebratory mood as we bore witness to the fastest race in history, we couldn't help rewinding 20 years to the crazed eyes and cannonball pace of Ben Johnson as he blasted Carl Lewis into oblivion. The stripping of drug cheat Johnson's gold and the erasing of his seemingly impossible time from the record books had sown the first seeds of doubt. A scab of heavy scepticism then formed over the intervening two decades as a succession of male and female 'fastest-on-earths' went the same way. As Andrew Longmore so eloquently put it in the *Sunday Times* in August 2008, sprinting had become 'a spittoon for sporting cynicism'. He then voiced both the hope and caution we all shared, stating that 'Johnson's reign as Olympic champion lasted barely a day in 1988. Athletics will pray the new world record and his [Bolt's] credibility survives for longer than that.'

Also in August 2008, Simon Barnes in the *Times* provided his own reason for rejoicing. 'Nothing can elevate sport higher than a sprinter. Nothing can bring sport lower than a sprinter. On Saturday, sport was elevated and the world rejoiced once again in the greatest race of them all.' Then Barnes, too, just couldn't stop the doubt flickering back in, unsettling his joyful return to innocence. 'Can you believe in a person who annihilates the world record, massacres a field in which six people ran sub-10, and does so without even trying?'

Like the journalists, none of us could help casting a suspicious eye at Jamaica but, at the same time, also had to concede Herb Elliot (Jamaican team doctor and member of the IAFF Anti-doping Commission) was right to point out that Johnson and Linford Christie – Jamaicans who earned gold for Canada and Britain – only failed dope tests running and training outside the country.

So far, Bolt has unfailingly tested clean. There have certainly been enough tests to catch him – during the Beijing Olympics he was selected to give blood samples so frequently he complained he'd have no blood left to run with. Perhaps we should simply accept the official version that it's his height – 6ft 5in – that marks Superbolt out; after all, no one this tall has competed at this level before. The height advantage translates into an 8ft stride that takes just 41 steps to reach the 100m finishing line, while lesser men such as fellow Jamaican and former world record holder, Asafa Powell, has to make do with a 6ft 10in stride and another five steps to cover the same distance.

We all want to believe in sporting heroes and if the already fabled race turns out to be a fix, it will be a crying shame. If the official version turns out to be the truth, then it will be a crying shame, too, because the enormity of Bolt's achievement has been tarnished by the cheats that went before him.

As Superbolt was winning everything at the Games, Britain's Christine Ohuruogu was finding redemption winning gold in the 400m after a 12-month ban for three missed drugs tests. Meanwhile, 400m hurdles defending champion Fani Halkia was testing positive for the banned substance methyltrienolone. Halkia, of course, denied taking a banned substance, and asked for her 'B' sample to be tested. It duly tested positive the next day. Win some, lose some.

De Coubertin's noble words back in 1896 seem curiously antiquated in today's cut-throat sporting world, yet they perfectly encapsulate the honest 'struggle' that should be the cornerstone of sporting endeavour. Cheating makes a mockery of that essence because the triumph is fraudulent and achieved at the expense of the meaningful and honest experience of struggle.

The Boston Marathon may not receive the same worldwide, headline-grabbing attention of the Olympic diva event but perhaps nothing captures the futility of winning by cheating than the story of Rosie Ruiz. Rosie 'won' the event in 1980 but, in reality, never ran it; she simply registered and joined the competitors from the crowd with a mile to go, sprinting to the finish in record time.

The relationship between sport and drug use has a long and inglorious history but nowhere is it as systemically dysfunctional as in the world of sprinting. It is a union that has drained a wonderful spectacle of all semblance of credibility and integrity. When Ben Johnson was stripped of his 1988 Olympic 100m title and world record of 9.79 seconds for taking steroids, it would be another 11 years before American Maurice Green equalled that time. Green, who retired last year after winning world and Olympic titles, has constantly had to deny accusations that he used drugs. Justin Gatlin, Tim Montgomery, Marion Jones – all great Olympians and world record holders – have all been outed as cheats in recent years.

Similar rumours have swirled round women's sprinting. Pat Connolly, another former Olympian, claimed at the 1989 Senate hearings on the greatest sprinter of her generation, Florence Griffith-Joyner, 'Florence's face changed ... Her muscles bulged as if she had been born with a barbell in the crib ... it was difficult not to wonder if she was taking some kind of performance-enhancing drugs.'[1] When Flo-Jo, the former goddess of the track, died suddenly in 1998 at the age of 38 of asphyxiation following an epileptic seizure, most couch critics were convinced it was down to earlier chronic steroid use.

There are few more captivating sporting events than the 100m sprint. Its brevity, less than 10 seconds, and simplicity – a straight line between two points – provides a purity and clarity of focus that other sporting events cannot match. But it is also brutal; one one-hundredth of a second can be the difference between fame and obscurity. There is something primal about it. There are no tactics, no complicated game plans or special skills, just massive power and blistering speed. You can train night and day, you can lift the heaviest weights imaginable, but if you don't have the requisite amount of fast-twitch muscle fibres, you will never amount to anything in the world of sprinting. It is, in short, a stark Darwinian world. The ultimate accolade – the holy grail of 100m sprinting – is the title 'world's fastest'. This is the sporting title with the clearest direct biological link to our evolutionary past. Thus there is an aura and mystique that accompanies the owner of the title 'Fastest on Earth' as we continue to evolve. The fastest in the 100m today can not only be the fastest in a given race, in a given year, but the fastest human our species has ever produced. And because of the purity of such a claim, it attracts particular calumny when cheats win.

On 30 August 1987 when Ben Johnson faced Carl Lewis in the final of the 100m in the World Athletic Championships in Rome, the Seoul Olympics were still a year away but the rivalry between the two was intensifying by the day. Carl Lewis was the brash, urbane American and current Olympic champion with film-star good looks; Ben Johnson was the shy Canadian with the speech impediment. The pair hated each other and made little effort to disguise the fact. Coming into the race, Johnson and Lewis between them had recorded nine performances under the 10-second mark. Both had shown they were capable of breaking the world record of 9.93 seconds held by the American, Calvin Smith. However, the hype that attended the two main protagonists masked the fact that this was also the fastest group of sprinters ever assembled for a 100m race. An audience of 580 million tuned in to watch.

When the gun went off, Johnson exploded from the blocks leaving everyone in his wake. Johnson was known for his quick starts; Lewis, with his smooth, long stride, was expected to pull him back as the race unfolded. With 30m to go, the race was over. Johnson – like Bolt 21 years later – was not going to be caught. As he hit the finish, the clock recorded a time of 9.83, a full tenth of a second faster than Calvin Smith's world record. To give some perspective on this performance, the world record had only seen an improvement of two one-hundredths of a second in the 15 years between 1968 and 1983.

The Lewis–Johnson rivalry dominated proceedings coming into the 1988 Seoul Olympics. Little were we to know at the time, but the final of the 100m sprint would go down as the most infamous of all time and shape both the future of sprinting and also the sport of athletics itself. The race was as spectacular as the hype of the build up. Johnson again blasted out of the blocks and left everyone for dead. His time of 9.79 seconds was not just another world record but seemed to redefine the limits of what humans might be capable. His time broke the 20-year-old Olympic record set by Jim Hines in 1968. Carl Lewis, the reigning Olympic champion, was a distant second in 9.92 seconds. Incredulity and euphoria, however, were swiftly followed by a stiff dose of reality as Johnson tested positive for the anabolic steroid Stanozolol and was stripped of his gold medal.

Rumours that Johnson was not 'clean' had dogged the athlete

for years and now the doubters were vindicated – the cheat had been caught. The legitimacy and integrity of the 100m had been brought into disrepute but sanity and integrity was quickly restored; Carl Lewis was declared the winner and all was now well. Or so it was believed.

In an interview in 1996, Johnson acknowledged that he had taken steroids but suggested that others on the starting line that day were equally guilty. At the time these claims were dismissed as the remarks of a man with a grudge. However, it has now emerged that four of the athletes in that final failed drugs tests. Dennis Mitchell was banned for two years in 1998 after testing positive for excessive levels of testosterone. His defence was that he had drunk five bottles of beer and had sex with his wife four times the night before giving his urine sample. Desai Williams was implicated by the Canadian Government's inquiry into the use of performance-enhancing drugs in 1989. He later admitted to using steroids. Following the final, Linford Christie failed a drugs test for the stimulant ephedrine, but was cleared on appeal after convincing the panel that he had inadvertently taken it when drinking ginseng tea. He was banned for two years, however, in 1999 after testing positive for nandrolone. In an interview with Duncan Mackay in the *Guardian* in April 2003, Carl Lewis admitted that he had failed three drugs tests during the 1988 US Olympic trials and that these had been covered up after the American Olympic body conveniently accepted the story that he had innocently taken a herbal supplement.[2]

As a drug cheat, there was always something naïve and child-like about Ben Johnson's involvement with steroids. The former world's fastest was like a kid caught with a hand in the sweetie jar desperately pleading innocence. It was all so obvious. For a start, there was the body, or more particularly the shoulders. We were led to believe that Johnson had beefed himself up with the help of a vigorous weights programme. In no time, he went from muscular to Incredible Hulk proportions. Suddenly, he looked like someone had stuck a bicycle pump into his body and forgot to stop pumping. And then there were the eyes. As Carl Lewis famously put it in his autobiography, *Inside Track*, 'I couldn't get away from those yellow eyes. The bastard did it again.'[3]

The issue of cheating, especially drug use, arouses conflicting emotions depending on the sport. Our feelings can range from a 'flog 'em then hang 'em' reaction when it comes to sprinting, to an ultra-liberal 'well, if they're all at it, it makes no difference anyway . . .' when it comes to cycling. Part of the difficulty is in confronting our own experiences of cheating and also our own guilt. Cheating in golf in any form is deemed not just unacceptable but a cardinal sin and a lifetime ban is mandatory. Other sports, like cycling and athletics, take a more forgiving view as is shown in the recent success of Christine Ohuruogu. There is a scale of cheating in sport. Some instances merit a life ban, others a fine or a short ban. While one may view all cheating as 'sinful', the reality is that the context is everything and that these contexts often reflect very different states of mind.

Consider these two instances. In 1994, Schumacher was on the verge of winning his first Formula 1 world championship. The title was his if Britain's Damon Hill did not beat him in the final competition in Australia. During the race, however, his Benetton car suffered a terminal fault and it looked as though he would lose the championship. Schumacher seemingly had other ideas. As Hill passed, Schumacher's Benetton swung into Hill's Williams car, taking both competitors out of the race and ensuring that the championship was his. Schumacher was blamed for the incident by many knowledgeable observers but the race stewards judged that it had been a 'racing accident' and took no further action.

In 2004, Marion Jones, the American sprinting superstar, dared the US Anti-Doping Agency to charge her after the Bay Area Laboratory Co-operative (Balco) steroid scandal and suggested they back off if they did not. She proclaimed that she had never failed a drug test in her life. In May 2007, Jones admitted that those proclamations were untrue and pleaded guilty to lying to federal investigators about her use of banned drugs from 1999–2001. She was subsequently jailed for six months.

One might argue that these are both incidents involving cheating but they have very different psychological dynamics. Schumacher's is a spontaneous reaction to a situation – albeit a dangerous one. Jones's is a premeditated, well-orchestrated guerrilla campaign of deceit and lies. One is perhaps able to understand Schumacher's shunt. Like a trip outside the penalty area, it could be thought of as a moment of 'madness' in the heat of battle. Even though ludicrously dangerous and wrong, it is perhaps forgivable. The Jones saga, however, is altogether more disturbing both for its premeditated nature but also its relationship to notions of guilt and remorse.

While Ben Johnson stained the pre-eminent male event for two decades, top of the women's cheat list is undoubtedly Marion Jones, the erstwhile superwoman of world sprinting, who, prior to her drug bust, was America's greatest athlete. Her story is as sinister and disturbing as it is desperately sad, for the scale and scope of her deceit was truly breathtaking.

Marion Jones' choice of a career in athletics can be viewed as a means of dealing with a traumatic childhood by transforming perceived rejection and abandonment into worldwide fêting and acceptance. However, paradoxically, it would appear that she unconsciously sabotaged that process by becoming a drug cheat because at a fundamental level the one person she couldn't convince regarding her greatness was herself; deep down, it would appear, she simply couldn't buy into her own myth.

Understanding what states of mind are involved in drug-taking is crucial as it has profound significance for sport as a whole, for without 'fair play', sport ceases to be sport in any meaningful sense. Critical to our understanding of these states of mind is the notion of guilt. It is a uniquely human experience that is at the heart of our relation to each other in the sense of being concerned about our actions and their effect on others. Facing up to and bearing feelings of guilt facilitates the process of repairing that which we have damaged or hurt. In a wider context, a sense of guilt binds society together by operating as a restraint against transgressions towards each other. It is, in its most basic form, an unspoken bond to 'do as you would be done by'.

The use of performance-enhancing drugs suggests an idea of inadequacy, of a belief that somehow the person is not quite good enough. One way of dealing with this dilemma is to withdraw into a state of self-sufficiency. Once this retreat has been made away from the perceived emotional dangers that other humans represent, a relationship with inanimate, performance-enhancing drugs probably feels like a much easier world to bring under control. By abusing the boundaries of 'fairness', however, and mistrusting the world around them, such athletes, at an unconscious level, also compound their corrosive sense of being and accentuate an already poor self-image. Cheating thus becomes a way of suffering in silence.

Coming into the 2000 Sydney Olympics, Marion Jones was the queen of women's sprinting and hot favourite to take home a bag full of medals. The world around her suddenly imploded following her win in the 100m when news emerged that her husband, the US shot-putter, C.J. Hunter, had tested positive for nandrolone in competition in Oslo in July. Ron Rapoport, in his biography of Jones, *See How She Runs,* recounts how 'Marion and C.J. cried for hours ... It wasn't true, he told her. He would never do a thing like that, not ever ... Marion looked him in the eyes and knew he was telling the truth. She had no doubts. None. She would stick by him, she told him. She had complete faith in him.'[4]

Hunter predictably denied all charges, despite the fact that the tests revealed levels of nandrolone a thousand times over the legal limit. It later emerged that he had failed four other drug tests earlier in the season. In June 2001, Marion Jones announced that instead of sticking by Hunter, she was divorcing him, citing irreconcilable differences. The ruthlessness was astonishing. Hunter, no longer able to collude with the enormous deception, was expendable and simply cast out.

By July 2004, Hunter had testified to the Federal prosecutors that Marion Jones had been using banned performance-enhancing drugs when she won her five medals at the Sydney Olympics. He further added that he had injected her with banned substances and seen her inject herself. As the furore gathered momentum following Hunter's positive drug test, Jones came under intense pressure. Fortunately, as Rapoport wrote, '. . . there was one solid rock she could lean on for support – her coach.'[5] And Marion herself supported the view, 'He was just incredible . . . He convinced me we weren't going to let anything pull us down.'[6]

In May 2008, that coach, Trevor Graham, was charged with making 100 telephone calls to a Texas-based dealer in performance-enhancing drugs within a two-year period. He was alleged to have referred at least eight of his athletes, including Jones and Montgomery, to the dealer, Mexican-born Angel 'Memo' Heredia, so they could get hold of steroids, EPO and growth hormones.

By August 2008, Trevor Graham had been found guilty of perjury by a court in San Francisco. He was deemed to have lied to agents investigating the Balco scandal. Graham, ironically, had initiated the investigation himself when he anonymously sent a syringe containing a previously undetectable steroid to the US anti-doping authorities in 2003 (allegedly to get back at Tim Montgomery in a row over money). He was coach to both Montgomery and Justin Gatlin – both convicted drug cheats – as well as Jones. Perhaps this is what Marion meant when she called him 'the solid rock' she could lean on for support.

When C.J. Hunter was first implicated in the failed drug-test saga, Victor Conte (founder of Balco) – described by Rapoport as a nutritionist working with many Olympians – came quickly to Hunter's rescue suggesting that Hunter was taking an iron supplement and that the manufacturers hadn't cleaned their machines properly when switching from one product to another and that this probably caused the contamination.

In 2004, Conte was interviewed on television and admitted supplying Marion Jones with banned drugs. Jones denied the allegation and filed a $25 million defamation suit against Conte. It was subsequently settled out of court. In 2005, Conte pleaded guilty to conspiracy to distribute steroids and money laundering in a deal with federal prosecutors.

Marion Jones had always presented herself as vehemently anti-drugs and when the US Anti-Doping Agency started to investigate, she went on the offensive, daring them to charge her and boasting that she had never failed a single test. In 2004, in her autobiography, she went further and devoted one whole page, written in large red letters, to a denunciation of her involvement with drugs: 'I HAVE ALWAYS BEEN UNEQUIVOCAL IN MY OPINION: I AM AGAINST PERFORMANCE-ENHANCING DRUGS. I HAVE NEVER TAKEN THEM AND I NEVER WILL.'[7]

Following the Doping Agency's investigation, Jones was tried and pleaded guilty to lying about her use of steroids prior to the Sydney Olympics. She was convicted on 11 January 2008 and sentenced to six months in prison followed by two years' probation and community service for lying to the federal prosecutors investigating the use of performance-enhancing drugs.

In the introduction to his 2001 hagiography of Jones, Rapoport wrote, 'She drew me into her circle, put me in touch with her family, friends, former coaches and team-mates and spoke into my recorder at such length that finally on a rainy day at the North Carolina State University track in Raleigh, we looked at each other and laughed. I had no more questions and she had no more answers.'[8] In other words, he had no more questions because he knew all there was to know about Jones. But throughout the writing of the book, Marion Jones was, in fact, taking performance-enhancing drugs as was her then husband with the full knowledge of her coach Trevor Graham and supported by her nutritionist, Victor Conte. What does this tell us about her relationship with her biographer, Rapoport? Might she have used him to promote a myth about herself? If she didn't feel guilty that she duped Rapoport and abused his trust, why not? If she didn't feel guilty about cheating to win, why not?

If we switch 'god' to 'goddess', John Steiner's analysis of Oedipus at Colonus may throw light on Jones' state of mind. 'As he raises himself to the stature of a god, it becomes less and less appropriate for him to feel guilt. Gods are familiar with wrath but they can admit no wrong and guilt is foreign to them.'[9]

But how do such gods get that way? The infant's regular and constant interaction with the mother lays the foundation for trust. If all goes well, and the majority of experiences are positive, the child will develop trust, faith and confidence in those around them and this will become the cornerstone of their relationship to the wider world. However, if there is a significant disruption to that early containing environment – as in Oedipus's case – then trust can be compromised with potentially profoundly damaging consequences. Although the individual may seem to be adapting well at later stages of development and achieving success, the fundamental fragility of that core trust often remains invisible. Such individuals may never feel safe enough to put anyone but themselves first. For the anti-social personality, others are only ever a means to an end. For healthy guilt to come into play, there needs to be concern for others.

Donald Winnicott, a famous paediatrician and psychoanalyst, suggested that 'crime' was a reaction to deprivation and belonged to the childhood stage of dependence. He believed that the anti-social person had an early experience where something good (love and affection) was taken away (in fantasy, stolen) and that the anti-social act is an attempt to take it back. In other words, delinquent athletes steal the adulation/medals that they believe to be their due. Thus in a curious way there is a perverse logic to the unconscious need to cheat, a kind of justice in making good the deprivation experienced earlier in life.

Like many of our sporting giants, Marion Jones' childhood was something of a mess from a relational point of view. Her formidable physical and athletic prowess gave her the opportunity to transcend those difficult beginnings. However, athletic prowess may only suppress psychological distress, rather than resolve it. The internal legacy of those unresolved childhood dilemmas would later come back to haunt her.

Marion's mother, also called Marion, had already experienced a failed marriage – from which she had a son called Albert – when she met George Jones in 1972. Marion was born three years later. Apart from being a much older man, George was serially unreliable. Soon after they married and moved house, he upped and left. So began a pattern of unexplained comings and goings that continued until Marion's mother divorced George. Her mother then met Ira Toler, a retired postal worker. Toler, according to Rapoport, was much more than a father figure to young Marion. He effectively became her mother, as Marion senior was working as a legal secretary. Tragically for Marion junior, Ira died of a stroke when she was 11 years old. What made things even more difficult was the fact that her brother, Albert, was living with an uncle in Belize at the time. She told Rapoport that, after the death, she felt something was missing in her life.

It is more than likely that the absences and unreliability of her parental figures played a significant part not only in her early life but in the dramas that would later follow. It would seem Marion transferred a lot of her need for stability on to her elder brother, Albert. Her sporting gifts allowed her to integrate with Albert's friends and Albert came to see Marion as a younger brother. This led to some identity issues; Marion, according to her mother, found little girls too soft and so always preferred playing with boys. Might this indicate that she had already forsaken 'softness' for 'hardness' in her psychological make-up? By being invulnerable, Marion would not need to rely on others. Hardness was to be Marion's real rock on the road to both sporting greatness and hubris.

Susanna Abse, Director of the Tavistock Centre for Couples Relationships, claims that narcissists, 'because they are damaged and fearful, feel that the only safe way to operate is to put themselves at the centre of their universe'. She goes on to explain, 'These ruthless feelings are generated by a belief, sometimes deeply unconscious, that if they don't behave ruthlessly they will be done for by the other. As largely a defensive mode of relating, designed to protect the self from threat and pain, the defensive strategies are employed to protect the self from the knowledge and experience of vulnerability.'[10]

Rapoport recounts that, as a young child, Jones was enthralled by the wedding of Prince Charles and Diana Spencer in 1981. She asked her mother why a red carpet was rolled out for them and when it was explained that it was because Charles and Diana were very important people, Marion asked, 'Well, when I go places, why don't they roll it out for me?'[11] Marion Jones' whole athletic life might be understood as an all-consuming pursuit of that red carpet and the validation of her worth.

It might be suggested that Marion Jones took herself as the love object as a defence against the pain of loss and betrayal. She became 'number one' and everyone else became mere support acts. She fell in love with an image of herself walking the red carpet and there was no room for others on it. Like Narcissus, she fell in love with her own fantasy image and embarked on an ultimately sterile and deathly embrace. When Jones' husband would no longer collude with her dark, hard lie he was dumped. As for her biographer, he was simply duped along with every one else.

Sporting biographies often suffer from an all-too-familiar misconception, namely the tendency to interpret sporting success as a *resolution* and transcendence of tough childhoods. Rapoport describes how Jones had, from a very early age, an exceptional ability to focus on the job in hand, a quality Jones, herself calls 'living in the moment'.[12] This conjures up notions of that special sporting state of mind, 'being in the zone'. One of Jones' early reminiscences from childhood brilliantly illuminates this. 'I was always interested in whatever we were doing at the time . . . But I can't remember one specific moment with a friend. I really don't. Not as a child.'[13]

Those whose personalities develop what is known as 'a dismissive attachment style' are often found to lack real memories of relational incidents. These lack of interacting vignettes from childhood are important because, far from exhibiting a talent for being 'in the zone', they indicate a little girl predominantly preoccupied with herself and unable to connect meaningfully with other children. The precocious self-confidence in a young child – especially one who had suffered as many losses and absences as Jones – is no more than a defence against feelings of helplessness and inadequacy.

How might all those early difficulties have affected Marion Jones and how might they have contributed to her final denouement? One of the fascinating things about psychoanalysis is that the past can be seen alive and well in the present. It is a kind of invisible living history of our pain and sorrow. Our best efforts to keep this history locked away (rather than resolved) are only ever partial successes; the so-called Freudian slip is always there to remind us that there is another self at work behind the scenes.

Despite the incongruity of Jones' tale, it does have a chilling symmetry from a psychoanalytic perspective. In search of affirmation of self and attempting to make good her early deprivations and losses, she chose cheating and criminality.

Winnicott wrote that experience was traumatic if it was incomprehensible and beyond the child's grasp. The losses and absences that characterised Marion Jones' early life were surely beyond her comprehension. But like all young children, she would have manufactured an explanation for these events, erroneous though that explanation may well have been. It would most likely have centred on her part in the orchestration of proceedings. In other words, what have I done to make things unfold this way? Why do the people I love keep leaving (mother, father and brother), dying (Ira Toler) or show no interest in me (father)? Her astonishing success as a sportswoman provided the antidote to being unworthy, unwanted and uninteresting. It was her way of getting on the red carpet. Being applauded and appreciated was confirmation of her success, her goodness and her very existence. But it was a Faustian pact; without the winning, there was no applause. To be certain of winning, she needed to take drugs for, ultimately, she had no real belief in her own self-worth.

The tragedy of Marion Jones' story is that she ended up exactly where she started. She started with loss, helplessness, inadequacy and apparently no conscious guilt; after a stellar athletic career, she ended up back at the beginning. Her successes (medals) were taken away; she lost her reputation, her money and temporarily her freedom. Perhaps more importantly, she inflicted a potentially traumatic loss on her own two young children. The chilling symmetry is that she has unwittingly re-enacted an unconscious fantasy that the reason she suffered so many losses and absences as a child was because she was a bad person.

Is it possible that Jones, and other drug cheats, feel no guilt whatsoever? Freud, writing in *Civilisation and its Discontents* (1930), tried to address this issue. He came up with the then radical new idea of unconscious guilt, that the patient's self-sabotaging behaviour was evidence of an unconscious need for punishment to neutralise unconscious feelings of guilt. Such individuals have a tendency unconsciously to inflict suffering on themselves to defend against such feelings of guilt on a conscious level.

By taking banned performance-enhancing drugs, Marion Jones was engaging in both self-damaging and self-sabotaging behaviour. She may consciously have believed she would get away with cheating and breaking the law; like many who place themselves at the centre of the universe, she may have felt she was above the rules. However, once she transgressed, she invited the possibility of being caught. Her behaviour would eventually lead her to being imprisoned and shamed as an unworthy fake. Strange though it may seem, from an unconscious point of view, it was as if she preferred to face imprisonment than face her own guilt.

Why should guilt be so unbearable? The answer to this question brings us full circle. Internally, the individual has such a low self-opinion and fragile sense of self that he or she cannot accept any wrongdoing or criticism without feeling completely worthless. Sadly, despite the aura of invincibility she so carefully created, it would appear that at a deeper, unconscious level Jones probably never really believed in either herself or her myth and eventually sabotaged success to confirm her worthlessness.

Many have argued that sprinters are getting close to the limit of what is physically possible in a 100m race. The next potential minefield is gene therapy. Recent experiments with mice have produced substantial improvements in strength, speed and endurance.

There are no certainties and short cuts to dealing with the problem of drug cheats because sickness in the psyche equates to sickness of spirit and that is not a state confined to sports. Top class sport, because of the kind of demands it makes on the individual and the kind of 'psychological' rewards on offer, attracts more than its fair share of the psychically troubled. As such, there will be many more Ben Johnsons and Marion Joneses to come. Such athletes choose the hard body, protecting the omnipotent fantasy that they're invulnerable even if it involves lying and cheating.

With Marion Jones and other drug cheats, things quickly spiral out of control. Athletes as a group are particularly resistant to help and treatment, perhaps believing that they may lose strength by exposing insecurity and anxiety and allowing someone in to help them. A close analogy is the story of Samson, who believes he'll lose his strength if his hair is cut (the fact he does lose his strength just confirms the power of belief). Such athletes generally prefer to rely on themselves, feed off their own achievement, and – in the most extreme cases – see no boundaries as to how success is achieved. Some, instead of seeking help and treatment for anxiety, eating disorders, performance inhibition, depression or other neuroses, indulge in ritualised, superstitious behaviour as a means of managing the unmanageable. Others may take things a little further and cheat to fast-track success.

Freud emphasised that the resistance to treatment stems from doubts about self-worth. What Freud was trying to understand was why 'patients cling to their disease.'[14] He suggested that the symptoms of a disease represented a sort of deal. The symptoms were the price the patient paid for being spared more painful feelings. 'It is hard for the ego to direct its attention to perceptions and ideas which it has, up 'til now, made a rule of avoiding, or to acknowledge as belonging to itself impulses that are the complete opposite of those which it knows as its own.'[15]

Returning to our latest superhero, is it self-love or simply relief at not failing when Usain Bolt preens and struts as he nears the finishing line? Narcissus was said to be the most beautiful male on earth. One day, when he became thirsty, he sought out a stream to drink in but as soon as he saw his own reflection, he fell hopelessly in love. When he tried to kiss the object of his desire, the face disappeared. It seemed as if it had simply run away. Although he grew ever thirstier, spurned Narcissus refused to touch the water in case he drove his love further away. He eventually died of thirst and self-love, staring at his own reflection.

In a *Times* article in August 2008, the new superhero, the mythical archer sending bolts from the blue, is quoted as saying, 'I pray each night [for God] to keep me strong. They say He helps them who help themselves.'

Ian Williamson's Casebook – Michael

A few years ago a boy was referred for psychoanalytic treatment because he had been caught hacking into the school's computer system with intent to change his grades from mediocre to excellent. He had done this via his housemaster's computer. What was extraordinary was that he had set out to gain the housemaster's trust in order to carry out the scam so it was in no sense an impulsive act but had all the cunning of a Marion Jones guerrilla campaign. This was his second brush with the school authorities, having been expelled from another school for dealing drugs.

Most of what he expressed in the early months of treatment was anger; anger that he had been caught and anger that others were doing the same things and getting away with it. The boy made endless rants about injustice and the system being screwed, and about his contempt for those in authority over him. I became frustrated and concerned that he seemed unable to see or feel the inherent 'wrongness' of his actions and, more importantly, to locate any sense of guilt.

It took a long while before Michael could feel any sense of remorse for his actions and even longer before he could reveal the insecurity and sadness that lay beneath his behaviour. Through time, a much more complex picture emerged. Far from being a teenager hell bent on anarchy, he was beset by extreme anxieties about himself and his self-worth. His peer group relationships were precarious and intensely rivalrous. He quickly became paranoid at the slightest difficulty in a friendship, fearing plots and betrayal. He felt unable to acknowledge his real worth instead focusing solely on his peers' alleged superiority. He painfully admitted during one session to repeatedly watching the Godfather films before going out. The images and feelings associated with the part of Michael Corleone acted like a social Viagra and gave him the necessary confidence to be potent in the group. He would imagine what Michael Corleone might say or do and then act accordingly. Corleone, of course, was an anti-hero, a ruthless operator, who removed anyone who got in the way of his wishes and desires. At other times, Michael carried round a picture of Brad Pitt in his back pocket which would be used, like the Corleone image, to boost his flagging self-esteem. Armed with these tools, he could compete. He was now a genuine 'player'.

The flaws in this strategy were self-evident, as he himself recognised. If it worked, he would be in a constant state of anxiety fearing he would be found out. He dreaded being outed as an impostor; someone so pathetic as to have to pretend to be someone else. But, of course, pretending to be someone else did little or nothing for the real Michael, so in a way all his achievements felt completely empty and meaningless.

The key to Michael's difficulties was to be found in his early experiences. Two in particular stood out as being crucial. His mother had had cancer when he was two and there was some doubt as to whether she would survive. As a consequence, he went to live with his aunt for eight months. A year after his mother recovered, she became pregnant and the severity of her medical history meant that she remained in hospital for the last three months of her pregnancy. Both these traumatic events were central to an understanding of the breakdown in Michael's trust in those around him and in the wider world. His experience of losing his central attachment figure – his mother – eroded his trust in relationships.

It would be wonderful to write that Michael recovered and went on to lead a successful life but, sadly, therapy is full of failures; sometimes therapists get it wrong but, more often, the power of the need to repeat the trauma is too great. As trust between Michael and myself grew and feelings of guilt began to emerge, Michael suddenly broke off treatment. Without a phone call or a message, he stopped attending his appointments. It was as if he needed to show me what it felt like to be abandoned and let down.

I heard nothing more from him until several years later when I received a letter saying he had joined the Royal Marines. Like Corleone, the Royal Marines were a perfect 'hard' home for a hard anti-hero. By choosing a career in 'defence' (defence of the realm) Michael chose the route of reinforcing his defence against softness and vulnerability. In a way, this is what athletes often do by turning against the soft, vulnerable parts of themselves. Michael chose the Marines; Marion Jones and Ben Johnson chose another form of deception.

4

THE ICE MAIDEN

Sporting rivalry – the deadliest of games

*'If one cannot be the favourite oneself, at all
events nobody else shall be the favourite.'*

Sigmund Freud

On 6 January 1994, around 200 people gathered in the Cobo
Arena in Detroit to watch the triallists for the US Olympic
figure skating team going through their final practice
routines. As the crowd's favourite, Nancy Kerrigan, stepped off
the ice, a man rushed towards her with a police baton and,
seconds later, the sound of metal on bone echoed round the arena.
The assailant rushed down the hallway to a set of locked doors,
used his head as a battering ram to break through the Plexiglas,
and escaped into the city.

Great sporting rivalries evoke a passionate intensity that is
often irrational, sometimes frightening but never less than
gripping. The greatest rivalries provide the seminal moments in
each sport: the bitter and brutal battles between Muhammad Ali
and Joe Frazier; the timeless tennis tussles between iceman Bjorn

Borg and explosive John McEnroe; and the seemingly suicidal jockeying for Formula One supremacy between Ayrton Senna and Alain Prost.

The reason such contests engage us so intensely is because they appeal to something powerful inside us all. We have all experienced the extra-competitive and emotional edge that comes with battling our closest rivals. On the football field, it's invariably the nearest neighbour – Celtic/Rangers, Liverpool/Everton, Roma/Lazio – that provides the spiciest encounter.

At the heart of all sporting rivalries are intense, often extremely aggressive feelings allied to an almost pathological need to be 'the special one', the top dog. These feelings are invariably set in granite in the dynamic of early sibling rivalry. The hate, the love, the competition we feel towards others is nurtured not only in our relations with parents but with our siblings. Within the family, this rivalry can at times feel as murderous as that between Cain and Abel but most of us manage to control it even if we never fully resolve it. An awareness of this dynamic helps us understand the elements that drive intense sporting competition.

The arrival of a younger brother or sister shatters the comfortable and secure feeling of 'specialness' or 'onlyness'. With the arrival of a sibling, a small child's emotional world becomes immeasurably more complex and fraught as he/she experiences a threat to his/her very existence. Of course, the new arrival faces problems of their own, too, as the physically stronger, more skilled older sibling is a far more experienced rival for parental preference. Athletic rivalry can be understood as an extension of this primitive battle to become the favoured child. In *Madmen and Medusas*, Juliet Mitchell starkly sums up, 'When a child is replaced by a sibling, initially this feels like annihilation; "murder" is the reaction of the fittest.'[1]

In the sporting arena, 'winning' is the psychic equivalent of achieving that goal. For most of us, failing to achieve victory may be experienced as no more than disappointment and irritation. For someone with powerful unresolved sibling issues, however, the spectre of failure may well be a trauma too far which needs avoiding at all costs.

Most rivalries end when the final whistle is heard; there are handshakes and an exchange of shirts, irrespective of the hype and bile beforehand. Occasionally, however, the thin veneer of civility and decency cracks to reveal a darker and more primitive side, namely the wish to eliminate the other by foul means or fair. In this chapter, we'll examine what is going on when rivalry becomes a matter of life and death and an ice skater – Tonya Harding – is implicated in a plot to have her main challenger taken out of the Olympics with the help of a retractable baton.

At the time of the incident, Nancy Kerrigan's career was seemingly peaking perfectly in time for the Lillehammer 1994 Olympics. An extremely talented child skater, she had won a bronze medal at the 1992 Albertville Winter Olympics, finished second in the World Championships and had won the Nationals in 1991. Her poise and grace on the ice, together with her media-friendly skills, made her the darling of the press and public as well as the early favourite for the Lillehammer Games.

In their book *Thin Ice*, Frank Coffey and Joe Layden outline the facts surrounding Tonya Harding's childhood: that she came from a broken home, lived in a trailer park in Oregon and was nobody's darling. The family was desperately poor and her mother, LaVona, was widely reported as abusive (although she has vigorously denied this admitting to only once hitting her daughter with a hairbrush). Her father, Al, drifted from job to job and was plagued by health problems while Tonya's own fragility manifested itself in asthma, a condition often associated with stress. Harding had started a new school almost every year and moved home 13 times by the time she was 16. She did, however, have one thing going for her: she was a hugely talented, athletic but erratic skater who had eyes fixed firmly on the 1994 Olympics. After two decades as an amateur, the 1994 Cobo Arena meeting was the competition she had to win to make the Olympic team, secure her place in history and make a lot of money.

In the run-up to the competition, Harding was in bullish mood. There were no platitudes about 'If all goes well . . .' or 'Hopefully . . .' Instead, she boasted that she would win the National title and then the Olympic gold. Harding was thought by many to be a better skater than Kerrigan but her inconsistency showed in head-to-head competition where her rival had a 7-2 edge. Thus, despite Harding's confidence going into the championships in Detroit, Nancy Kerrigan was still the clear favourite. Many assumed Kerrigan's classic good looks and poise was the product of blue-blood stock but, in fact, her upbringing was blue collar. But Kerrigan had what Harding must have yearned for: secure relationships, a stable family supporting her and huge popularity.

Following the attack, Nancy Kerrigan was rushed to hospital where an initial examination showed that the blow had badly bruised, but not seriously damaged, the muscle above the right knee. The attack, however, threw the championships into turmoil. Kerrigan would not only be unable to compete in the competition, she also risked losing a guaranteed place in the Olympic team. With Kerrigan now out of the way, Harding put in a near flawless performance to take gold in the championships and secure her spot on the Olympic team.

Kerrigan recovered from the attack quickly and was back in training within 10 days. Then, in an unprecedented move, the US figure skating officials controversially decided that since Kerrigan's injuries were the result of a criminal assault rather than a skating accident, she would be permitted to compete at the Olympics in Lillehammer, demonstrating that having favourites was not confined to the family home. Up until then, it had been an unshakeable policy of all US Olympic team selection that competitors had to qualify at trials and even greats such as sprinter Carl Lewis had suffered as a result of the policy. The officials, however, had a groundswell of popular opinion behind them and the decision may also have been influenced by the fact that nine months earlier, tennis star Monica Seles had been stabbed by Gunther Parche in an attempt to remove her from competition so that Steffi Graf could return to the top of the world tennis rankings.

There was wild speculation about who could have wanted to injure Kerrigan. Noting the fact the attack had targeted her take-off and landing leg, newspapers were quick to suggest it might be the work of a rival or a deranged fan. It was not uncommon for top female skaters to get hate mail and stalkers. Tonya herself had reported receiving a phone threat only two months prior to the US championships and had subsequently hired a bodyguard for protection.

Within a week, the drama took a decidedly bizarre turn. The police announced they were now looking for an Arizona bounty hunter named Shane Stant in connection with the assault. Stant turned himself in and made a surprising confession, claiming that the attack was part of a plot involving Tonya Harding, her husband and her bodyguard. According to Stant, Harding had been involved from the beginning and had invented her own phone threat to make Kerrigan's attack look part of a pattern.

The extraordinary sequence of events hints at something beyond the intensity of athletic competition. Harding's attempt to eliminate Kerrigan from the competition, if true, may have been an expression of a desperate need to feel not just special but 'the most special'. This is a significant distinction because the feeling of being special can be a shared experience – I can win one day and feel special but someone else will be special the next time – but the need to be 'the most special' can only belong to one individual. The need to be 'the most special', the need to annihilate all rivals, is the credo of the top champion.

Within three weeks of the attack, four men had been arrested by the police and one of them, Shawn Eckardt, told the FBI that the plot had been hatched with Harding's husband, Jeff Gillooly, in order to remove Kerrigan from the competition. Eckardt and Gillooly had been friends since childhood and the former later implicated Harding in the plot. The Olympic Committee, having already resolved the tricky dilemma of Kerrigan's selection, were now faced with the problem of what to do about Harding who was being drawn ever closer to the scandal. The committee decided to exclude her from the team but changed its mind when Harding's lawyers threatened them with a $20 million lawsuit.

The investigation was gathering pace as both Kerrigan and Harding arrived in Lillehammer. Harding was accompanied by her trainer, her choreographer, her lawyer and a whole host of media representatives, the closest the skater had to a supportive family. Harding and Kerrigan both requested separate training times but this was denied and they eventually met on the ice on 16 February. The tension between the pair was palpable as they sat at opposite ends for the team photo. When Kerrigan was asked about the extent of their relationship, she replied to the effect that there was no relationship. The stage was set for the ultimate showdown, dubbed the 'Battle of Wounded Knee II'.

Some 204 million viewers tuned into the CBS coverage of the Lillehammer Olympics, making it the most watched Winter Games ever. After the opening day's short technical programme, Kerrigan led from world champion, Oksana Baiul of the Ukraine. Harding, meanwhile, had been out of sorts and was back in tenth spot. On the final day, Kerrigan again skated flawlessly and, with bated breath, commentator Scott Hamilton, assuming the gold was hers, told millions of viewers, 'Olympic dreams *do* come true.' The fairytale, however, turned out to belong to the 16-year-old world champion, Oksana Baiul, who shaded it by one-tenth of a point.

Harding improved marginally to eighth place but her final performance was flawed. After sobbing uncontrollably, she went across to the judges to show them her broken lace. Astonishingly, she was allowed to restart her performance. Bad luck, poor preparation ... what did this broken lace signify? Great sporting contests are often decided by the appearance of something defining yet inexplicable: a burst tyre; the broken string of a racket; a slip on the turf. Perhaps what Harding was protesting about, from an unconscious point of view, was that something important in her life had been broken and needed fixing and that it simply wasn't fair that once again another girl was being allowed to be the 'special one'. Whatever the reason, Kerrigan went home with silver while Harding went home with nothing to face charges of conspiracy to interfere with the investigation of the assault on Kerrigan.

In the aftermath of the competition, Kerrigan's mantle of civility and grace slipped as she complained that the judges hadn't noticed the perfection of her performance, nor Baiul's mistakes. Harding's skullduggery quite possibly plunged Kerrigan back into a primitive family scrap. She had previously donned the elder child's guise, hiding her competitiveness and rivalry beneath a social façade of being the nicest and best behaved daughter. Her attack now took the moral high ground in the sibling battle but the subtext was still 'I deserve it more'.

In his book *Born to Rebel,* Frank Sulloway states that the position in the family is overwhelmingly the most influential factor in determining later development. Sulloway suggests that, throughout history, we can discern a pattern of the eldest being the competitive, dominant, conforming conservative; while the later-born are literally 'born to rebel', questioning the old guard and creating new paradigms. Kerrigan revealed herself to be adept at using the elder child strategy in her war with her ice skating 'siblings'.

Ian Williamson's Casebook – Charlie

Charlie, aged five, had been having a great deal of difficulty settling into his first class and his exasperated parents sought help because other children had been complaining of him hitting and biting them. Charlie was the eldest of three. His younger brother, Harry, was 3 years old and his sister, Natasha, 18 months.

The usual practice concerning younger children brought to the consulting room is for the parents to help them get settled and then leave. Charlie arrived with his parents but, because of difficulties with childcare arrangements, they also brought Harry with them.

Charlie was clearly a confident and eager little boy. He made straight for the toys and started arranging the wild animals into groups. I asked if he knew why he was coming to see me and he nodded without looking up. Harry, meanwhile, climbed down from his mother's lap and attempted to join in the play. In doing so he accidentally(?) knocked over a group of animals. Charlie stood up and immediately cussed him: 'You stupid idiot. I hate you.' Charlie then pushed his younger brother hard in the chest, sending him sprawling and smacking the side of his head against the table. Harry screamed out with the pain and shock but Charlie appeared unperturbed, standing over his younger brother like a boxer over a felled opponent.

The mother rushed to Harry's aid, picking him up and cradling the sobbing child on her lap. Father, meanwhile, was reprimanding Charlie and demanding an apology. Charlie remained silent for a moment but eventually mumbled a reluctant 'sorry' under continued pressure from his father. Both parents were visibly shaken and apologised profusely for Charlie's behaviour. They insisted the boys really did love each other and at home Charlie couldn't be a more loving brother.

I suggested to Charlie that he seemed to have some very strong feelings about Harry messing with his toys. Charlie looked up at me and nodded his head affirmatively.

I asked Charlie if he minded staying with me for a little bit without the rest of the family. He appeared genuinely relieved when his parents left the consulting room and quickly resumed rearranging the wild animals in a circle, explaining that they had to be this way to keep other animals out. He went on to show me that the animals outside the circle all wanted to get inside to take all the food. I made the obvious link to Harry trying to get inside his space and messing things up. Charlie stopped for a moment and said that Harry was always messing things up and that he constantly cried for attention whenever Charlie tried to stop him from spoiling his games. Charlie complained that invariably he was then blamed for upsetting Harry by his mother who insisted that they play together.

As he was informing me of the sibling drama, Charlie's play with the animals grew increasingly aggressive. The beasts were now fighting and Charlie was lost in his play, battling to keep the intruders out. Some were killed and thrown across the room. After several minutes of intense play, Charlie stopped, looked at me and said that he had got rid of the bad animals now. I said that he must sometimes wish he could get rid of Harry like that. He agreed and added that he didn't like having a brother but that his sister was OK.

Intuitively, it is hard to view this consulting room drama as anything other than a 'murderous' sibling confrontation. Harry's arrival had made a mess of Charlie's life and he would like to rid himself of his rival's presence. This symbolic acting out is expressed through his play with the toy animals. However, the drama in the consulting room also displays the parental denial of hostilities and, by not acknowledging them (or at least not being open to their possibility), the conflict is driven underground.

Four men eventually served time in prison for the assault on Kerrigan: bounty hunter Shane Stant; his uncle, who drove the getaway car; Harding's bodyguard, who'd hired Stant; and Harding's ex-husband, Jeff Gillooly, who engineered the crime. 'Team Harding', Tonya's motley surrogate family, failed her just like her real family always seemed to and duplicity, as always, shot the 'family' to pieces. Initially, after his arrest, Gillooly tried to protect Harding but on learning that his ex-wife had already testified against him to the FBI, he changed his story and said that she had known all about the plot from the outset and had approved it.

In a plea bargain agreement with the Multnomah County Court, Harding pleaded guilty to hindering the investigation and was sentenced to three years' supervised probation, a $100,000 fine, a $50,000 donation to a fund to benefit the Special Olympics, $10,000 court costs and 500 hours' community service work.

The question whether Harding actually planned the assault remains unproven. However, the US Figure Skating Association held a nine-hour hearing in which it was decided she had intentionally contravened the concept of sportsmanship and fair play in relation to the assault on Nancy Kerrigan. In short, Harding 'had prior knowledge and was involved prior to the incident'.[2] As a result, she was stripped of her 1994 title and banned for life from USFA events.

Prior to this extraordinary event, Harding had won the US figure skating championships twice and had been runner-up in the 1991 World Championships. To all intents and purposes, she was enjoying a glittering career. But the pressure of top-class sporting competition is relentless in exposing cracks and insecurities in the psyche. Whatever possessed this talented young woman to cross the line in such a way? And does an unbearable and destructive envy of Nancy Kerrigan tell us something fundamental about the nature of sporting rivalries, why they flood some athletes and not others? Money and fame are just the most obvious, superficial aspects of the picture but there is something deeper and more primitive at work.

As mentioned earlier, Tonya did not get the best start in life. Her family was at the bottom of the heap and, within that family, Tonya was at the bottom, the youngest of five children. The attack on Kerrigan, if Harding had indeed been involved in the planning, can be seen as an attempt to take pole position in her mother's affections but, if this was the case, it was certainly a desperate throw of the dice.

The template for the sibling drama is most clearly seen in the Cain and Abel story, our earliest tale of fratricide. Cain was Eve's first son and Abel her youngest. It was the latter's lot to take care of the flocks while his older brother cultivated the land. The way the story is told in the Bible, it is God's favour the children seek, but we easily recognise the contours in relation to a parental figure – God the Father. 'In the course of time, Cain brought to the Lord an offering of the fruit of the ground, and Abel brought of the firstlings of his flock and of their fat. And the Lord had regard for Abel and his offering, but for Cain and his offering he had no regard.' (Genesis 4:3-4)

What happened next is as rich a description of the passions of sibling rivalry as one could hope to find. 'Cain was very angry, and his countenance fell. The Lord said to Cain, "Why are you angry, and why has your countenance fallen? If you do well, will you not be accepted? And if you do not do well, sin is crouching at the door; its desire is for you, but you must master it."' (Genesis 4:6-7)

The question why the Lord would favour one of his children over the other, though fascinating, is not our concern here. What is important is the issue of Cain being displaced as the family favourite. God effectively tells Cain to get on with his life and not let the destructive passions of sibling rivalry engulf him. Unfortunately, the strength of Cain's feelings do overwhelm him with disastrous consequences. 'Cain said to Abel his brother, "Let us go out to the field." And when they were in the field, Cain rose up against his brother Abel and killed him. Then the Lord said to Cain, "Where is Abel your brother?" Cain replied, "I do not know: am I my brother's keeper?"' (Genesis 4: 8-9)

God becomes angry with Cain and tells him the ground will no longer yield to him and he must be a fugitive and a wanderer. When Cain protests that being 'hidden from God's face' is more than he could bear and he fears he would be slain without his father's protection, God says, '"Not so! If anyone slays Cain, vengeance shall be taken on him sevenfold." And the Lord put a mark on Cain in case any who came upon him should kill him. Then Cain went away from the presence of the Lord, and dwelt in the land of Nod, east of Eden.' (Genesis 4:4-15)

In essence, Cain killed his brother because he couldn't bear the fact that he couldn't be number one. It is a story that speaks of the intensity of the rivalry between siblings, and the genesis of many famous sporting rivalries often have their roots in these unresolved passions. The wish to be the parent's favourite, the number one, can be a bloody battle at the heart of which are murderous feelings and the wish to annihilate the rival. The sporting lexicon is full of the vivid imagery of this brutal and bloody conflict. The opposition were 'crushed'. He was 'ruthless' in his demolition of his opponent . . . and so on.

Perhaps above all sporting rivalries, the Ayrton Senna/Alain Prost Formula One motor racing battles stand out both for the ferocity of their mutual hatred but also because of the terminal nature of the end game. Senna was a great driver whose legendary status was assured when he became deified following his premature death at the age of 34 after a crash in the San Marino Grand Prix in May 1994. But it was his battles with Alain Prost that really caught the public imagination.

The rivals were generally depicted as opposites. Senna was the charismatic, colourful Brazilian; ruthless, obsessive and impulsive. Prost was softly spoken, controlled and nicknamed 'The Professor' because he was the calculating master-tactician. Their hatred of each other was no media fiction. Prost was alleged to have said, 'Metaphorically, Senna wanted to destroy me.'[3] Their races certainly seemed to hint at times at something more literal than metaphorical. Their 1988 battle at Estoril is just one example. At the end of the first lap, Prost tried to overtake Senna as they were passing the pits but Senna would not give way and instead swung wide and tried to force Prost into the pit wall. Prost accelerated and just squeezed past. Those who were there that day say that less than 15cm separated them from potential disaster. Commenting on the race afterwards, Prost said, 'Ayrton, I didn't realise you wanted the championship that badly.'[4]

Nothing epitomised their antipathy more than their confrontations at Suzuka in 1989 and 1990. Both men qualified on the front row of the 1989 race but Prost got away more quickly and Senna was left chasing for most of the race. With six laps remaining, Senna raced into the fast left-hand bend just before the pit chicane in an attempt to pass his foe. Prost was determined not to let Senna through and closed the gap. The two cars slid to a halt in the middle of the track their wheels locked together like the horns of beasts. As both men had failed to finish, Prost climbed out his car, believing that the championship was his. Senna, however, eventually managed to rejoin the race and went on to pass the chequered flag first. This was not the end of the drama, though, as Senna was disqualified for rejoining the race at the wrong place. An appeal followed but Senna was fined $100,000 and received a suspended six-month driving ban. Prost was rewarded with the world title.

On the back of this perceived favouritism (Senna believed that the President of the FIA, Frenchman Jean-Marie Balestre, had favoured his fellow countryman), Senna made it clear that the following season he would exact revenge at some point. That point curiously came at Suzuka again. On the morning of the race, Senna effectively threatened Prost, telling the assembled press that if Prost were to get to the first corner before him and try to move inside, he would not make it. Sure enough, that is exactly what happened; finding Prost ahead of him at the first corner, Senna rammed him off the track. Senna became world champion but this time the FIA took no action claiming it was a 'racing incident'.

What made the Prost/Senna rivalry so intense was their willingness literally to risk their lives rather than lose to their hated adversary. Sadly, Senna eventually did lose his life while leading the San Marino Grand Prix in 1994.

Freud is rightly credited with having brought to light the importance of sibling rivalry. Writing in *The Interpretation of Dreams*, he claimed that he had never known a man or woman who did not dream of murdering his or her siblings. 'Children are completely egoistic; they feel their needs intensely and strive ruthlessly to satisfy them – especially against the rivals, other children, and first and foremost against their brothers and sisters.'[5]

Freud himself was haunted throughout his life by his rivalry with his first playmate, his nephew John, 18 months his senior; and also far more importantly by the death of his younger brother Julius. 'I greeted my one-year-old brother [who died after a few months] with adverse wishes and genuine childhood jealousy . . . that his death left the germ of self-reproaches in me.'[6]

In sibling battles, Freud observed, 'The elder child ill-treats the younger and maligns him and robs him of his toys; while the younger is consumed with impotent rage against the elder, envies him and fears him.'[7] In another of his works, Freud put it even more succinctly, 'If one cannot be the favourite oneself, at all events nobody else shall be the favourite.'[8]

Juliet Mitchell's notion of familial feelings of 'murder and madness' is consequent upon a failure to manage the sibling universal rite of passage. A successful resolution marks the entry by the child – and thus the adult he or she becomes – into a more collaborative and co-operative world. Others can now be friends and colleagues rather than rivals. But when the passion of sibling rivalry is not mediated, then paranoia, violence and persecution become the cornerstones of the psyche: suspicion reigns, conspiracy abounds. In short, rivals are seen as forever plotting to steal or take over.

The 1972 battle for the World Chess Championship between the American, Bobby Fischer, and the Russian, Boris Spassky, possessed all of those ingredients – persecution, paranoia, conspiracy and suspicion – and more. It was a psychological drama worthy of a Hitchcock thriller played out to a global audience. Fischer was the first Westerner seriously to threaten the Soviet dominance of a game that symbolised for the USSR the superiority of Communism over Capitalism.

Fischer was fully aware of the political importance of the match and this just seemed to accentuate his reputation for being an eccentric, intransigent, uncommunicative and unco-operative loner. Initially, he refused to fly to Reykjavik until all his demands regarding playing conditions had been met (the US Secretary of State, Henry Kissinger, even had to intervene at one point to encourage Fischer to go and play). Whether this was a deliberate tactic or not is unclear, but it undoubtedly had the effect of unsettling Spassky.

Fischer eventually arrived late, missed the opening ceremony, lost the opening game and forfeited the second saying that the film cameras were distracting him. Fischer continued to make complaints about the chairs, the noise, the chess pieces and the audience. Such was his state of mind that he seriously considered forfeiting the match and returning home. At this point, however, Fischer's paranoia and tyrannical demands seemed to start working to his advantage as Spassky became increasingly unsettled by the eccentric behaviour. The third game was played in a back room away from the cameras and Fischer won. Although the rest of the games were played in the main hall, this break effectively turned the match and Fischer went on to dominate proceedings. By the end of the 20th game, Fischer only needed one point from the last four matches to win. Spassky knew he was beaten.

The match should have been the beginning of a great chess career but, instead, it was the end. Fischer's defeat of Spassky marked the pinnacle of his chess career but arguably its effect psychologically destroyed him. Extraordinarily, after all the drama and success of this battle, Fischer defaulted his title in a scheduled match in 1975 against the Russian challenger Karpov without even playing a game and he did not play another competitive chess match for 20 years. He refused endorsements, turned down lucrative offers and demanded extraordinarily exorbitant fees to play exhibitions.

Fischer was undoubtedly a chess genius but he was also a troubled man. His father and mother divorced when he was two (there was also some doubt about who his biological father was) and he and his elder sister, Joan, were brought up by their mother. He became US chess champion at the age of 13 and went on to win the crown eight more times. At the time he was assessed as having an IQ higher than Einstein. In everything he did, he found confirmation that he was indeed 'the special one'.

At 16 he dropped out of school and, at the same time, his mother moved out to pursue her medical studies. He allegedly slept in all three beds in rotation, keeping a different chessboard with a game – and battle – in play by each. Clearly, the youngest member of the family, the 'baby,' was mightily indulged and expected things to go his way.

In the match with Spassky, Fischer's psyche resembled that of a three- or four-year-old: obsessive, argumentative and controlling over his environment and those around him.

The fact that Fischer's chess career – and, in many respects, his life – effectively ended after the match might suggest that his chess genius, and the feeling of superiority that came with it, was hijacked by the imperative psychological need to protect an illusion of 'eternal specialness'. One suspects that he was also aware, at least from an unconscious point of view, he could lose that mantle if he continued to play. Having destroyed Spassky and therefore cemented his psychological position as number one, perhaps he was unwilling to put that position at risk again. Maybe chess and the world title meant so much to him that he couldn't bear the prospect of losing it. In sporting terms, he retired undefeated after one contest. Once he had forfeited the title to Karpov, he became ever more reclusive and paranoid, and died aged 64.

Returning now to Tonya Harding, the critical question that

needs addressing is why she reputedly crossed the line that separates internal from external reality and allowed sporting rivalry to spiral out of control.

Tonya was clearly unfairly handicapped from the beginning with a life marked by violence, poverty and instability. Such a background was rare among an élite skating world which was more generally populated by privileged girls, bred for greatness. This probably only accentuated Tonya's feeling of not being good enough. Finding herself among a new 'family' of well cared for, well supported and wealthy siblings, the search for confirmation for goodness, worthiness – indeed, specialness – would have become increasingly strident. Psychologically, these needs could probably only be ameliorated by 'winning'.

It is likely that the specific details of her early life, and particularly the relationship with her mother, hold the key to the drama of 'Wounded Knee'. Tonya and her mother fought constantly. The chaos of family life reached new levels when Tonya, aged 16, returned home one day to find that her mother had left with all the furniture. In a later interview, she said, 'I stayed with my dad . . . mom didn't want anything to do with me.'[9]

A damaging, complex and disturbing dynamic continued to be played out between mother and daughter throughout her career. LaVona, as mentioned earlier, is contentiously documented as being physically abusive. What would appear to be in less doubt is that she frequently verbally put Tonya down and told her that she would never achieve anything in life.

Coffey and Layden, in their book, *Thin Ice*, recount a conversation between Tonya and her coach Diane Rawlinson in her hotel room soon after Tonya had received a phone call from her mother chastising her for coming sixth in a New York competition:

> 'Mom said that . . . um . . . she goes: "So I heard you missed your combination. You know you didn't get any credit at all for that."

'And I said, "Mom!"
'And she goes, "You did terrible, you know that! You
sucked!"
'And I said, "Mom, I got half a credit for it."
'She goes, "So the rest of the programme sucked also . . ."'[10]

Coach Rawlinson recounts that as Tonya reported the conversation to her, she seemed less like a woman on the brink of
national athletic prominence and more like a frightened and
wounded little girl. After the conversation, Tonya apparently sat
motionless on the bed, wringing her hands and staring into space.

Skating was more than a passionate interlude in Tonya's life.
When she was skating and winning, she could be someone else. The
applause of the crowd and marks from the judges drowned out the
voice of her mother berating her for never being any good. Beating
her rivals gave her a fleeting feeling of being number one, of being
the best. Her mother's constant denigration would inevitably leave
Tonya not only with a sense of not being good enough but also an
overwhelming grievance that the world was not fair.

The other side of constant denigration is that somewhere a
fantasy entity is created that one measures oneself against; an
invisible being who represents the benchmark of what is good
and special. Much as Harding's mother put her down, somewhere in LaVona and Tonya's minds there existed an idealised
fantasy daughter better than Tonya could ever be; a sister that
Tonya could in no way ever compete with or emulate. Nancy
Kerrigan probably became, in Harding's mind, the embodiment
of that imaginary sister, a sister who stood between her and
salvation through winning. James Golden, who later became
LaVona's husband and Tonya's stepfather, commented that if
Tonya had had the charisma and charm of Nancy Kerrigan, she
would have been on top a long time ago. To Harding's mind,
Kerrigan was probably not just a sporting rival but rather the
embodiment of everything that Tonya could never be, thus
probably evoking hatred and envy in equal measure.

When the experience of envy is excessive, it can be extremely destructive and can evoke a need to 'destroy' the envied or steal the thing most envied. Pathological envy is at the extreme end of the spectrum and a central part of the psychological dynamic behind celebrity killings. This kind of narcissistic pathology requires an endless supply of admiration, adulation and affirmation. But being feared or derided can also provide the fuel in this search for attention and applause. If fame cannot be had, notoriety is next best. The gap between grandiose fantasies and dreary and humiliating reality becomes emotionally insupportable. By destroying a celebrity, the killer destroys the object of their pathological envy. Mark Chapman asked John Lennon for his autograph and then shot him four times in the back hours later. If he couldn't be John Lennon then nobody else could be either.

Despite Harding's protestations to the contrary, she was never realistically capable of competing with Kerrigan from a psychological viewpoint because, in her mind, Kerrigan was probably not just another competitor but a representation of the perfect fantasy sister of whom she was deeply envious.

The physical and emotional mistreatment LaVona reputedly administered would have left an indelible mark on Tonya's internal world. As well as a poor self-image allied to a lack of trust in herself and others, the reality was probably that in Tonya's mind she was forever doomed to lose in competition with her mother's fantasy daughter. Try as she might to succeed, at heart she believed she was undeserving of that success and unconsciously sabotaged her best efforts. But if she wasn't worthy, then she didn't want anyone else to be either.

What now of Nancy and Tonya? Kerrigan married her manager, Jerry Solomon, and together they produced several successful ice shows. She skated in a variety of exhibitions and ice spectaculars and is involved in a number of charities.

Deprived of being able to skate professionally, Tonya Harding, meanwhile, continued to plough a seedier furrow while still searching for that illusive feeling of 'specialness'. A video of her wedding night was sold by her ex-husband Jeff Gillooly, and pictures of her appeared in *Penthouse* magazine. She tried her hand at singing, backed by a band called The Golden Blades, but soon gave it up after being booed and pelted with plastic bottles. She married Michael Smith a short time after her final break-up with Gillooly and was divorced a few months later. She has been arrested for assaulting her boyfriend, Darren Silver, with a hubcap and driving while intoxicated.

Tonya now fights her own battles. In 2002, she turned to professional boxing and 15.5 million viewers tuned in to see her beat Bill Clinton's accuser, Paula Jones, on *Celebrity Boxing*. Three years later, in a *Boston Globe* feature, Stan Grossfield records attending a press conference prior to another celebrity fight. The promoter, who happened to be Tonya's godmother, insisted that no reporter asked questions about Nancy Kerrigan. Unfortunately for Tonya, it remained top of the media agenda and, as usual, was the first question out.

Grossfeld describes Harding, now 35 years of age, as still having piercing blue eyes 'but her 5ft-1in frame is bulked up more than her listed 125lb. Her biceps look like telegraph poles and she is dressed in black.'[11] In a rambling interview, Harding reflects on her new boxing career but Grossfeld senses that she would rather not get into the ring at all. She has already had her nose broken, she has a migraine and she's been sick with bronchitis and 'flu for months. Grossfield detects a hint of sadness as she speaks. 'I do a lot of things for kids . . . I back anything about kids . . .'[12] But the media, she says, won't let anyone forget about Nancy. Like Cain, Tonya has been marked and driven into the land of Nod, east of Eden.

5

DADDY'S GIRL

The Svengali syndrome – fathers stalking the tennis court

'The wisest men follow their own direction
And listen to no prophet guiding them.
None but the fools believe in oracles,
Forsaking their own judgement. Those who know,
Know that such men can only come to grief.'

Euripides, *Iphigenia in Tauris* (414-412 BC)

In 1981, at the age of 16, Andrea Jaeger was ranked number two in the world on the professional tennis circuit, and two years later scorched her way to the Wimbledon final without dropping a set. The nation, and the world, collectively licked its lips at the prospect of a changing of the guard. It was clearly only a matter of time before Jaeger eclipsed the achievements of the giants of the game, Chris Evert and Billie Jean King.

Unfortunately, the Wimbledon final didn't quite live up to the billing. From the outset, Jaeger appeared surprisingly listless against Martina Navratilova, an opponent she'd beaten just a few weeks earlier at Eastbourne. The first set vanished in a 6-0 blink of the eye. We put it down to nerves – she was, after all, still a teenager. Things would improve as she settled into the game; we just had to wait.

Things did improve – marginally. But Jaeger still lost the second set 6-3. Fifty-four minutes after arriving on court, she was back in the locker room wondering what had hit her. Nerves clearly had got the better of the young pretender. Or so we believed.

Twenty-two years after that final, in an interview with the *Observer*'s Victoria Lee on 29 June 2003, Jaeger revealed for the first time the real reason she lost one of the most one-sided Wimbledon finals ever seen. The revelation came when Lee mentioned that the previous evening she'd had a conversation with a reminiscing Martina who had told her, 'There were some difficulties with Andrea's father, particularly that Wimbledon. It wasn't an easy time for her. Probably for her the court was sort of a refuge in bad times. No matter what was going on in your life, that's where you could get away from it and hopefully play well, despite it all. Sadly, that was the case with some of the women with abusive fathers. It was the only place they were safe – until the match was over. I think it was a difficult match for Andrea because of that.'[1]

Martina's reflection on the match seemed to free something in Jaeger and she opened up on events that led up to her humiliating defeat. Just before Wimbledon, Jaeger claimed she had damaged a thumb diving on grass ('I loved to dive on grass, which I thought was fun'[2]) and subsequently had had to adjust her grip. 'The day before the final, my dad had insisted I practise and I didn't want to because my thumb was really painful by now. We had . . . erm . . . a heated discussion [she laughs] and I guess he didn't realise the extent of the injury.'[3] Later that evening, with no sign of the argument abating, Jaeger found herself locked out of the home her father had rented for Wimbledon fortnight.

Seeking sanctuary, bizarrely, she knocked at the door of

Navratilova's rented home further up the street. It was at this point Jaeger seemed to clam up, unwilling to reveal what went on inside. When Lee switched tack and asked whether Andrea thought she would have won the match if she hadn't had the disturbing row with her father, Jaeger replied, 'Yeah, maybe. Who knows? All I know is that I was playing the best tennis of my life at that Wimbledon.'[4]

Five years later, in an interview with Peter Robertson of the *Daily Mail* in April 2008, Andrea Jaeger went considerably further, claiming she had actually deliberately thrown the match. She also claimed that the fight with her father had an altogether different cause. 'The afternoon before the final, my dad saw an empty crisp packet in my room which I wasn't supposed to have. He also asked me about something he heard that happened in the locker-room. I refused to answer. If I'd told him some of the things I encountered on the tennis circuit, he'd have hurt people and pulled me out of that final. Over the years, I took a few beatings from my father to protect players and staff.

'Dad was so angry that I would choose to protect them and not answer his question that I thought he was going to get his belt. I said I was sorry, grabbed my bra and my wallet and ran outside, aware Dad wouldn't hit me in public. I wanted to order a cab, so I went to the flat next door where Martina was staying. I was upset and kept pounding on the door and ringing the bell until Martina's trainer, Nancy Lieberman, opened the door and took me to the kitchen. Martina was sitting in the living room. She glanced round at me briefly with a look on her face to say that I'd interrupted her preparation for the final. She stayed seated and didn't look at me again. I couldn't have done that in her position, but all I thought at the time was: "I've changed her routine and affected her. I can't go out and try in the final now." Martina missed her chance to help her neighbour who was suffering in order to fulfil her desire, so I had to make it right. I gave up my desire to give someone their help.

'I went on court in complete peace knowing that giving the match away was the right thing to do. I had to look myself in the mirror for the rest of my life. It meant more to Martina anyway. God knows the truth. I knew the truth. I emailed Martina three years ago to say it doesn't take away from her win, but she never replied. Had I tried fully, would I have won? I don't have that answer.

'During the match, I missed balls on purpose. I hit right to Martina and when I was getting whipped in the first set 6-0 . . . I tried to look upset about it. I glanced at my dad. He knew something was wrong because I never got nervous and always started great.

'I needed to make the second set closer and I did, but not close enough to worry Martina. At changes of ends, I didn't want to look at the crowd. I felt bad that I wasn't giving them the best match as the fans were so good to me over the years, but I also felt that if they knew what had happened they would understand.

'When Martina won the second set 6-3 – and the match – I was happy for her. She walked around with the trophy and everyone wanted her picture. In the press conference, I said she played too well.'[5]

Two years after the thrown final, Jaeger retired from the game with a persistent shoulder injury aged just 19. As the next 'greatest player ever', she hadn't even made it out of her teens.

Jaeger's explanation of events is as extraordinary as it is confusing. Perhaps both events happened – the refusal to practice and the forbidden consumption of crisps. Perhaps it's a case of memory playing tricks. Whatever the cause of the row, the most important aspect however is the bullying, threatening presence of her father. Andrea may have been defeated by Martina but perhaps she was struggling to beat a greater adversary and her defeat was, in fact, a victory for revenge.

Like many women tennis stars, Andrea was coached by her father, Roland, a Swiss-German strict disciplinarian and former boxer who introduced her to the game at the age of eight. From

Jaeger's account, it is clear he regularly resorted to the belt.

Jaeger's story sadly is an all-too-familiar one in women's tennis. The litany of dysfunctional fathers and their tennis-playing daughters is long and shows no sign of abating. Jennifer Capriati's father once tellingly joked about making her do sit-ups in her cot and confessed to pushing her into professional tennis at the age of 13 because he knew she might burn out early but, by that time, she would have earned plenty of money.

Steffi Graf's father reputedly kept her isolated from other women on the tour and was famed for embarrassing her in public. Jelena Dokic's father wins hands down, however, when it comes to stealing the daughter's headlines. On 30 May 2009, ABC News reported, 'The father of Australian tennis star Jelena Dokic faces eight years in jail after he was charged with threatening to kill the Australian ambassador in Serbia with a grenade launcher.' His arrest had been reported by journalist Reko Rennie in Australia's *Sport and Style* magazine on 7 May 1999. The article read, 'Serbian police reportedly found two illegal bombs and a hoard of guns when they searched the house of tennis dad Damir Dokic after his arrest over threats against the Australian ambassador in Belgrade. Mr Dokic was detained overnight after he threatened to "fire a rocket" on the ambassador's car. He was angry after his daughter, tennis star Jelena Dokic, revealed details of her violent upbringing in *The Age* this week. One of the revelations was that the bruises noted by coaches and competitors during her early career were the result of abuse from her father.'

Rennie went on to catalogue earlier Damir Dokic misde-meanors such as being evicted from a tournament in Birmingham for being verbally abusive at matches, and subsequently being caught drunk, lying in the middle of a road. 'In 2000, Mr Dokic was removed from Wimbledon grounds after a drunken rage where he smashed a broadcaster's phone. A couple of months later, he was thrown out of the US Open for abusing staff about the $10 price of a meal of salmon.' Damir subsequently moved the family back to Serbia, claiming, according to Rennie, that the 2001 Australian Open Draw has been rigged.' Five years later, however, Jelena returned alone to Australia. According to Rennie, at the time 'Mr Dokic said he would drop a bomb on Australia and kidnap his daughter'. The strain of their relationship eventually took its toll as Jelena dropped from number 4 in the world to 450 and, in August 2005, at the age of 21, Dokic stopped playing altogether, resolving to get away from her father once and for all. 'I had to sort myself out. I had dropped down so far and my personal life was a mess.'[6] The 'sorting out' took four years and she only returned to tennis in 2009, reaching the quarter-finals of the Australian Open and making a winning return to Australia's Federation Cup team.

Jim Pierce's treatment of his daughter Mary was possibly the most brutal of all. According to Pat Jordan in a feature in the *Sporting News* on 15 November 1993, 'Jim Pierce coached his daughter in the same way Attila the Hun exhorted his troops.' Wikipedia would seem to back the view, stating, 'During her first few years on the tour, Pierce was known for the behaviour of her father, more so than her performances on court. Jim Pierce . . . often shouted abuse at her opponents during matches. On one occasion when he was sitting in the stands, he notoriously screamed, "Mary, kill the bitch!" He was also reportedly often verbally and physically abusive to Mary during practice sessions and after defeats.'

The Wikipedia entry on Mary Pierce continues to chart the stormy relationship: Jim punching a spectator in the French Open in 1993 (and being subsequently banned from all Women's Tennis Association Tour events for five years); Mary dropping him as her coach and placing a restraining order on him; Jim becoming embroiled in a knife fight with her bodyguard; and Mary eventually paying Jim US$500,000 to leave her alone when he subsequently sued her, claiming he'd been promised 25 per cent of her earnings.

In the *Sporting News* story, Jim Pierce admitted to training his daughter eight hours a day, sometimes until midnight. 'For 7 years, 8 hours a day, I hit 700 serves at Mary . . . My young son slept by the net. I wouldn't let Mary leave until she got it right. Sure, she cried.'

Top-class sports are filled with stories of heroic endeavours and extreme behaviour in the pursuit of success and fame but there is nothing quite so disturbing as tales of budding tennis players seemingly stalked by their own fathers. These young women are usually adolescent in age, if not developmentally, when they first come to our attention and their journeys seem to follow a familiar trajectory; having had their lives co-opted by fathers in pursuit of fame and fortune, they are coached, controlled and often badly mistreated.

Although we won't be discussing titillating tabloid tales of lesbian relationships on the circuit, it would hardly be surprising, with fathers such as these, to find a higher than usual incidence of single-sex relationships in tennis. If this is the case, it could be purely genetic coincidence, of course. But it's also possible such athletes have either been scared off other male partners, have never quite grown out of an unconscious feeling no other male will match up to Daddy, or perhaps it has something to do with the risks involved in bringing a rival into the world who will vie for Daddy's affection. For those not actually coached/bullied by fathers, a similarly skewed view of men is provided in the commonplace sexual harassment of vulnerable young female athletes in training camps. One survey by *Sports Canada* in 1995 found 20 per cent of respondents from national teams admitted some sexual involvement with their coaches and almost half of these said they had been forced to have sex before the age of 16. [9]

In this chapter, we will call the persistent and insidious over-reaching of familial boundaries the 'Svengali Syndrome'. Svengali was a fictional character in George du Maurier's 1894 novel *Trilby,* who hypnotised Trilby into becoming a great singer and then continued to do so to sustain his performance. The term Svengali in common usage today, serves as the stereotype for any coach who exercises domination over a performer (especially female). It seems particularly apposite, therefore, when referring to hypnotised daughters on the tennis court who serve as extensions of their fathers' narcissistic wishes.

L. Jon Wertheim, in his book *Venus Envy*, provides the perfect description of the archetypal dysfunctional tennis father: 'He has often quit his full-time job to manage his daughter's career. He usually shoves his wife deep into the background. In many cases, he was an athlete of modest distinction who never quite fulfilled his promise.'[10]

In one of his last published papers in 1967, 'The Location of Cultural Experience', psychoanalyst and paediatrician, Donald Winnicott, located the ideal of parenting to be in providing children with an early holding environment in which the child 'will find his or her own self and will be able to exist and to feel real. Feeling real is more than existing; it is finding a way to exist as oneself, and to relate to objects as oneself.'[11] The apparent simplicity of this statement belies an enormously difficult task for parents – how to nurture a child's sense of independent identity, and crucially not bleed into them their own emotional anxieties and failed hopes. A healthy developmental trajectory for a girl therefore requires parents who contain and think about her mental state as separate and distinct from their own feelings and desires.

In the most dysfunctional daughter-father tennis relationship, however, the child's developing self is taken over and exploited by fathers often in order to gratify their own conscious and unconscious needs. By getting into their daughter's minds, such fathers colonise (or 'hypnotise'), making their children extensions of their own desires. If the girls are lucky and talented, they may have the consolation of becoming famous and financially successful. But even for the lucky ones, what is the cost to their sense of self? As Jennifer Capriati discovered when she quit the game, 'If I don't have tennis, who am I? What am I?'[12] Many of these tennis players are thus sentenced to living their lives in a half-light, waiting endlessly to be properly born.

Ian Williamson's Casebook – Jenny

It is quite normal for parents to ring an analyst to talk about the problems their children might be having before actually making a commitment to therapeutic treatment; however, the tone and manner of Jenny's father's call was worrying and a foretaste of things to come. On the phone, he said that I had been recommended as someone who might be able to help his 17-year-old daughter who was suffering extreme bouts of anxiety and sleeplessness. He said he was sceptical about therapy and wanted to make it clear that she was highly intelligent and was expected to do very well in her exams. He did not want her to get involved in anything that would jeopardise these exams. He further added that he wanted to meet me to find out exactly what I would be saying and doing to Jenny. I tentatively suggested that as she was 17, a better way forward might be for me to see Jenny on her own and then see her with him and his wife to discuss how we might go forward. At this point, he became quite agitated and let me know in no uncertain terms that Jenny was not allowed to see anyone without his say so. I reluctantly agreed to see him and his wife for the first meeting.

That first meeting was both difficult but illuminating. The father said very little about his daughter but asked endless questions about the therapeutic process and how it might affect her. He said the school had recommended that she see someone and that he wasn't sure there was anything much wrong. Surely, he added, all teenagers were difficult.

I asked the mother for her thoughts. She said she had been concerned for some time as Jenny seemed cut off and miserable. Jenny had very few friends and didn't seem at all interested in boys. The father irritatedly brushed aside his wife's concerns saying that she worried too much about everything and wasn't a good judge of Jenny's state of mind. He then said something that caught my attention. 'I've heard some therapists exploit their patients and I'm not going to let that happen to Jenny.' I asked him to explain exactly what he meant so I could understand his concern. He was unable or unwilling to elaborate further but instead restricted himself to saying enigmatically that he had read things in the papers. What had caught my attention was his concern about exploitation. Was this a genuine concern or an unconscious expression of his fear that he himself was exploiting Jenny? We ended the meeting with an agreement that I would be allowed to see Jenny for three assessment meetings and we would then reconvene to discuss how to move forward.

The meeting left me feeling distinctly uneasy. The mother was clearly worried and had been for some time but seemed to have no voice in the family. The father was, to all intents and purposes, controlling Jenny's life. I suspected he treated Jenny in exactly the same way as he treated his wife.

The day before I was due to meet Jenny, I had a distressing call from her mother. She tearfully revealed that things at home were unbearable. Her husband was putting Jenny under intense pressure academically. He was constantly on at her about her homework and would scream at her if she got average grades. This had, she said, been going on for years. Jenny had no life other than work. The mother then added as an afterthought that she thought her husband was too involved in Jenny's life. At the end of our conversation, she asked me not to mention the call to her husband.

Predictably, Jenny arrived at the meeting with her father. She seemed very uneasy about coming to the consulting room without him. The meeting took on a pattern that was to become familiar – I asked Jenny a question and she dutifully answered it. She neither initiated any dialogue nor expanded on any of the questions. I asked her if she was happy and she said that she didn't know. She seemed flat and lifeless. She only came to life when I asked her about her school work. She said she was terrified of getting poor grades but was unable (unwilling?) to elaborate on why that was. I suggested that getting poor grades might disappoint her parents. She said that her father wanted her to get into a top university to study medicine. I asked if this was what she wanted. She looked bewildered by my question and took a moment to respond that her father thought 'it was a profession where you could make a real difference'.

Our two further meetings followed a similar pattern. Jenny seemed unable to make a connection with her own thoughts or feelings, let alone articulate what they were. At the end of sessions, I was left with a striking feeling of a young woman without a sense of herself.

Jenny's father came to the review meeting on his own; he said his wife was busy and that Jenny said she didn't want to come. He quizzed me in detail about what Jenny had said and gave me his thoughts on his daughter but he seemed disinterested in my reflections on the sessions with his daughter. He then launched into a monologue about his own life, especially his own academic disappointments. He said he had wanted to be a doctor but his parents had sent him to the wrong school. At this point, it became evident that individual treatment for Jenny would not be the way forward. This father was not going to let go. He had far too much of his own unfulfilled dreams and hopes tied up with his daughter's development. My suggestion that they attend family therapy to try to resolve Jenny's difficulties was a much more palatable option for the father. I later heard that their attendance at family meetings was sporadic and largely unproductive but that Jenny had got the grades to get into medical school.

While most parents provide care and nurture the development of the dependent and powerless child, in the case of the disturbed boundaries between the 'tennis couple', the relationship is often unpalatably close to the husband-wife relationship. In the Pat Jordan interview in the *Sporting News* referred to earlier, Jim Pierce, discussing his turbulent relationship with his wife, states, 'We fight like dogs, but I sleep with my wife every night. When we have sex, the next morning I say to my wife, "Do you like the things we do in bed?" She says, "Yes." I say, "Do you trust me to do the right things in bed?" She says, "Yes." Then I say, "Well, why ain't I good enough to coach Mary then?"'

Jim Pierce's rather odd explanation is littered with the kind of confusions that lie at the heart of the relationship between dysfunctional fathers and their tennis-playing daughters. Pierce seems to be saying that his ability to do the right things with his wife in bed is qualification enough for coaching his daughter. But a more coherent explanation is that he is expressing anxieties about his own potency and worthiness. Anxieties that he hopes coaching his daughter will dispel.

The myth of Echo and Narcissus can be usefully conjured up here to highlight the tennis court's distorted father-daughter relationship. Echo was a beautiful nymph devoted to the pursuit of woodland sports who had one failing: she always had to have the last word. Falling foul of Juno (Queen of the Gods), Echo had the ability to initiate conversation (to speak first) taken away, leaving her only ever able to reply (echo). Along with her 'voice', she effectively had her identity stolen.

When Echo first saw the beautiful youth Narcissus, she immediately fell in love with him and desperately wanted to talk to him. Lacking the power, she had no choice but to wait for Narcissus to make the first move. But Narcissus could not see her as he only saw his reflected self. Devastated by the disappointment, Echo lived the rest of her life out in mountains and caves. Grief and sadness shrivelled her because she lacked a voice and could only mimic.

If one takes Narcissus as a father instead of a romantically-linked peer, the myth holds its own mirror up to the disturbed nature of these tennis relationships which follow the romantic model rather than conforming to the healthy paternal-protective model. Narcissus cannot see his daughter because he only sees his own reflection; Echo loses her voice and identity because she is merely an extension of her father's narcissistic wishes.

With the exception of Steffi Graf, none of the tennis stars we discuss in this chapter have married: the Williams sisters remain single and childless, as do Mary Pierce, Jelena Dokic, Jennifer Capriati, Maria Sharapova and Andrea Jaeger.

In all these cases (apart from the Williams sisters' mother, Oracene Price), there is either virtually no mention of mothers or they are spoken of as shadowy presences, also seeming to lack a voice of their own. Perhaps as L. Jon Wertheim believes, the father 'shoves his wife deep into the background'.[13] Whatever the reason, when the mother goes AWOL, an otherwise unprotected child only has the father to go to.

Early in the twentieth century, Jung introduced the term the 'Electra Complex' to describe the daughter's early relationship with her father. 'A daughter develops a specific liking for the father, with a correspondingly jealous attitude towards the mother. We would call this the Electra Complex.'[14] Although the Electra Complex is rarely referred to these days – and has never managed a place in the zeitgeist corresponding to the mother-son Oedipus Complex – it does provide a starting point in understanding a dangerous tipping point between healthy and unhealthy father-daughter relationships. At the point where the daughter grows jealous of her mother's romantic intimacy with her father and becomes her love rival, it is crucial that fathers don't abuse those boundaries and collude in creating a distorting romantic model.

The father's relationship is massively affected by the quality and shape of the mother-daughter relationship. If the mother is strong and controlling and the father weak, the daughter has two problems: the father is not able to provide her with a masculine role model; and, unable to stand up to the mother, he cannot assist his daughter in differentiating and separating herself from her mother.

More relevant to our discussion, however, is the opposite problem: the weak/passive mother married to a controlling husband where both mother and daughter are dominated. In the latter case, the mother's passivity does not provide the daughter with a model for genuine feminine independence and the conse-quences can be disastrous. Linda Schierse Leonard refers to such women as 'puella aeterna' (the eternal girl)[15] and describes them as psychologically stuck as dependent daughters even though they may physically be mature women. Such women tend to have a weak sense of self and readily accept the identity that others project on to them. Leonard claims those that marry often do so to authoritarian men and become the image of the woman that the men want.

Perhaps the most successful and controversial of the father-daughter tennis partnerships is that between Richard Williams and his daughters, Venus and Serena. The Williams sisters are unusual among the tennis-playing daughter-father fraternity in the sense that their mother has played, and continues to play, a significant role in their lives. Acknowledged as being the backbone of the family, she has been a strong presence in the upbringing of her daughters. What isn't clear is whether she had reservations about the master plan her then husband, Richard Williams, conceived to create tennis superstars of her daughters.

The relationship between the Williams sisters and their father is well documented and the intriguing difference in this case is that there are two daughters rather than one. Richard Williams himself would appear to be a larger-than-life character and, from the stories told about him, possibly also something of a 'Walter Mitty' fantasist, forever telling extraordinary tales about himself and his activities. L. Jon Wertheim in *Venus Envy* describes one particular Richard Williams flight of fantasy before a big tennis tournament in Palm Springs, California, in which he tells the assembled press that he is looking into buying the Rockefeller Center for $3.9 billion. He also claims to have purchased the air rights over India and will make millions charging planes to fly over this space. He next suggests a casino in the Bahamas has offered him $250,000 a night to sing and another $250,000 if he can coax Venus to back him up on drums. Harmless fun one might think, but such flights of fantasy pre-date his celebrity status and suggest a man frustrated by his own modest achievements as well as confused regarding his identity.

According to Wertheim, Williams told people he was a star athlete at school, a fine footballer, an outstanding basketball player (so good that he was offered a try-out with the New York Knicks) and also 'the greatest golfer in the state of Louisiana'[16]. Wertheim is unable to verify the validity of these stories. Williams' high school football, basketball and track coach from that time, Leonard Barnes, says he had never heard of Williams, nor had the journalist Jim McClain, who covered high school sports at the local newspaper.

One of the central underlying dynamics of these father-daughter tennis relationships is the inadequacy and insecurity of fathers who unconsciously seek a confirmation of self through their daughters' sporting achievements. This dynamic provides the psychological glue between the couple: the father's negative feelings about himself being ameliorated by his daughter's outstanding performance. In order to control or stabilise that corrosive sense of self, he needs to control his daughter. His daughter, in turn, needs to succeed because she has learned, ever since she can remember, that this is the way to gain father's love, attention and approval and thereby validate her own self-worth.

The extent to which this relationship can be controlled by the father is illustrated by a story Wertheim tells about a final played between Venus and Serena at Key Biscayne in 1999. He cites a source close to the family saying that Richard Williams gave his daughters explicit instructions that Venus was to win in three sets. Despite playing superbly going into the final, the sisters made 107 unforced errors as Venus won 6-1,4-6,6-4. Wertheim quotes Lindsay Davenport, a rival tennis star: 'I thought Serena was playing better tennis going into the match, but personally I thought Venus was going to win for outside reasons'.[17] Richard Williams has always vehemently denied ever giving instructions regarding which of his daughters should win a match and there has never been any firm evidence to contradict his claim.

Before the tennis success of Venus and Serena propelled him to wealth and stardom, Richard Williams seemed a complex character with a facility for being economical with the truth and volatile both as a husband and a father. He was born to a single mother and claims he was the son of a Louisiana sharecropper but even this is disputed by one of his childhood friends, Arthur Bryant. Bryant told Wertheim, 'He ain't no fucking son of a sharecropper. Only thing I ever saw him raise was his fork to eat the vegetables someone else raised. '[18] Richard Williams did not know his father well; in fact, his father rarely came home, preferring to spend time with his girlfriend down the street. Richard eventually married a woman called Betty Johnson and the relationship, before the couple separated, produced five children – two daughters and three boys. According to their eldest daughter Sabrina, the marriage was stormy and volatile and, even back then, he was telling tall stories about himself. She recounts to Wertheim that her father told her that he went to UCLA and played for the Los Angeles Lakers professional basketball team. She vividly remembers her embarrassment and shame when fathers of her girlfriends told her that it was all a lie. She then makes a crucial point while trying to explain the reasons behind his story telling. 'Richard – I don't call him Dad – is a manipulator. He likes to think he can make people believe what he wants them to.'[19]

It would certainly seem to be the case that Richard made his other daughters, Serena and Venus, want what he wanted. What is curious historically, in the light of his depiction as a father devoted to his children, was the fact that he allegedly abandoned his previous family both physically and financially. Sabrina told Wertheim that when he quit the family to start a new life with Oracene, his ex-wife, Betty, was working two jobs to keep the family afloat while one of his sons, Ronner, served time in prison for second-degree armed robbery, and another, Richard Jr, for firearm offences. Sabrina claims another sibling lived briefly in a homeless shelter. What is significant is that there is no evidence of long hours spent on the tennis court with any of the children from his first marriage.

Richard Williams met Oracene Price when they were young and had a son, Gabriel Mukuku, before the couple went their own ways and she married Yusuf Rasheed and he married Betty Johnson. Oracene had three daughters with Rasheed who died before she returned to Richard Williams and remarried.

Richard Williams has an interesting tale to tell about how he discovered tennis, claiming he had his epiphany watching the Romanian tennis player, Virginia Ruzici, receive a cheque of

$35,000 for winning a tournament. He told his new wife Oracene of his plans and that they needed to have two more daughters whom he would turn into tennis players. They duly did just that. As Wertheim astutely notes, they already had three daughters at the time so why didn't he raise Lyndrea to be a tennis star as she was only one year old when Venus was conceived?

Of course, the truth is that it is highly unlikely that there was any such master plan. The reality was probably a little more mundane. Like Sharapova's father, the realisation that his daughters had wonderful athleticism allied to the potential to make money, captured his interest. His daughters' success clearly also raised his own standing.

The story told by coach Rick Macci to Wertheim leaves no room for doubt regarding Richard Williams' enormous authority over his daughters and his determination to make his dream a reality. Richard, according to Macci, noticed that Venus and Serena, aged 14 and 12 at the time, had a tendency to run away from the ball. Richard became angry with them and demanded that they stand opposite each other 3ft from the net and then try to hit each other's heads with the tennis ball. They hammered balls at each other until eventually Venus hit Serena hard in the chest. Their father nodded approvingly as Serena tried to hold back the tears.

The hard-nosed athlete may well remind us no wimps ever get to the highest step on the podium; 'tough love' is what forges champions. We would argue, however, that 'forged' is a particularly apposite word here, suggestive of malleability and a lack of choice; these were not adults but young, vulnerable adolescents still growing and developing. They may well have had dreams of winning tennis tournaments, but primarily they are likely to have pursued the dream initially because they loved (or were fearful of?) their father; not to carry out his wishes was to risk further punishment and the forfeit of his love and approval.

I guess the question most of us would like to ask is: why didn't the 14-year-old Venus tell Richard to go to hell like most adolescents would? Why were Venus, and her younger sister Serena, so compliant?

According to Wertheim, on 7 February 1999, Oracene went to hospital for treatment to three broken ribs. She initially told the sheriff that she had sustained the injury through running into a door handle but, when pressed, replied, 'I know you know what happened and I am fearful for my daughters' careers.'[20]

This wasn't the first time that the police had had to intervene, according to Wertheim. Two years earlier, Oracene called saying she was being threatened with a gun. When the authorities arrived, she claimed the dispute had been resolved. When Richard Williams was interviewed, he explained he had been simply playing around with a pellet pistol, acting out a screenplay he was writing.

By the end of 2000, Richard and Oracene Williams had separated and were divorced in 2002 citing irreconcilable differences. The family has understandably closed ranks on these events but one cannot help wondering what effect these incidents had on the girls and how many other similar events perhaps went unreported as they grew up.

In the course of a wide-ranging interview with Paul Kimmage for the *Times* in 2008, Maria Sharapova tells a remarkably similar story. Like Richard Williams, Sharapova's father, Yuri, had little contact with his father who died when he was young. She tells Kimmage a painful story from her youth, ostensibly to illustrate the difficult sacrifices she has had to make on her way to becoming a champion but it is also significant in highlighting how her father ignored her pain in pursuit of his own dream. On her way to tennis practice with her father, she remembers falling and cutting her hand. The cut was bleeding and she was crying. She pleaded with him to take her back to the apartment. He refused and eventually screamed at her, 'Stop crying, Masha! You are going to practice.'[21] She was six years old at the time.

Maria Sharapova's father started coaching her at the age of four. When she was seven, he took her from Russia to the Nick

Bollettieri Tennis academy in Florida in pursuit of fame and fortune. Having made the sacrifice, Maria had to cope with another disappointment; the academy said she was too young and told her to come back in two years. Kimmage reports that the young Maria didn't cry or complain but the next two years were about survival. Maria's mother had to stay behind in Russia because of visa problems and only joined her two years later. During that period, Maria only spoke to her mother every six months. Effectively, her mother had been silenced. We don't know what impact her father's one-tracked pursuit of his dream had on Maria, nor the cost of the separation from her mother. No doubt Yuri would point to the fact that his daughter became the world's highest-earning female athlete and her fame and fortune has been paid for by *his* sacrifice.

Kimmage tentatively suggests that while these stories may on the surface seem heroic and character-building, they might also be thought of as abusive. 'It's a pretty big call for your father to make,' Kimmage comments to Maria. 'To take you away from your home at that age.'

'Yes,' she says in reply, 'it's a crazy sacrifice, crazy, and I see a lot of young kids in the same situation right now when I go back to the academies.'

'Some might say that the decision to impose that hardship on your only child is almost abusive,' suggests Kimmage. Sharapova acknowledges the difficulties but ducks a real answer. She says that with the success (financial and sporting) she has had, she would do it again.

Later, Kimmage quotes from Sharapova's weekly blog from September 2007. 'I know it's tough for my fans to handle my losses as it is for me. But let me point something out. I didn't leave my mom at the age of seven for nothing. I didn't spend six hours a day practising in the Florida sun at the age of nine for nothing . . . I didn't sleep in little cots for three years, eating oatmeal out of a packet while playing in the middle of nowhere for nothing. All this has helped me build character and there is no better asset

than being able to stand up for yourself.'[22] Sharapova's protestations are revealing but they are incorrect. She didn't leave her
mother; her father took her away from her mother. She didn't
choose to practise six hours a day in the Florida sun; her father
made that choice for her.

What is transparent for both the Williams sisters and
Sharapova is that the motive and drive to success initially came
from the father and not the child. It is not a father supporting
a daughter's choice but rather a father shoe-horning his
daughter into his own dream. The fact that the drive later
predictably becomes internalised and self-fuelling in the
daughter does not alter the inescapable truth that it did not
originate in her nor was it chosen by her. There is not a hair's-
breadth of difference between Svengali's hypnosis and Yuri's
total control of his daughter. As Sharapova herself makes clear
to Kimmage, she didn't have a choice when her father took her
to America. This raises fundamental questions about the
sanctity of a daughter's identity and autonomy. It also raises
very difficult questions about abusive behaviour. If we accept
the parent's role is one of nurturing, do we only cross the line
into child abuse when we physically lock our daughters in a
cellar for a decade and sexually abuse them as in sensational
cases such as Josef Fritzl? The truth is that emotional
manipulation – unconscious or otherwise – is more mundane
but nevertheless can be extremely damaging.

Dr Fred Wertz, chairman of Fordham University's psychology department, speaking to Wayne Coffey about Jennifer
Capriati in the *New York Daily News* in July 2007, commented,
'When someone that young has such an incredible level of talent
and promise and the whole world identifies them with it, it can
short-circuit the natural process of identity formation. The result
is you see yourself in one way, doing one thing. Other options
don't even compute.'[23] The crucial question when considering
whether such a rigorous tutelage is abusive is whether the athlete
pursues the sport for herself or to please her father so that he loves

her. If it is the father's choice and there is no mother to soften and mediate the father-daughter relationship, then things can quickly spiral out of hand.

As the young person moves into adolescence, her mind and body undergoes changes; the upheaval is enormous and has a major impact on the sense of self. Moving into peer groups and severing umbilical ties with parents are an essential part of this process, if complex and painful. This invariably involves enormous conflict and is often accompanied by extreme states of anxiety. The process may be turbulent and painful but it is also a critical developmental stage in moving from childhood to adulthood. The emerging, fledgling adult sense of self inside the child, protected and guided by the parents, has to learn to stand alone. The difficulty of negotiating this stage is what largely accounts for the chaos of adolescent life.

If, however, the child's sense of self has been co-opted by the father from an early age, and the mother is chased into the background, how does the adolescent girl negotiate the transition to adulthood and independence? This is where Winnicott's description of the ideal object of parenting becomes of paramount importance, for if the child does not have the opportunity to 'find a self', then how is she ever properly to separate? The Svengali relationship is damaging because in place of what should be the daughter's true sense of self is the father's sense of who he wants his daughter to be, plus his own thwarted hopes and dreams. What is then created can be seen as an alien self. As Jennifer Capriati implied so movingly, now that tennis is over, who is Jennifer Capriati?

There is one further distorted consequence of this 'colonisation' of the daughter's mind. As her experience of herself is synonymous with what the father wants her to be, and her own true self is unexplored, she is now inextricably tied to him. The daughter's normal need to separate and develop is experienced as a threat by both parties. Co-dependency becomes a way of life – he is nothing without me and I am nothing without him.

Richard Williams has made much of the fact that his

daughters have much more to their lives than tennis. Despite the occasional absence from the tennis circuit, however, neither Serena nor Venus have shown any inclination to retire, even though they are now the relative seniors on the tennis circuit. There is little evidence of either of them wanting to separate from their father and go their own way; no other 'marriage' has yet materialised. Instead, Wertheim describes the sisters as 'fiercely, almost pathologically, loyal to their father'.[24] When Richard Williams, in turn, is unable to attend tennis tournaments, he reputedly speaks to his daughters as often as once an hour.

The added twist in the Williams saga is that the daughters are in competition with each other, both at a literal and metaphorical level. As mentioned earlier, it has often been rumoured – but never substantiated – that Richard even decides the outcome of their head-to-head matches. If this is the case, then he is able to play each off against the other, making one his favourite one week and, like a fickle Greek god, then withdrawing favour to bestow on another. By having three in the relationship, a permanent Oedipal/Electra struggle continues to be played out.

In *The Wounded Woman*, Linda Schierse Leonard discusses a type of woman she calls the 'Armoured Amazon' who has her feminine identity damaged in pursuit of a masculine identity. The Amazons, according to legend, were reputed to be fearsome warriors, prepared to remove their right breast so they could shoot arrows more efficiently. This physical damaging of their feminine identity is perhaps the key to understanding our father-controlled champions. The tennis daughters can be seen as incarnations of the mythical Armoured Amazons, unconsciously identifying with the masculine (strength and power) at the expense of the feminine. The modern tennis Amazon takes on 'the characteristics that are generally associated with the masculine disposition' and thus 'identifies with the power aspect of the masculine. At the same time, she renounces the capacity to relate lovingly, a quality that has traditionally been associated with the feminine.'[25]

The problem for such women is that they become trapped in

'Amazon armour', cut off from their feminine identity. One way in which this Amazon armour is expressed is through what Leonard calls 'the superstar daughter' whose life is devoted to success and achievement and primarily driven by the desire to compensate for the father's lack of identity and success.

Jennifer Capriati had a father who says he trained her from the cot and then managed her career. Capriati's interview with Wayne Coffey quoted earlier is a salutary reminder of the price these young women pay. Now approaching her mid thirties, her life is at a bleak crossroads. Racked by debilitating injuries that signalled the end of her tennis career, Capriati is battling the psychological fall-out from a life groomed for tennis stardom. She confesses to suffering from depression and feels suicidal at times (although she reassures Coffey that she has never made any actual attempt at ending her life).

'When I stopped playing, that's when all this came crumbling down. If I don't have tennis, who am I? What am I? I was just alive because of this. I've had to ask, well, who is Jennifer?' But she also confides in Coffey that even when she was winning she had low self-esteem. 'If I was at the height of my game, beating Serena Williams, I was on top of the world, but something was still missing inside . . . I'm still struggling to find out what that is.'[26] Beating Serena was the only way of possibly winning Daddy's approval and validating herself. No wonder she is still struggling to find the thing (a sense of independent self) missing inside.

The prognosis for these young women is not good from a psychological point of view. The distortions of self and the dysfunctional nature of their relationships mean they are ill-equipped to go forward in any meaningful way. Despite the fame and riches these young tennis stars reap, it's hard to think of any other sporting activity that exacts such a heavy psychological price. They give their heart to their father but he wants their soul. Their vulnerability and childlike innocence make them susceptible to being exploited and manipulated, consciously or unconsciously, by Svengalis for the father's greater glory. From the young Sharapova's six-hours-a-day practice sessions, thousands of miles away from her mother, to Capriati's mythical sit-ups in the cot; from Jaegar's father's rant at losing a match, to Mary Pierce's father's alleged physical abuse . . . all have suffered enormously for their moment of fame. And when they are all used up before they reach 30, what then? The abuse, the bullying, the exploitation will have become internalised and fill the space where there should be a confident secure sense of self. With no tennis to define their being or give meaning to life, they will be cast adrift in search of another Svengali figure to lead them through the wilderness. Leonard believes this path invariably leads to difficulties with depression, emptiness and loss of meaning because identification with success and achievement cannot compensate for the lack of a secure sense of identity.

Andrea Jaeger explained to Andrew Longmore in the *Sunday Times* that she was almost relieved when she suffered her career-ending shoulder injury. 'When I got injured, to be honest, I was relieved. Everyone was applauding me for playing tennis but when I was injured I thought, finally, I can go and be me.'[27] She gave all her money to setting up the Little Star Foundation which supports young cancer patients and, at the age of 41, became Sister Andrea, an Anglican Dominican nun. After prodigious success as a tennis player, and coping with an enforced early retirement, Andrea Jaeger has forged a new and independent path. Some atheists, however, might argue that her 'marriage' to Christ is no more than a capitulation to the most powerful Svengali of all.

6

HE'S MA BOY

Cycling away from death –
the will to win as a defence against loss

*'But at my back I always hear
Time's winged chariot hurrying near.'*

Andrew Marvell, *To His Coy Mistress* (1651-52)

In his fledgling professional cycling career, Lance Armstrong displayed an innocent naïveté, riding his bike like a man possessed. Well built for a professional cyclist – a legacy from his earlier triathlon days – there seemed to be no tactics about his style, just full-on, win-or-die-trying endeavour. Armstrong was a young, brash American, aggressive and talented enough to become the youngest rider to win a stage of the Tour de France at the age of 21, but the odds were stacked against him taking it further in a sport dominated by Europeans.

By the age of 25, Armstrong was still a decent pro cyclist, though by no means a great one. Then, in 1996, any dreams he had of progressing further were obliterated with the discovery that he had aggressive testicular cancer that had spread to his lungs, abdomen and brain. According to one expert, Lance had a 3 per cent chance of survival. His racing team Confidis pledged to continue to support him and then pulled the plug while he was in treatment, reasoning – perhaps understandably – that he would never race again. It might have made business sense but it was a sickening betrayal of a man in the grip of a potentially fatal illness.

Two surgical procedures – one to remove the cancerous testicle and another to remove two cancerous brain lesions – were followed by four bouts of intensive chemotherapy. It was during this darkest period that Armstrong's almost superhuman competitive spirit seemed really to kick in. He firstly declared himself a cancer survivor rather than a victim and founded the Lance Armstrong Foundation to battle the disease. Then he went out and became the greatest cyclist the world has ever seen.

The Tour de France is often cited as the world's most gruelling competition: a 2,500 mile, three-week race in which lung-bursting French mountain climbs in freezing rain alternate with 60mph chases across parched plains in scorching temperatures. Armstrong described it as a 'contest in purposeless suffering'.[1] Every day, competitors race around 100 miles at mind-numbing speeds. One bad day, one momentary loss of concentration, a puncture, a crash or a stomach bug can end a rider's chance of success. And yet, incredibly, Armstrong didn't just win one Tour, he won seven consecutively, surpassing the achievements of all other cycling giants.

According to Johan Bruyneel, Armstrong's manager, Lance nearly killed himself training for his first successful 1999 Tour de France. While most other riders were resting in the winter off-season, Armstrong and his team-mates were riding Alpine and Pyrenean switchbacks in freezing rain and snow, seven hours a day. All the work paid off. Armstrong won, leading from start to finish at a record average speed of 40.2km/h.

In *It's Not About the Bike*, Armstrong likened fighting cancer to a bike race, albeit with a very different destination; there was the pain, the suffering, the time checks and progress reports. But the cancer required him to up his game. He couldn't afford to lose concentration or focus for, if he lost this contest, he'd be dead.

In a curious way, no one could have been better prepared for both his epic battle with cancer nor with the Tour, for Armstrong's life had already been a series of guerrilla wars: from childhood to adulthood, Lance had been David battling real and imaginary Goliaths.

Victory over adversity and misfortune, the triumph of life over death is central to any understanding of Armstrong's extra-ordinary success and his resurrection through physical activity and will. Carl Jung's notion of the 'compensatory nature of opposites' provides some initial illumination in understanding this bottomless will to win – the idea that conscious activity can be a way of compensating for unconscious deep-rooted traumas and anxieties. The intensity of Armstrong's will to win would seem to have been laid down in early childhood with the help of his mother, who taught him to dominate and control difficult experiences.

Regarding these early beginnings, Armstrong wrote, 'The main thing you need to know about my childhood is I never had a real father, but I never sat around wishing for one either . . . I never had a single conversation with my mother about him.'[2] Armstrong may claim that his father quitting on him when he was two years old had no impact, but Jung might think differently. Linda Armstrong, when referring to the abandon-ment in her own autobiography (*No Mountain High Enough: Raising Lance & Raising Me*), sets the tone, impatiently dismissing the subject by stating that 'that dog' had 'been walked'.[3] It is a curious phrase, both tidy and convenient, suggesting that you don't talk about unpleasant subjects more than you have to; you simply move on. Simple though the statement is, the subtext is more complex, for psychological issues cannot be simply told to go away; they constantly have to be 'walked'. And if they're not 'walked' consciously, then they are likely to 'walk' the person unconsciously, or, in Lance's case, 'ride' them. As Jung himself warned, the real emotional significance of early trauma is that, although it may well remain hidden from consciousness, the emotion never wears out but repeatedly forces itself back on to the conscious mind. 'The explosion of affect is a complete invasion of the individual. It pounces upon him like an enemy or a wild animal.'[4]

The reality of life is that its greatest battles are often waged against the phantoms of the past. Such phantoms, however, are unlikely to have ever encountered a tougher adversary than Armstrong. As Dr Ferrari, his trainer, pointed out, 'Lance does not admit weakness . . . it's not a possibility.'[5] Armstrong's mother, from an early age, instilled in her son a belief that all setbacks should not be felt as defeats but as challenges to be overcome. Armstrong expressed this in his own inimitable way: 'Pain is temporary. Quitting lasts for ever.'[6]

Taking his mother's mantra as his rosary enabled Lance to hold uncomfortable feelings at bay. Such resistance helped hugely in his mental battle with cancer and unquestionably contributed to making him a great athlete. However, childhood values are almost always tied up with the need for love and parental approval; Lance is likely to have believed that by adhering to his mother's credo, he would please her and, in return, be loved more.

The reality, as every teacher and GP will confirm, is young children need to be encouraged to talk about difficult issues and are quick to sense 'no-go' areas. By not encouraging a dialogue about his father, his mother may have effectively vetoed the topic and, in so doing, Lance is likely to have absorbed the message not to talk about painful issues.

Linda Armstrong and Lance's father, Eddie Gunderson, were both 17 when Linda became pregnant. They were both inexperienced adolescents overwhelmed by the situation they found themselves in. It is clear, reading Linda's account of their relationship, that Eddie was too immature to be a responsible husband, let alone a father. To complicate matters further, Linda herself came from a poor family and had a father who was an abusive,

philandering alcoholic. It is not altogether surprising therefore
that she found male relationships difficult to trust or sustain and
has married and divorced several times. Linda's family dynamics
were complicated to say the least. In her autobiography, she
mentions her father beating her mother and abandoning the
family for another woman. She also describes how relieved she
was when he went off to fight in Vietnam.

For Lance, just as there was life after losing his father, so there
would be life after 'death' and, as before, the way out would not
involve looking back. When questioned about his battle with
cancer, Armstrong willingly conceded that a major part of his
recovery could well be down to his own mental fortitude. Like
most sportsmen, he's happy to accept that a gritty, positive
attitude can help overcome physical illness. What he is perhaps
more resistant to is the flipside; that physical illness or traumatic
events can create negative psychological fall-out.

It is certainly the case that most medical practitioners believe
there is often a very strong link between mental and physical
states. So what happened to those inescapable feelings of
rejection? And what of the poisonous feelings Lance must have
harboured at the harsh hands of his stepfather, Terry Armstrong?
His stepfather, we are told by Linda, was particularly strong on
discipline and regularly 'paddled' his stepson (which she goes on
to say is 'a coy way to say "hit and keep hitting"'[7]). Lance himself
even makes a rare admission that these beatings 'didn't hurt just
physically, but also emotionally'.[8]

In *It's Not About the Bike*, Armstrong provides his own sound
reason for not looking back. 'Athletes don't have much use for
poking around in their childhoods, because introspection doesn't
get you anywhere in a race . . . ' He does then, however, tellingly
concede, 'But that said, it's all stoked down in there, fuel for the
fire.'[9] Jung couldn't have expressed it better.

All the sporting greats have a phenomenal will to win that
might be considered pathological if it wasn't creatively channelled
into sport. The iconic American football coach, Vince Lombardi,

is credited with the oft-quoted paean to victory, 'Winning is not everything; it is the only thing.' He is also credited with branding as 'subversive drivel' Rudyard Kipling's famous lines regarding treating the two imposters, triumph and disaster, the same. But Lance's will to win was of an altogether different order for he had an even greater imperative as each victory symbolically took him further from the Grim Reaper concealed in the pursuing pack. The prognosis of almost certain death catapulted Armstrong into a super-human league and the more titles he won, the greater the distance he may have unconsciously felt he was putting between him and his most dangerous adversary.

After clinching his fifth Tour in 2003, Armstrong returned to the team bus with the leader's yellow jersey and was observed storming up and down the aisle punching the seats while screaming, 'No one trains like me. No one rides like me. This jersey's mine. I live for this jersey. It's my life. No one's taking it away from me. This fucking jersey's mine.'[10]

Armstrong's primary unconscious drive to victory, to possess the 'jersey', can be viewed as both victory over death but also wreaking revenge on those who came to 'steal' his mother. The outburst encapsulates the intensity of Armstrong's life-or-death need to win and perfectly exemplifies Lombardi's credo that victory is simply all there is for certain individuals. Wearing the yellow jersey can be seen as symbolically signifying Lance's victory in the Oedipal battle that earns him his place at his mother's right hand. The chivalric symbolism is redolent of Arthurian knights wearing their queens' colours into battle.

On one of the occasions when Lance and Terry Armstrong came to blows, Lance was expelled from the house and Linda was instantly filled with remorse and guilt as she felt she had betrayed him and taken the wrong side. When, eventually, the stepfather was finally sent packing, Lance confesses to feeling initially confused, as he had seen other kids at school falling apart at the seams and needing to see counsellors when their parents divorced. But 'I had a party, you know, because it's such a load off my back.

I got confused because I thought, "Well, man, what is wrong with you?" This tears kids up and yet we're kicking this guy out and [I'm] ecstatic.'[11]

Like Lancelot, Armstrong was prepared to fight to the death anyone who tried to take Guinevere/the jersey from him. It is perhaps the intensity of the Oedipal struggle that provides the raw energy – 'the fuel for the fire' – and makes the will to win non-negotiable. The role of the father can be viewed as an unwelcome intruder in this triangulation, likely to fuel paranoid-like anxieties. The intensity of the will to win is often intimately connected with the resolution, or lack of it, of the Oedipus Complex. The need to keep the parents separate and lay sole claim to the mother (by symbolically reclaiming the yellow jersey) may well have been the unconscious driving force behind Lance's athletic endeavour. No father in the following pack was ever going to get in front of him again.

The psychoanalyst, John Steiner, claimed that when the child becomes aware of a third person penetrating his exclusive bubble, an idealisation of the mother often follows, allied to an underlying feeling of grievance and resentment against the father. This, he says, is a paranoid solution to be contrasted with the healthier situation where the child is able to recognise and accept the parents' relationship.

In adulthood, Armstrong once again experienced the psychological trauma of the intruder in the most real and life-threatening way imaginable. He was 'caught' by cancer which started in one of his testicles and had to be removed through surgery as part of his treatment. If Armstrong is about anything, it is *'cojones'* ('balls'). His cycling feats and, indeed, his life can be understood as a recurring confirmation of potency. Those who question the legitimacy of his cycling achievements by suggesting he took performance-enhancing drugs are, in effect, questioning the truth of his potency.

In an early Tour of the Mediterranean race, the young gunslinger was involved in an apocryphal run-in with Moreno

Argentin, one of the Italian dons of the sport and a former world champion. As Armstrong rode up on to his shoulder, a surprised Argentin asked the upstart what he thought he was doing and then confused him with someone else, calling him Bishop instead of Armstrong. The error was instantly interpreted as a slight and Armstrong proceeded to shout abuse at Argentin while vainly attempting to get past him. Later, in the cyclists' compound, Argentin screamed at Armstrong's senior team-mates that their colleague needed to be taught manners and to respect his superiors.

A few days later, Armstrong entered the Italian Trophée Laiguelia, a one-day race that was supposed to be an automatic win for Argentin as it was an unwritten rule of pro cycling that veteran cyclists were to be respected in their home country, in front of their fans and sponsors. Predictably, Armstrong ignored protocol, went after Argentin and this time won the battle.

Taking on male authority figures (fathers) has been the leitmotif of Armstrong's life. Even during his illness, he often challenged his male doctors, placing more trust in the nurses who cared for him. What he found was that he had an almost infinite capacity to bear pain, endure and thereby overcome opponents. And in the Tour – a 'contest in purposeless suffering' – he found the perfect arena.

According to Armstrong, 'What makes a great endurance athlete is the ability to absorb potential embarrassment and to suffer without complaint. I discovered that if it was a matter of gritting my teeth, not caring how it looked, and outlasting everyone else, I won . . . If it was a suffer-fest, I was good at it.'[12] A legacy of Terry Armstrong's 'strong arm' fathering was that Lance learnt how to endure. The fact that Terry Armstrong eventually left the family added another valuable layer to Armstrong's psychic armour. Despite the pain and hurt he suffered at Terry's hands, he eventually outlasted him and won. And, in typical Armstrong fashion, he used his battle with cancer as another training camp in which he stretched the pain threshold to super-human limits. Like the stepfathers in his life, Terry

Armstrong and John Walling, cancer was another unwelcome intruder and, in typical fashion, Lance went to war and won.

Deep into his chemotherapy, Armstrong's body was deteriorating fast and he had taken to shuffling round the ward in his dressing gown, pushing his IV stand. He was due to have an MRI scan on his brain at the children's hospital that was located about a mile away through a tunnel connecting the two facilities. A nurse arrived with a wheelchair but Armstrong decided he was going to walk. 'I told her we would be taking the tunnel to Riley [the hospital] on foot, even if it meant walking all night. LaTrice didn't say a word . . . I shuffled through the tunnel, there and back. I looked like a stooped, limping old man. The round trip took over an hour. By the time I got back to my bed, I was exhausted and damp with sweat, but I was triumphant.'[13]

Daniel Coyle in *Armstrong's War* tells another tale that highlights this phenomenal capacity to bear pain that was honed in his cancer treatment. On the night before the start of the 2003 Tour de France, Armstrong found himself unable to walk. His hip, which had been injured in a crash three weeks earlier, had become jammed in its socket but Armstrong was due on stage imminently for the opening ceremony. Unable to climb even one stair, he went to the team bus and asked for his chiropractor, Jeff Spencer. There was no time for a medical assessment or even a cautionary X-ray. Instead, he asked Spencer to pull his leg as hard as he could. The sound, according to Spencer, was 'like a ten-inch dry tree snapping across a hollow log'.[14] Spencer thought he had broken something but Armstrong stood up, flexed the hip, tested it walking some stairs, thanked him and headed out for the opening ceremony.

Two other Coyle anecdotes also illuminate Armstrong's enormous physical strength and iron will. The first concerns two new riders to the Armstrong team who trained with him for a fortnight. As they wanted to impress, they rode up mountain after mountain, never complaining. They did everything Armstrong did and, at the end of the fortnight, both riders had injured their knees so badly they never raced again.

The second parable involves Armstrong's best friend and top 'domestique' (cycling's equivalent of a pace-maker), Kevin Livingstone. After the huge success of the first two Tour wins, Livingstone reasonably asked for an increase in pay. Armstrong refused, explaining that he wanted to use the money to sign more riders for the team. Livingstone quit and ended up riding for Armstrong's great rival, Jan Ullrich.

The first story illustrates Armstrong's determination and physical strength, but the second is even more revealing because it shows his single-mindedness in putting winning before all else.

In the numerous books on Armstrong, a complex and sometimes contradictory character gradually emerges: on the one hand, an impression is created of a ruthless athlete with a computer-like capacity to absorb painful information and block out negatives. And yet another Armstrong emerges between the lines: a sensitive and insecure soul, driven by fear, anger and no little paranoia. His ability to ignore negatives and move on was certainly selective and didn't extend to those whom he perceives to have crossed or slighted him. Armstrong readily admits to repeating the names of these perpetrators (or 'trolls' as he calls them) mantra-like for motivation during training and requested constant updates on their activities from colleagues. He doesn't explain what the nature of the slights or betrayals were, nor does he say why he was so hurt by them.

Sigmund Freud, writing in 1911 (*Psycho-analytic Notes on the Autobiographical Account of a Case of Paranoia* 12:3-79), suggests that long-remembered psychological slights or injuries are evidence of traumatic disappointments early in life and that vindictiveness and a capacity for revenge is an attempt to avenge those early traumas. Vindictiveness and the capacity for revenge are common components in the mindset of great athletes' will to win, providing fuel for the competitive fire. Such athletes may appear sanguine in public but privately they don't accept loss gracefully in Kipling's sense and they don't do dignity. Losing is not a feeling to be digested and reflected on but an opportunity to regroup and seek revenge. This is dramatically played out every week in post-match interviews in every sporting arena when managers or players blame the referee, cheating, the pitch, a crooked fixture list or anything else rather than themselves. Harold Searles in *The Pychodynamics of Vengefulness (Psychiatry 19;* 31-39) similarly stresses that vengefulness is often a defence against overwhelming feelings of grief, fears of separation and anxiety. The vengeful person would rather seek retaliation than passively tolerate grief.

Another 2004 Tour de France Coyle story encapsulates Armstrong's elephant memory for slights, as well as his vengefulness. A day after the extraordinarily difficult Alpe d'Huez mountain stage, the riders were supposed to have a quiet day before the last time trial. Armstrong had dominated the previous week and was set to win the Tour. It was customary on the Tour that the lesser riders would be left to contest the unimportant stages; to grab some glory for themselves and their sponsors. A group of eight riders broke away from the main group and, under normal circumstances, would have been left to fight it out. However, the whole complexion of the day's racing changed when an Italian, Filippo Simeoni, tried to move into the breakaway group. Simeoni had testified against Armstrong's doctor, Michele Ferrari, in a drugs trial in 2002. As well as admitting that he had used dope himself, Simeoni alleged that Ferrari provided him with EPO (Erythropoietin, a banned performance-enhancing drug) and instructions on how to avoid getting caught. When Armstrong had called him a liar in a French newspaper, Simeoni sued him for defamation of character.

As Simeoni started approaching the leading pack, Armstrong struck; there was history between them and slights to be avenged. Armstrong caught and passed Simeoni, then sat at the front of the breakaway group. The message was clear: Armstrong was not going to let Simeoni contest even a minor stage. Armstrong's team were astonished by his tactic. What was their team leader doing? He was already assured of winning the Tour and it was an unwritten rule of professional cycling that these routine stages be left to the lesser lights to contest. The other riders knew why Armstrong was at the front and pleaded with Simeoni to drop back, which he eventually did.

Versions of what was said between the riders differed somewhat. Armstrong claims he simply berated Simeoni for taking him to court and speaking out against his friend and trainer in the first place. Simeoni's account was somewhat different – he claimed Armstrong threatened to use all his considerable financial and legal resources to destroy him and his cycling career.

Armstrong's tactical move during the stage created dismay in the cycling fraternity. Much was said about the dignity of the yellow jersey having been sullied, and that Armstrong had shown a lack of grace and dignity. Floyd Landis, a team-mate of Armstrong's, got to the heart of the matter. 'If somebody fucks with him, he makes it clear that they shouldn't.'[15] Or as Deuteronomy 19;12 puts it, 'Life shall go for life, eye for eye, tooth for tooth.'

The problem is that while this siege mentality with its accompanying paranoia heightens the intensity of the athlete's will to win in vertical relationships (a world consisting of winners and losers), it creates a very inadequate basis for meaningful horizontal, life relationships. Coyle himself mentions that while researching his book, 'Throughout the season, Armstrong kept track of me, always letting me know he knew who I was talking with.'[16] The critical point about the siege mentality is that the need to win becomes a psychological imperative; it is a case of 'I have to' rather than 'I choose to'.

Armstrong's relationships with many older male figures, including coaches, tended to be tempestuous and Coyle tells another illuminating story about the young Armstrong that points to deeper, more complex feelings. When Lance was 15, he and his mother became friends with Rick Crawford who was, at the time, the nation's third-ranked triathlete. Crawford helped Lance with training and supported him and over the years became close to both Lance and his mother. There were tensions, however, particularly when they travelled as young Lance – used to getting his own way – was not the most obedient of young men.

On a trip to Bermuda, Armstrong rented a moped in Crawford's name and didn't return for hours, prompting a police search. Later that night, while fooling around during dinner, he broke some expensive dishes and glassware in the house they were renting. Crawford had had enough, lost his temper and tore Armstrong off a strip. Rather than be cowed and apologetic, Lance screamed back at him, 'Fuck you. You're not my dad.'[17]

According to Crawford, that was the end of the relationship. He wrote a letter to Linda Armstrong explaining the story and apologised for the incident. Despite Crawford's attempts to heal the rift, he was reputedly never invited into the Armstrong home again.

While Lance was perhaps questioning the legitimacy of Crawford's authority, at the same time, the wildness of his behaviour might also be seen as an unconscious cry for a real father to intervene, contain him and lead him out of the mother/son impasse. His constant head-to-heads with authority figures only further underlines this need, whether it is stepfathers giving him orders, or, later in life, God calling time on him. His lack of a father was both his strength and weakness. Far from being an irrelevance, the reality was that fathers – albeit absent and inadequate ones – played a very significant part in shaping Armstrong's career and relationships.

Despite the extraordinary way in which Armstrong has managed to transform adversity into triumph, there has been other collateral damage from difficult relationships, notably with colleagues and friends. Jonathan Vaughters, a former team-mate, made the observation, 'There is a pattern. People get close [to Armstrong] and then something inevitably goes haywire.'[18] Coyle claims that riders, coaches and even Armstrong's Best Man at his wedding, have all had disputes with Armstrong and have then been 'removed'. What is it that goes 'haywire'? According to Coyle, underlying the random and seemingly trivial nature of some of the fall-outs is the fact that each has failed to live up to Armstrong's expectations. Or to put it another way, Armstrong feels they have, in some way, let him down just like the 'fathers' in his life.

An important clinical report from the Anna Freud Centre by Marion Burger (1985) highlighted a study of 13 children at the Hampstead clinic who had lost their fathers through separation or divorce in the first five years of their lives and it was found to have a detrimental effect on their development. It was only when the mothers went on to have a lasting relationship with a man other than the father that the child was able to move on developmentally. She reported a 'protraction of the original narcissistic interference both in their self-development and in their sexual identity; they are adhesively (glued to) and ambivalently tied to the remaining primary object (mother)'.[19] In other words, without the presence of a father to lead the child out of the mother-child relationship, the child can be left enmeshed.

David Walsh in *Inside the Tour de France* describes the closeness between the young 21-year-old Lance and his mother, Linda. When they were out together, she would invariably introduce Lance as 'this is my baby, this is my son'.[20] Many onlookers found it hard to believe as Linda was still in her thirties. Lance meanwhile, according to Walsh, was amused that he and his mother were sometimes mistakenly taken for boyfriend and girlfriend.

In both Lance and Linda's autobiographies, there are numerous examples of their closeness. Perhaps the clearest symbol of this is the fact that Lance called his home in Texas 'Casa Linda'. At the very outset, Linda refused to let her husband hold Lance as a baby. She claimed he didn't support his head properly. The next marriage to Terry Armstrong – the disciplinarian, born-again Christian – seemed to disintegrate following major confrontations with Lance. Linda throughout her life always put Lance first – like the time she felt it only right to forego a medical operation so that it didn't clash with her son's athletic commitments. When Lance finally left home, she describes how she missed sitting down to candlelit dinners with him when they would tell each other about their day. And when Lance's father tried to contact him during his cancer treatment, she vetoed it, arguing that it would not be good for her son.

The central question from a psychoanalytic point of view is what Lance, as a boy, made of this. He states at one point that he was completely loved by his mother and that he loved her back and that this 'felt like enough for both of us'.[21] It would seem that 'the couple' shared a mutual interdependence and were sealed off from the influences and relational complexities of the outside world. It was as if the unspoken deal was that Linda would keep Lance safe and Lance would do the same for Linda.

In further trying to flesh out the idea of a 'will to win', it is worth reflecting for a moment on the symbolic nature of racing, and bike racing in particular. As Armstrong himself says, a bike race is an exercise in leaving others behind. The question that comes to mind from a psychoanalytic perspective is who exactly is being left behind. Coyle recounts the story of Armstrong and his team preparing a training ride up a crucial climb in the Pyrenees. Lance noticed that a rival team, T-Mobile, containing his arch rival Jan Ullrich, were riding up ahead. He and his teammates got into the team bus and drove on up the climb past Ullrich and the rest of the T-Mobile riders. When they were sufficiently far head, they got out of the bus and started riding. Armstrong wanted to make it clear to Ullrich that he would always be chasing, even on a training ride.

Ian Williamson's casebook – Jonathan

Jonathan was 10 when he was first sent for a psycho-analytic consultation. He had been referred by his school for disruptive, hyperactive behaviour and an inability to share, or join in, school activities. His father and mother had divorced when he was less than a year old and his father had gone to live in the United States. He now lived alone with his mother who couldn't comprehend why Jonathan behaved so badly at school and yet was a 'delightful, loving and helpful boy at home'.

It was only when we started to discuss structure and boundaries that a slightly more complex picture emerged. Jonathan was the centre of his mother's universe and clearly used to having things his own way. His mother rarely reprimanded him, preferring to negotiate or bribe him. She described him as having a temper if he didn't get what he wanted. She added that although he was confident in the day, he was frightened at night and usually ended up in her bed. She confided that she felt lonely looking after Jonathan all the time and that it was impossible to get a boyfriend as he was always so rude and confrontational with anyone she brought into the house.

I asked about his father and she informed me he had not contacted Jonathan since he left for the States soon after the divorce. She claimed Jonathan didn't miss him as he had been so young when his father left. She also added that she rarely talked about him for fear of making Jonathan upset.

My first meeting with Jonathan not only set the confrontational tone of our future appointments but it also made clear the nature of the Oedipal drama that would follow. Jonathan reluctantly followed me to the consulting room. Once inside, he tried to take control of both the room and the relationship, telling me how our arrangement would work and what the consequences would be for me if I didn't do as he instructed. I said that he seemed to want to be in control of our meetings, like he felt he was in control of his mother.

I let him make the running but a conflict quickly emerged over a game of catch. He couldn't cope with losing the game and demanded a replay. The replay ended the same way and he became even more furious. I made the comment that we seemed to be in a battle to see who was the best and that the prize was his mother, and that it made him angry when he lost because it made him feel like a little boy when he really believed he was the man in the house. He screamed that he hadn't lost the game, accused me of cheating and demanded that we play again. I told him that we had run out of time but we could continue next week. He became almost hysterical, screaming that he would decide when the meeting ended. I responded by telling him he knew I was the adult and in charge of the meetings. This was a mistake, as he knew no such thing. He believed that by sleeping in his mother's bed and successfully getting rid of potential suitors, he was in charge. He threw a small chair at me and ran out the room back to his mother.

His mother rang me several days later to ask what had gone on in our meeting as Jonathan had been highly agitated and obsessively insisting on playing catch since our last meeting. Subsequent meetings with Jonathan became increasingly fraught, tense and confrontational, and intensely rivalrous. The game of catch quickly lost any semblance of playfulness. It became an imperative and winning it carried a confirmation of domination and superiority. In his mind, he was the same or better than me; he couldn't accept that as a little boy he was unlikely to beat me, no matter how many times we played. It was painful to watch him struggle with the reality of his smallness.

Our meetings never really shifted gear and the treatment eventually broke down when Jonathan refused to come to subsequent meetings. I had sensed that this might happen. He decided to opt out and preserve the illusion of parity and occasional moments of superiority rather than face the truth of his position as a little boy in the presence of a father.

On further reflection, the treatment had little chance of success. Although his mother at one level wanted change, at another she was too caught up in a gratifying mutual interdependence and, without unravelling that knot, my attempts to get between them were doomed to failure.

What is also interesting is why Lance Armstrong chose cycling as his sport. Unlike Jonathan in the casebook above, who chose to slug it out with his rival face-to-face, or toe-to-toe, Lance opted for a less aggressive route to humiliate adversaries and leave them for dead by choosing cycling as his battleground. This allowed him both to follow his mother's mantra of accentuating the positives and, by not resorting to open aggression or quitting on the job, reassure her that he was not like her father or his.

Paradoxically, racing also means constantly being pursued and we know that being chased is the stuff of childhood nightmares and phobias and is also an essential part of childhood games. It is possible to think of a bike race in a similar way and, in doing so, we can rethink Armstrong's project from an unconscious point of view, as dedicating his life to never being caught or overwhelmed by fearful parts of himself. He himself admits in the introduction to his first autobiography, *It's Not About the Bike*, that he always does things fast and his ex-wife, Kristin, remarked in Coyle's book that as long as Lance was pushing himself to go fast, he didn't have to deal with emotions.

This idea of 'going fast' implies not only a sense of being driven by fear and anxiety but also the notion of being chased. If you are racing through life as fast as you can, there is no time or opportunity for reflection or processing experience. Armstrong and his wife both acknowledge that this mode of living effectively ended their marriage. As Kristin Armstrong succinctly put it in 2003, 'We've been together four-and-a-half years, and we've had six homes, three languages, three countries, one cancer comeback, three children, four Tour de France wins and one rise to celebrity. You're not supposed to cram a huge amount of events into such a small period of time.'[22] In a way, Lance was going so fast, the rest of the family got left behind.

Having survived cancer, Armstrong became even more consumed by moving relentlessly ahead and tellingly titled his second autobiography *Every Second Counts*. Having been caught and overwhelmed (almost terminally) by cancer, he was even more determined and focused on racing *faster*.

Armstrong – an intelligent and, in many ways, an insightful man – is not unaware of his obsession with speed and insightfully confesses, 'Self-examination has not always been my strength; for one thing, it takes too long and, for another, I have the suspicion that it's the old secrets in me, the cheats and slights of childhood, all melted down into one purpose, that make me turn the wheels.'[23]

As in his earlier autobiography, when asked why he wasn't more curious about his father, he replies, 'I've never wanted to look over my shoulder. Occasionally, friends ask me why I wasn't more curious about the past. "I don't like going backwards,"' I said, "It just creates a headache."'[24] Lance doesn't want to look over his shoulder and see what's chasing him and certainly doesn't want to allow unprocessed, difficult feelings to catch him.

In September 2001, Armstrong felt ill and became anxious that the cancer had returned. He experienced an enormous, swamping tiredness that was of an altogether different order to that which was part and parcel of his cycling season. He was sleeping 14 hours a night and it reminded him of how he felt when the cancer was first diagnosed. Understandably, the worry became overwhelming. For Armstrong, the only two markers he concerned himself in life with were his cycling speed and his blood levels. A combination of the two, he believed, always told him how he was doing.

What he may have missed, however, was the impact the forthcoming birth of twins would have on him, just two years on from the birth of his son, Luke. Subsequent tests revealed that physically Armstrong was OK, but the question of his profound tiredness remained unsolved. Armstrong came to the conclusion that he was doing too much – too much travelling, too many projects. But perhaps the constant activity, the travelling, projects, the training, was a way of coping with the seismic changes that were about to take place in the family. Might the tiredness have been a symptom of feeling depressed?

But, if this is the case, what could he have been feeling depressed about? Lance was now facing a multitude of new relationships and status changes. The role of father may now have assumed a new level of intensity, a role of which he had no positive experience. He was now thrust into the unfamiliar world where he would have to share the stage with three others for whom he would be responsible. By February 2003, just a year after the twins were born, Armstrong and his wife agreed to a trial separation. He would seem to have hit an impasse and that impasse was once again family. Although the details of his marriage break-up rightly remain private, it is hard to imagine that his need to keep coming first, and the speed he was moving at, did not have a major impact.

However much Armstrong protests the importance of his father, they were both unable to stay the course with their families and left early. Perhaps there is far more interplay between them, real or unconscious, than Lance imagines. As the family broke up, the next psychological challenge for Lance was what kind of father he would become. Would he be the absent, unreliable, philandering father of his childhood and fulfil Freud's prophecy of following in the father's footsteps, or would he make the transition to something better? It will inevitably be an enormous challenge but, if his history tells us anything, once he recognises the parameters of a challenge, there are none more determined to meet it. Today, he remains far more involved in his children's lives than his father ever was.

Once retired from cycling, Lance increasingly devoted himself to looking after the entire world 'family' of cancer sufferers. As he said in an interview with *USA Today* in June 2006, 'My mission is now bigger than winning the Tour de France.'[25] The task he has taken on is to beat the disease that almost killed him 10 years earlier. Instead of pounding mountains, he found himself pounding doors, lobbying Congress to increase funds to find a cancer cure, and raising awareness of the work done by the Lance Armstrong Foundation, Livestrong. On the website home page, the welcome banner states, 'At the Lance Armstrong Foundation we unite people to fight cancer believing that unity is strength, knowledge is power and attitude is everything.'

Sadly, no assessment of Armstrong's achievements or understanding of the man himself can be complete without addressing the persistent allegations of doping. At the time of writing this book, that is all they are – allegations. Despite having ridden for 15 years in countless races around the world, Lance never failed a drugs test. At the height of his success, he was tested 30–40 times a year (making him arguably the most drug-tested athlete in sport). Were all the negative results just luck? It seems inconceivable that if he was taking drugs, no one has come forward with substantive evidence, especially given the general antipathy towards him as an American dominating a European sport. It is also hard to believe that he would risk polluting his body in such a way after having gone through such pain and trauma in his fight against cancer.

So what about the question of why he was so much better after the cancer than before? Putting aside the mental factors that we have tried to address, Armstrong always had the physical equipment before the cancer. His heart is a third larger than that of a normal person. He also seems to be able to process lactic acid (the stuff that makes muscles burn out) more efficiently than other cyclists. What held him back was his attitude and build. He had developed too much upper-body muscle for a top cyclist from his triathlon days. The cancer decimated his upper body musculature and reduced his body weight by 20lb. This made a massive difference in the mountain climbs where body weight is the biggest problem. According to Armstrong, he was able to improve his times in the mountain stages by 10–12 minutes.

Jacques Anquetil was a cycling legend and won the Tour five times. He was frank about the subject of drugs, and has openly admitted to taking amphetamines. He is alleged to have ridden the Grand Prix de Forli without the use of any drugs for a bet to see what would happen. He won, but the suffering was apparently so great he said he would never do it again. Daniel Coyle tells an equally telling story about the great Tour champion Fausto Coppi. Coppi alleged in an interview on French television that all riders took drugs and that anyone who claimed differently knew nothing of the sport. The interviewer asked Coppi if he had ever taken drugs. Coppi is alleged to have replied, 'Yes, when necessary.' 'When was it necessary?' asked the interviewer. 'Almost always,' replied Coppi.[26] If Coppi is right and all cyclists are taking drugs, then the question regarding Armstrong is irrelevant; with or without them, Armstrong is the best there has ever been.

Armstrong's competition was of an altogether different order for his battle was with the Grim Reaper himself. The prognosis of almost certain death catapulted him into a war to become an immortal. His seeming triumph is of a mythic quality and yet the respite brought by his own back-to-back victories was always fleeting, a temporary respite from his internal struggles. Each time another Tour was secured, there was a brief illusion of having conquered the demons before he started training for the next competition. The need to reassert (and reassure himself of his dominance) always quickly resurfaced leading to a return to battle and all the suffering that it entailed. It is often a very thin line between what nourishes and what poisons.

Has he been enjoying his retirement? Maybe, briefly. Whatever, it didn't last long. Lance took up marathon running and managed to edge Dean Karnazes in the New York Marathon. He has had several high-profile relationships – with rock singer Sheryl Crow, fashion designer Tony Burch, and actresses Ashley Olsen and Kate Hudson. None lasted the course. His latest partner, Anna Hansen, is currently carrying his fourth child. It must be tough for any woman to live up to an ideal of a partner based on the selfless devotion provided by Lance's mother.

In September 2008, Lance announced he was getting back in the saddle. 'I am happy to announce that, after talking with my children, my family and my closest friends, I have decided to return to professional cycling to raise awareness of the global cancer burden.'[27] It doesn't, of course, have anything to do with an unrequited need to head the pack, prove his supremacy and win an eighth Tour de France. He also said a further motivation was finally to lay his own doping stigma to rest. 'There's this perception in cycling that this generation is now the cleanest we've had in decades, if not for ever, and the generation that I raced with was the dirty generation . . . So there is a nice element here where I can come with a completely comprehensive programme and there will be no way to cheat.'[28] Interestingly, Armstrong joined the Astana team who were kept out of the 2008 Tour because of doping violations.

If anyone seriously believed that Armstrong's return to competitive cycling would be a nostalgic shuffle around the roads of France to raise awareness of cancer, they simply didn't know Lance Armstrong. It was a cast-iron certainty that he would have checked out his physical capabilities with the precision of a microbiologist. He would also have sounded out the condition of all his main rivals. He would ride the 2009 Tour with an absolute belief that he could win it. To the chagrin of the sceptics, he took third place on the podium and proclaimed he'd be back next year with his own team.

7

JONNY BE GOOD

**Obsessional behaviour and specialist kickers –
sporting heroes in search of redemption**

*'The repetition compulsion . . . protects
the vulnerable self from potentially
traumatising experiences'*

David G Kitron in *The International
Journal of Psychoanalysis*

*FIFA World Cup qualifying round – England v Greece
Old Trafford, Manchester
6 October 2001*

The football fans who have arrived in bright sunshine
and expectation have created a carnival atmosphere
knowing the opposition are only here to allow Paul
Scholes, Robbie Fowler, Steven Gerrard and David
Beckham to express themselves expansively. Predictably,
the match doesn't quite unfold that way and, by the
second half, England have resumed their headless
chicken act. Three minutes of a generous four minutes of

injury time have passed with Greece 2-1 ahead. Unless there is a miracle, this particular Greek tragedy will end England's hopes of automatically qualifying for the Japan and Korea 2002 World Cup finals. Somewhat fortuitously, a free kick is awarded for a foul on 35-year-old veteran substitute Teddy Sheringham well outside the opponent's penalty area. David Beckham, the England captain, picks up the ball and carefully places it before launching into his customary short run up and leaning into the shot to generate maximum power. The ball arcs beyond the wall, curls and soars into the top left corner of the net. England escape by the skin of their teeth yet again.

Rugby World Cup Final – Australia v England
Telstra Stadium, Sydney
22 November 2003

Early in the first half of extra time, fly-half Jonny Wilkinson kicks England into a three-point lead and the advantage remains until late into the second period when the Australians pull level. Three minutes remain; one last chance for either side to strike the killer blow. England force their way into the opposition half, clearly manoeuvring towards a drop-goal attempt by Wilkinson. Australia, wise to the ploy, defend with manic intensity. Both sides are only too aware that this will be the decisive play of the game.

Seeing the Australians protecting the expected drop-goal, scrum-half Matt Dawson bursts through the centre, gaining precious ground. Wilkinson is by now screaming for the ball but captain Martin Johnson holds his nerve and takes it forward one last time. Johnson lays it back to scrum-half Matt Dawson, who offloads the perfect pass to Wilkinson. The Australian defence know what's coming and try to block the kick but Wilkinson, despite the extraordinary pressure, is pin-point accurate, as ever. The ball sails through the uprights, history is made and England win the World Cup for the first time.

These two seminal moments in sporting history showcase two athletes at the top of their game, united by a steely nerve and faultless technique. Neither athlete would claim to be the most skilful nor possess blistering pace, but when it comes to specialist kickers, they are peerless.

Greatness for David Beckham and Jonny Wilkinson is not down to exceptional genes nor special gifts, but rather a seemingly infinite capacity for endless repetitive practice. When everyone else has gone home, Beckham and Wilkinson will still be found at the training ground repeating kicks from different angles of the field. Endless repetition is the gift that marks them out and endless repetition is also the millstone round their necks. The obsessive practice may seem like a remarkable dedication to their chosen sport but, in reality, they are simply fulfilling the imperative of their obsessional personalities. And, in Wilkinson's case, the monster at the controls of his machine doesn't even give him Christmas day off.

Rituals, superstitions and magical beliefs are the rosary and supplications of sport. On 8 June 2008, in a football match in Ghana, two teams – the Wa All-Stars and Obuasi Ashgold – took to the field with just 10 men each and only brought their 11th on 15 minutes from time because an oracle had pronounced this to be the only way to win the match. Predictably, it ended in a goalless draw.

Finding a footballer free of superstition is a tall order. TV sports anchorman Gary Lineker admits that, in his playing days, 'In the warm-up, I would never shoot at the goal . . . I'd always change my shirt in the second half if I hadn't scored in the first, but I'd keep wearing the same shirt if I had scored. If I ever went on a bad run, I'd always get a haircut.'[1] England captain John Terry once scoured Barcelona's Camp Nou pitch

for a lost pair of lucky shinpads and ended up with about 50.
'I am so superstitious,' he has admitted, 'I've got to have the
same seat on the bus, tie the tapes round my socks three times
and cut my tubular grip for my shin-pads the same size every
game. I also drive to games listening to the same Usher CD in
my car.'[2] Adrian Mutu of Fiorentina and Romania is spared
such an assault course as he is apparently immune to bad luck –
'Curses cannot touch me because I wear my underwear
inside out.'[3]

The science of coaching is not exempt either from superstition.
In 1986, manager Carlos Bilardo, having borrowed toothpaste
from one of his players before Argentina's first successful match
in Mexico, insisted on continuing the routine all the way to the
final. Raul, the Spanish star, was reprimanded for turning up at
an international training session in a yellow t-shirt, a colour his
manager, Luis Aragones, believed unlucky. The French coach,
Raymond Domenech, meanwhile, is said to be influenced by the
star signs of players when he picks his team – Scorpios, such as
Robert Pires, being apparently a particularly high risk as 'they
always end up killing each other'.[4]

The rituals serve as amulets, protecting athletes from failure
in highly pressurised contests where 'fate' always seems to play
such a big part. It also shelters them from the fragility of their
bodies for such thoroughbreds know they are only one injury
away from early retirement. Most top athletes manage to confine
their superstitious practices to the sporting arena. For some,
however, the harmless preoccupation overflows in a far more
debilitating attack on other aspects of their lives. Paul Gascoigne
has admitted to returning often to his hotel when suddenly
overwhelmed by the fear that he's left the towels on the bathroom
rack in a marginally irregular fashion. In this chapter, we will
examine the extreme end of superstitious ritualistic behaviour,
when it becomes an obsessional neurosis or the more extreme
form of OCD.

David Beckham, the world's best-known footballer and style

icon, has openly admitted to suffering from OCD. He spoke out in 2006 about his addiction and confessed to rearranging hotel rooms and lining up cans of soft drinks to make everything orderly. 'I'll put my Pepsi cans in the fridge and if there is one too many then I'll put it in another cupboard somewhere . . . I'll go into a hotel room and, before I can relax, I have to move all the leaflets and all the books and put them in a drawer. Everything has to be perfect.'[5]

Maxine Frith fans the rumours further in an article in the *Independent*, reporting that Beckham wears white clothes to match his furniture, buys 30 pairs of identical Calvin Klein underpants every fortnight and insists on lining up his shirts according to colour. In the article, Victoria Beckham corroborates this behaviour: 'We've got three fridges – food in one, salad in another, and drinks in the third. In the drinks one, everything is symmetrical. If there's three cans of Diet Coke, he'd throw one away rather than have three – it has to be an even number.'[6]

Beckham has much in common with Jonny Wilkinson – both are, in a sense 'perfect' role models and 'perfect' ambassadors who show 'perfect' humility and dedication on and off the field. And both suffer from obsessional behaviour.

Paul Simpson, in a February 2008 blog on *Four Four Two* entitled *The Struggle for Sanity: Football, Depression, OCD*, reports that OCD is more frequent among people who leave school at 16, as most footballers do.[7] The fact that such athletes also often have to leave home at a very tender age to train at a higher level than that available in their home towns, compounds the difficulties they have to face early in life. In *Moments* (Macmillan, 2007), Cristiano Ronaldo recalls his despair at having to leave his family back on the Atlantic island of Madeira when he was just 11 so that he could attend soccer school at Sporting Lisbon.

Jonny Wilkinson holds a special place in the heart of the British sporting public. The man who kicked England to World Cup glory in 2003, like Beckham, is every mother's dream son – blond-haired, blue-eyed and hugely successful. Jonny has the body of a Greek Adonis and the looks of a film star. He never 'bigs' himself up, nor swears and will never be found exposed in the tabloids. He has a few lucrative sponsorship deals but has turned down fortunes, fearing anything that interferes with his pursuit of sporting perfection.

Jonny does the right thing all the time. He lives a monastic life that revolves around playing, resting, training and eating. If he has to miss a training session for any reason, he will double up the next day as he admits to not being able to rest until 'I have tamed the devil in my head'.[8] In an interview with Simon Hattenstone in the *Guardian*, he speaks frankly about his obsessions. The day starts with eight egg whites for breakfast followed by up to eight hours of kicking practice. He admits to training to the point at which 'my body is screaming at me and I feel like I'm going to be sick'.[9] Rob Andrew, then Newcastle's director of rugby, reputedly often hid the balls from him. And each day invariably ended with 13 fillets of chicken and a quiet night in.

Wilkinson is the most dedicated of rugby players and a walking testament to the power of discipline and goal-setting. Anything that distracts him from his pursuit of playing the perfect game and living the perfect life has been shed. Jonny Wilkinson, in short, lives a life beyond reproach.

When Jonny received the ball with 30 seconds to go in Sydney, his captain later said he wouldn't have wanted anyone else taking that last kick. The accolades and acclaim that followed sat uncomfortably on the shoulders of a man renowned for his humility, reclusiveness and obsessive training routines. No Bentleys, bling or braggadocio for Jonny; after the World Cup celebration in London, he caught the first bus home, no doubt to focus on the next training session. Wilkinson may be a superstar but, unlike many who enjoy the fêting, fame seems to be the price he has to pay for his obsession, rather than the reward.

In a *Times* interview with Robert Crampton in June 2004, Wilkinson admitted, 'I have always been fighting against myself.'[10] In television interviews, that is exactly how he appears: a man at war with himself, tortured by doubt and anxiety. But what is this war raging inside him? What is the anxiety? And what is the devil he has to tame with his obsessional kicking practices? In the Hattenstone *Guardian* interview already mentioned, he talks about a Peanuts cartoon that he used to have on his wall that perhaps encapsulates the man better than anything else. In the cartoon, Charlie Brown is walking around saying he is really worried because he has nothing to worry about.

If Carl Gustav Jung, one of the founding fathers of psychoanalysis, were treating Jonny, he would no doubt suggest that Wilkinson is in a war to eliminate his 'shadow'. In 1945, Jung gave his most succinct definition of that shadow as 'the thing a person has no wish to be'.[11] In other words, it is the sum of all the unpleasant qualities one wants hidden. Jung, however, emphasises that the shadow plays a hugely important role in the psyche by making us all human and fallible. 'Everyone carries a shadow, and the less it is embodied in the individual's conscious life, the blacker and the denser it is. If it is repressed and isolated from consciousness, it never gets corrected and is liable to burst forth suddenly in a moment of unawareness. At all counts, it forms an unconscious snag, thwarting our most well-meant intentions.'[12]

Wilkinson obliquely tried to get to grips with his dilemma in his 2008 autobiography, *Tackling Life*. 'Searching for the perfect, lasting results in a world of forever evolving and unforeseeable events has been a very expensive and unforgiving vocation at times.'[13] How he manages to control the uncontrollable is testament to the convoluted mind games the obsessive has to go through in order to cope with their anxiety. As someone intent on being in control, it is clear that the future – with its inherent uncertainties and unknowns – is dangerous ground and Wilkinson deals with it in a similar manner to visiting a palm reader; in order to allay his anxieties, he imagines someone coming back from the future to tell him how life unfolds and reassures him that it will all be fine. He has a dialogue with this imaginary person as a way of relieving himself of the anxiety of not knowing. 'My imaginary conversations kept me awake for hours as I convinced myself that I would of course succeed'.[14] Why, one might ask, is the future so frightening? And why is it so much more likely to bring failure and catastrophe rather than something good, unless he magically brings it into the present and controls – and thus disarms – it?

The issue of denying the 'shadow' or uglier aspects of oneself is worth dwelling on for a moment because, if successful, it allows one the glow of 'being good' or the illusion of 'being perfect'. The child's wish to be loved is a powerful motivation for being good. The secure child has a strong internal feeling of being loved for who he/she is rather than how he/she behaves. If, however, there is an excessive desire to please, it can be a sign of insecurity and deep-seated doubt regarding self-worth.

It is a feature of Wilkinson's philosophy that everything has to be earned (and, by implication, that perhaps he is inherently undeserving). He would also appear to be driven by a fear of letting people down. Following his shoulder operation in 2003, he sat down to assess his life and jotted down his goals in a little black book. 'When I examined the dreams that had already come true, I saw those accomplishments as the result of hard work. I had earned them. The ones which still eluded me I seriously hadn't worked hard enough'.[15] He also admits loving 'to sit down and chill out, but only if I feel I have deserved it'.[16] Speaking to Tim Adams of the *Observer* in June 2008, Wilkinson confessed that having such high standards sometimes made it a struggle to keep his head above water – '. . . if I said the wrong thing or laughed too much or if I didn't do enough practice, I would go under'.[17]

So why might he be so afraid of letting himself and other people down? Why might he need to earn the right to rest and relax? Are they both manifestations of insecurity and a fragile sense of self? But there is also an absence of relatedness in his explanation. The training rituals and obsessive practice could be seen as ways of bolstering a fragile self-image and, crucially, they are all under his control and do not involve anyone else. His lifelong dedication to being the best necessitates that he eliminate all the 'shadow' aspects of himself.

There is no question that Wilkinson's obsessive pursuit of perfection in his sport and his need to exert total control over every aspect of his life has exacted a heavy price. His obsession has taken him to the point of self-destruction. Endless hours of goal kicking practice has damaged his groin, wrecked his back and torn muscles up and down his legs, requiring him to learn a whole new kicking technique. The rest of his body has also suffered; following his World Cup-winning drop-goal, he endured one serious injury after another for the best part of three years. A fractured facet in the left shoulder was followed by a haematoma in the upper arm, ligament damage to the left knee, an appendix operation, a hernia operation, a torn adductor muscle in his groin, medial ligament damage to the right knee, a lacerated kidney and – following the 2007 World Cup – another shoulder operation. His monastic lifestyle, obsessive kicking routines and dedication to rugby self-improvement would seem to be proving too much for his body.

In those dark days of interminable injury and rehabilitation, there was a great deal of doubt as to whether Wilkinson would ever play again at the highest level. His autobiography, written in conjunction with his fitness coach and friend Steve Black, reads in many respects like a medical manual. He describes, by his own count, at least a dozen serious injuries, each one followed by a redoubling of his efforts in the gym and on the practice field.

Despite the honesty and thoughtfulness of his reflections on his life, it would seem that he might have missed a fundamental systemic problem – his head seems to have been ignoring messages sent out by his body. Indeed, mind and body would appear to have parted company like a married couple in the throes of a painful divorce and unwilling to communicate with each other. Perhaps the blocking of such messages is deliberate.

Whatever the truth, the fact remains that, since 2003, Wilkinson has played hardly any rugby but has instead spent most of the time tending to injuries.

The obsessive practice and physicality of his play may be exacting too high a price but Jonny is clearly unwilling to make any concessions. This seems a curious act of negligence from a man dedicated to perfection. Might it be possible to imagine that Wilkinson's bravery is, in fact, a kind of unconscious self-harming? It would certainly appear that the drama being enacted is resulting in serious damage and that perhaps the real injuries that need tending are those in his psyche.

Wilkinson's glorious resurrection came against Scotland in the 2007 Six Nations Championship. A try, two conversions and five penalty kicks were an astonishing return given that the man had hardly played any rugby in the previous three years. One expected celebration and relief, but that has rarely been the case with Wilkinson. Kevin Mitchell, writing in the *Observer*, described his post-match interview as a 'masterclass in anxiety'.[18] The reality is that what Wilkinson seeks is perfection, but what he really needs is redemption. Wilkinson would appear to suffer from what Freud would call obsessional neurosis and, like all obsessives, the really important contests and relationships are going on in the mind; the result of the game is just a part of a much bigger, more complex picture.

Speaking to Donald McRae in the *Guardian*, Wilkinson admitted, 'The problem with me is I always think I should have done better. I felt that after the World Cup final and the same goes for my whole career. But it's the only way to go about this job — and life itself.'[19] He also confesses, 'I always needed to push my expectations way above those of everyone else, but as people started to expect more of me, it got harder and harder. If I beat my expectations it was, for me, nothing — that was where I should be — but if I failed it was crazily painful and lasted so much longer.'[20]

At one level, Wilkinson's comments are innocent enough;

after all, he is a dedicated, world-class athlete, with high expectations. But dig a little deeper and a more complex picture emerges. The point he is making is that the result of the game has little to do with how he feels about it. He is effectively saying, 'I have won the World Cup, the pinnacle of my career, but I do not feel ecstatic because I did not play the perfect game . . . ' (he even claimed that the actual winning kick wasn't very good and was more of a miskick). As he didn't play the perfect game, he can only take limited pleasure from it and must practise more until he achieves perfection. But perfection, as we all know, is impossible. This paradox provides the starting point of our enquiry into the tortured relationship between the obsessive and his sport.

Dissatisfaction with personal performance, even in victory, has been the pattern of Jonny's life. Iain Spragg and Adrian Clarke in *The Jonny Wilkinson Story* (Carlton Books, 2004) describe how, on an England Under-21 tour to Australia, having roundly beaten a New South Wales team by more than 70 points, Wilkinson sat inconsolable in the changing room for having missed a tackle that resulted in the one try England conceded. The pursuit of perfection, especially in sport, may arguably be a legitimate goal but to extend it to a 'way of living' as he suggests (' . . . it's the only way to go about this job – and life itself . . . ') is a philosophical journey that can only end in disappointment and failure. The experience of perfection, even if it was attainable, is but a fleeting moment in the passage of time and can never be a state of mind. Wilkinson's impossible quest is both to win the game and play perfectly. As he acknowledges, however, the pursuit of the latter has taken precedence over his enjoyment of the former.

If anyone doubts the persecutory nature that accompanies the obsessive state of mind, consider the feats of another famous sporting giant, runner Ron Hill. At the peak of his career, Hill won both the European and Commonwealth marathons but is now more famous for holding the world record for running on consecutive days. Ron has run every single day since 20 December 1964 and has so far totted up 150,000+ miles – a distance equal to circumnavigating the world six times. Nothing has stopped him, not even a head-on car crash in 1993 when he broke his sternum and damaged his heart. 'Luckily, I'd run that morning and I recovered sufficiently the next day to be let out. In the evening, my mother and my wife went out to do the weekly shop, so I walked down to a level stretch of road and ran a mile and walked back. I didn't tell them I was running. I did that for a week, and then started to build up again . . . The same year, I had a bunion operation. I ran a mile a day in a plaster cast, in a specially adapted shoe you get from hospital. That was more embarrassing than difficult, because I was going so slowly.'[21]

The daily run fulfils a basic imperative for Hill; it is not about the act of running itself nor even the enjoyment of the run. Hill's ritualistic imperative to run is not dedication but part of a compulsive need to appease some internal demand. It is about the fear that something terrible will happen to him if he misses a day. One day, of course, this extraordinary record will eventually come to an end – and then what? It is a very perilous sense of self whose very foundation depends on the completion of a daily run.

The historical origins of obsessional behaviours have their roots in early religious life. Some writers have claimed that intense religiosity can at times predispose devotees to obsessive scrupulousness and compulsive behaviour. This was particularly evident with religions that encouraged the suppression of sexual urges and often involved compulsive, ritualised acts of cleansing or self-mortification. In the Middle Ages, those who exhibited blasphemous, sexual or other seemingly 'sinful' thoughts were thought to be possessed by the devil and the accepted treatment was exorcism – a process of driving out the devil (Wilkinson's taming 'the devil in my head'). H. F. Ellenburger in *The Discovery of the Unconscious: The History and Evolution of Dynamic Psychiatry,* noted that sixteenth-century Catholic theologians used the word 'obsessio' to describe a state where alien thoughts and tendencies from outside occupied an individual (in other words, the infiltration of one's body by demons). Early attempts to make sense of these conditions may appear far removed from today's more complex understanding, but they share a common thread in identifying the notion of sin and associated feelings of guilt. The compulsive activities of the obsessive are performed to drive out similarly unpleasant, debilitating thoughts. To the healthy, such ritualistic tasks can seem peculiar and pointless but, for the sufferer, the routine and content are critically important because they ward off threatening anxieties.

Wilkinson himself confessed to Owen Slot and Matt Dickinson in the *Times*, 'I am a classic obsessive, classically driven. As a kid, I was one of those people who shoots paper in a bin and thinks, "If I miss this one, I'm going to die."'[22] He went on to explain, 'I have always had six kicks at the end of a training session. Normally, I put six through the posts and think job done. But if you miss one you have to start them again. And if you miss one early, then you think, now you are really pissing me off. An hour-and-a-half later I can be starting the whole session again.'[23]

His earlier reference to feeling like he was drowning is illuminating. One might dismiss his anxiety about dying if he missed a basket as a generalised fear that we all experience. But for some obsessives, the fear of death can be a completely different order of experience to the general, vague and depressing prospect of life coming to an end one day.

Over a century ago, Pierre Janet provided the first real insight into the stages of what is now defined as OCD and his writings on the subject are as relevant today as they were then. He described the first phase as a 'psychasthenic' state in which a patient is tormented by the conviction of being imperfect, despite reassurances from other people that his tasks have been performed well. He labelled the second stage as 'forced agitation', a state where repetitive and excessive behaviours are prevalent and where there is an exaggerated need for precision and perfection (and intense anxiety when the person falls short). The third stage he called 'obsessions and compulsions', in which obsessive ideas are carried close to, or beyond, the boundary with delusion (for example, when certain anorexics see themselves as 'fat' while in reality being dangerously thin).

Obsessive-compulsive treatments have clearly long held interest for psychoanalysis. In the early twentieth century, Freud attributed obsessive-compulsive behaviour to unconscious conflicts, which reveal themselves as symptoms. Thus, for Jonny the obsessive kicking might be thought of as a symptom of an unconscious conflict.

Central to the pathogenesis of obsessive-compulsive psycho-pathology is the pivotal moment when the person is faced with an experience, feeling or thought which arouses a level of anxiety that cannot be managed. In order to control this distress, the person separates the feelings from the idea that is troubling him and reconnects the feelings to other things that are not in themselves compatible – running for Ron Hill, kicking for Beckham and Wilkinson. In this way, the situation can be managed, although it is not resolved.

The other problem with this particular coping strategy is that there is inevitably a sense of 'a job half done'. As a result of the false connection, those outlets of repression become obsessions and compulsions. Because there is no real resolution, the feeling of anxiety attached to the seemingly 'innocent' pursuit becomes increasingly charged. The momentary relief that comes with completion is quickly transformed back into an imperative to repeat. In Shakespeare's *Macbeth*, however many times Lady Macbeth washes her hands, she can never quite manage to wash away her own deep-rooted sense of guilt at encouraging her husband to murder the king. Earlier, while playing host to King Duncan, she calls on evil spirits to 'stop up th'access and passage to remorse . . .' (Act I, Sc 5).

The guilt, however, does not have to be as extreme as complicity in murder. Someone, who, as result of a disturbing early experience, thinks that sex is 'dirty', might similarly end up compulsively washing their hands to cleanse themselves of their 'dirty' thoughts. In Lady Macbeth's case, she cannot simply 'stop up th'access'; guilt overwhelms her and she commits suicide. In the less extreme example, the hand washing similarly does nothing to affect the disturbing thought that sex is dirty in any real sense and invariably leads to ever more compulsive hand washing – the paranoid, obsessively sterilised room that American newspaper magnate Howard Hughes inhabited comes to mind. Because of this false connection between feelings and ideas, there can only be momentary relief and no resolution, just a strong sense of incompleteness, and the need therefore constantly to repeat the ritual. It is the sense of incompleteness and the wish for completeness (perfection) that drives the compulsion.

Critical to an understanding of the obsessive's state of mind is the fact that the compulsive acts are not guided by objective needs or results but by the technical requirement of absolute scrupulousness. Returning briefly to Lady Macbeth, while her husband returns to his chamber once he has committed the murder of Duncan, his wife returns to the murder scene and meticulously smears the sleeping grooms with Duncan's blood. Everything must be done correctly, everything must aspire to perfection. Lady Macbeth cannot be just another noble's wife, she must be Queen. Wilkinson cannot bear to be just another good kicker, he must be perfect. For the obsessive, the question asked every day is: 'Have I done everything I can to move my life forward?' And the answer is inevitably: 'Not enough, and so I must do more.' Because the source of the anxiety is never addressed but, instead, momentarily exorcised, it makes such obsessional states of mind so unrelenting and persecutory.

Jonny Wilkinson's obsession with kicking started very young and quickly became the centre of his life. What is rather curious and surprising is that no one seems to have been overly troubled about his kicking obsession. According to Spragg and Clarke in *The Jonny Wilkinson Story*, he was already working on his kicking technique as a toddler, knocking toilet rolls round the living room. In the Robert Crampton *Times* interview mentioned earlier, Wilkinson describes the beginning of his obsession: 'My mum would drive me to a rugby club and sit in the car for hours while I kicked because I had a bad day at school. My parents knew that if I didn't have peace of mind, I'd be horrendous. I would be inconsolable. There was nothing they could say that would make it better, not "You'll be fine tomorrow" or "Next time you'll be great."'[24]

On another occasion, as a teenager, having spent five hours kicking balls about the field, his mother reasonably suggested they return home. Jonny became upset because he hadn't got to where he wanted to be. Allegedly, she sat in the car for another hour-and-a-half until he got it right. As Spragg and Clarke note, 'His search for perfection left him with little time for other interests.'[25] Without the slightest hint of irony, Wilkinson confesses that what 'made me so happy' was practising every lunch hour at school and throughout the holidays. An interesting by-product of this obsession was that he got to keep control of his mother.

These childhood memories, detailing ever more extraordinary feats of devotion to his kicking practice, do not seem to have struck anyone as either odd or worrying. On the contrary, they are talked about in reverential tones, hinting at the idea that genius was at work, rather like the discovery of a precocious musical talent. In fact, it was probably nothing of the sort. At the very least, this young boy would seem to have been in a certain amount of distress; distress that he kept at bay by endless compulsive kicking practices. One wonders what those around him might have made of it all if his compulsion had been hand washing rather than kicking. Wilkinson acknowledges how his training and kicking practices became addictions that were essential to help alleviate his anxiety. 'Without my daily fix, there would be huge conflict in my mind between my desire to let go and a voice which told me I wasn't yet ready or that I should be doing more'.[26] His parents understandably decided, as most caring parents would, that as this was the thing that made their boy happiest, they would build their lives around it.

Following Freud's logic, it seems that Wilkinson's kicking obsession is only partially connected with the game he plays; it is simply his way of managing other deeper-seated anxieties. What did kicking a ball through rugby posts have to do with making a bad day at school manageable, and why would he be 'horrendous and inconsolable' if he couldn't practise his kicking? What was it that made him 'so happy' when he was able to practise during lunch break at school instead of playing with friends? Was it because he got better at it or because he now had more time to take control of distressful, unmanageable feelings? These questions are crucial to any understanding of the obsessional state of mind and answering them also sheds light on Wilkinson's dilemma.

There is something fundamental missing in Wilkinson's explanation of how he managed upset. Most children who have bad days at school turn to their parents for comfort and support; a chat or a cuddle might be enough. Despite the fact that his mother was clearly devoted to him, drove him to the rugby club and waited hours in the car, from the evidence of Wilkinson biographies and interviews, it would seem she was unable to provide enough comfort to make the 'inconsolable' consolable. It would appear that nothing she – nor his father – said had a balming effect on his emotional state. Only a lengthy kicking practice managed that job. His kicking routines (routines he could control) seem to have replaced people (whom he couldn't control) as containers of his anxiety. But it is also clear that the acute nature of his anxieties made the ritualistic practice a matter of urgency as he 'must have peace of mind' or he couldn't cope.

His use of the word 'inconsolable' is also instructive. What is it that he is inconsolable about? 'Inconsolable' describes an extreme state of emotional pain; a feeling more usually associated with terrible loss. It is not the usual way of describing a bad day at school. So where might this feeling come from?

Panic attacks often accompany obsessive/compulsive states of mind and they have been part of Wilkinson's life since he was a child. Speaking to Lina Das of the *Sunday Times*, Jonny claims he only got his first uninterrupted night's sleep when he was eight years old. Before that, he spent most of his nights worrying about his mini-rugby and about school. When he wasn't at school, he was worrying about going back to it. 'I had a chart where I crossed off the hours one by one and I'd start to panic when there were 112 hours to go.'[27]

Wilkinson talks about the genesis of his panic attacks in his earlier autobiography, *My World*, describing the almost paralysing levels of anxiety that gripped him before games even as a 10-year old. Wilkinson says he regularly suffered panic attacks on the morning of the game. He would cry and be consumed by a strong urge not to go through with the game. He would also invariably be sick on the way to a game. Interestingly, he says that it was the fear of losing and terror of letting himself down that overwhelmed him.

To the adult eye, the intense level of anxiety Wilkinson experienced seems markedly disproportionate to the minor significance of the actual junior games he was playing and even Wilkinson himself must have been aware that other boys were not enduring the same level of emotional persecution. Why was this small boy putting himself through such an ordeal and, perhaps more importantly, why could his parents not help him? With the benefit of hindsight, it is possible to answer at least part of the question. As a self-confessed control freak, the intense pre-match anxiety was clearly connected with his inability to control the multitude of uncertainties involved in a team game of such complexity. A significant feature of obsessions and compulsions is the need for control and when that need for control is threatened, panic can set in. This is also what happened to Wilkinson as an adult during the years of injury-related purgatory. His injuries began to threaten both his state of mind and the routines on which his life depended. By understanding the dynamics of the panic attack, it is possible to get some sense of the origin of his obsessive thinking and the intensity of his devotion to his kicking obsession. The one area of the game he could control was when he was in possession of the ball with the posts in front of him.

It is also worth reflecting for a moment on the symbolism of his relationship with a ball. Like Beckham, Wilkinson has probably spent more time with a ball than he has with any one individual in his life. So what is the nature of that relationship and what is its purpose? Watching children play with toys, one is struck by how they use them to act out imaginary dramas and solve internal problems. For Beckham and Wilkinson, their toy is the ball and they are hard at work trying to sort out a relation to it. There are many things going on at an unconscious level but, first and foremost, they are trying to get it to do exactly what they want, just like a small child trying to control his parents. The object doesn't move of its own accord so they are able to be precise about how they connect with it; they are searching for the perfect connection. However, there is a certain amount of aggression involved because they are kicking the ball hard. The other interesting quality of the relationship is the fact that they are kicking it away; the phrase 'kicked into touch' comes to mind as a description of getting rid of something or someone. In short, there is a mini drama going on about a problematic relationship; a washing of hands. This drama includes issues about control of a loved one, anger and absence. But the central drive underpinning it all is the need to be in control.

Ian Williamson's casebook – Billy

Billy was 11 and had been referred for treatment because of his compulsive, obsessional behaviour. His parents described him as a boy full of anxiety about 'everything' and unable to enjoy any aspect of his life. At school, he was something of a perfectionist in both his behaviour and his academic work. At our first meeting, he regaled me with an endless list of anxieties which effectively amounted to a generalised worry about being alive. He was pale-looking, his fingernails were bitten to the quick and he had the distracted look of someone preoccupied with important matters.

What he was preoccupied about was an overwhelming need to get everything right both at home and at school. Allied to this general anxiety was a preoccupation about his bedroom – or more specifically the things in it – as well as his bedroom windows. Everything in the room had to be in the right place and windows always had to be closed. As he began recounting how much time he had to spend going back to the room to constantly check, he broke down in tears. Although he was unable to resist the compulsion to go back and check time after time, he was simultaneously worried that he was going mad. The skin on the tips of his fingers was broken from the constant attempts to tighten the window locks.

This particular case gives us a wonderful insight into the persecutory nature of the obsessive/compulsive mindset. The intense anxiety of 'something being moved' had become attached to the idea of things in his bedroom staying in the same place. There was the same false connection with the closed windows. The fear of something being stolen had attached itself to the idea of burglars and the need for windows to be checked and rechecked. What had to be sorted out was the nature of the right connection. The difficulty with exploring Billy's compulsions was the lack of a narrative and it was difficult to identify any meaningful coherent story. Billy couldn't shed any light on why he had to do his checking and rechecking, only that he had to do it. This is the world of the obsessive – lifeless, repetitive and apparently meaningless, a life devoted to the management of extreme anxiety.

There was a breakthrough of sorts when Billy's mother rang to recount an incident that had occurred the previous night. Billy had become hysterical when his mother had gone out for the evening leaving him with the family babysitter. Billy had remonstrated with his mother, however, demanding she stay with him. Because of the level of his distress, his mother seriously considered changing her mind but her husband insisted they keep to their plan. Billy was apparently still in a rage when she returned some three hours later.

Ashamed and embarrassed by his outburst and behaviour, he was understandably reluctant to talk about it at our next meeting. It gradually emerged that what Billy really wanted was to stay in the same place as his mother. He wanted to be in control of her coming and going. The compulsive checking of things in his bedroom was a way of compensating for the impossibility of making good this wish to keep her where he wanted her. Later meetings revealed that he had been deeply affected by the birth of his younger brother, whose arrival he had connected with his mother going out and coming back with a rival. It emerged, through time, that the compulsion to check the windows had a link with his strong antipathy towards his brother. I made the comment that when he was angry with his brother, maybe he wished that a burglar steal him and that his need to constantly check that the windows were closed was a way of warding off his guilt at having such nasty thoughts. The piecing together and making sense of the narrative relieved him enormously and, in time, his obsessions and compulsions diminished and eventually disappeared during treatment.

Franco De Masi wrote a seminal paper on the psychodynamics of panic attacks in the *International Journal of Psycho-Analysis* in 2004. In it, he outlines the grim physical experience of a panic attack and suggests possible causes for such extreme states. He describes the attack as an eruption of unpredictable and intense anxiety felt entirely in the body. This eruption is accompanied by an acute sense of suffocation (or drowning, in Wilkinson's case). It has much in common with persecutory terror. The expectation of a catastrophe (future experience) – for example, a plane crashing – is experienced by the individual in his present experience as the plane actually crashing. De Masi goes on to explain how those who suffer from panic attacks are convinced that their death is imminent even though at another conscious level they know that it is not. The panic somehow overrides their capacity to be rational. He suggests, therefore, that the panic attack, while experienced bodily, is primarily a phenomenon of the mind.

The fact that the anxiety that initiates the panic can override the conscious mind suggests a weakness in the structure of the sense of self. The mind can normally contain anxiety and treat it for what it is, but if the anxiety is such that it cannot be contained, then it spills over into the body and is experienced as a deadly panic. Masi uses the term 'psychic skin' to describe this container for anxiety; a sort of protective barrier. In a panic attack, the 'psychic skin' leaks and the boundary between inside and outside is lost; as a consequence, the anxiety floods into the body (Wilkinson's drowning, perhaps). One function of the rituals and the compulsions of the obsessive are concrete attempts to create a containing structure, something equivalent to this 'psychic skin'.

Dr Fredric Busch, in an article on the *Psychodynamic Treatment of Panic Disorder* in *Primary Psychiatry*, explains more clearly the relational aspects of panic attacks. Research observations suggest that those who suffer from panic disorders often have difficulty with angry feelings and fantasies. A vicious cycle arises in which the child's anger is felt to threaten his all-important tie to the parents.

This then increases anxiety in the sufferer about the security of his dependency on them and snowballs to the uncontrollable onset of panic attacks. The panic attack averts the experience of anger and compels attention to the patient's distress. Busch also suggests that certain individuals are more susceptible to the onset of panic attacks because they are temperamentally fearful and prone to anxiety about separation and anger. As a consequence, they are often anxious about their attachments and are especially fearful of rejection and abandonment.

The picture now becomes clearer. Could it be the panic attacks that have bedevilled Wilkinson's life have their origin in both temperament and also in fears about his anger and aggression? Wilkinson has made much of his extreme, almost crippling levels of anxiety, especially before a game. This is evidence of what we would understand as a fragile self feeling under attack. Rugby and kicking provide a perfect arena and outlet for both the aggression and the anxiety. As he perceptively revealed to Lina Das in his *Sunday Times* interview, 'I suppose the key for me in any kind of people relationship is to realise that I'm not dealing with a ball.'[28]

There is another crucial aspect to this most curious of mindsets. While at a conscious level Wilkinson is obsessively engaged in making himself into the best rugby player he can be, at a deeper psychological level he is battling with a demanding internal figure for acceptance and validation; in psychoanalysis it is known as the 'superego'. This kind of superego demands unquestioning devotion, total compliance and servitude and is only satisfied by perfection. The struggle to satisfy the demands of the superego have dictated the shape of Wilkinson's life and taken an enormous toll on his body. He has stated many times that he dreads the day when he has to stop playing – and no wonder. When time is called on this illustrious sporting career, will he follow Ron Hill's lead but, instead of pounding the lonely road daily, be seen banging balls over the rugby posts late into the night in a forlorn quest to quell the inner demons? He is implicitly raising an important question: when does sporting dedication – an optional and chosen state of mind – slip over into the compulsory one of obsessional behaviour?

What is the superego and how does it become so powerful and demanding? Everyone breaks rules or does things that they feel guilty about. The voice that calls us to account is the superego or conscience. Freud conceived of it as an internal, regulating authority. A healthy person has a superego that helps him become a social being by making him feel guilty when he does something wrong or behaves badly. However, the qualities of tolerance and forgiveness are behind the spiritual idea of redemption. Things get difficult when the internalised superego is excessively harsh, demanding and destructive. The main consequence then is that there is a mountain of guilt waiting to be heaped on the individual for any perceived failure, transgression or act of disobedience. At its absolute worst, suicide or even murder can seem like the only way to silence the remorseless assault on the individual's sense of self as Lady Macbeth discovered.

In the Simon Hattenstone interview in the *Guardian*, Wilkinson stated, 'I believe in the 24-hour video camera, the idea that you can hand a video of your life to anyone at any time and be happy with it. I live as if I am being watched the whole time and I believe I am.'[29] When Hattenstone asked the obvious question regarding who it is that is constantly watching him, Wilkinson replied without hesitation, 'a higher being'. This begs the obvious question of who or what is this 'higher being', who is it videoing his life and for what purpose? Perhaps the answer is that it is Jonny's superego and it is scrutinising him for any imperfection in thought and deed.

Wilkinson elaborates on this idea of 24/7 video surveillance in another *Guardian* interview with Donald McRae and unwittingly highlights its purpose, which is far from benign. He imagines that anything he does that makes him less than proud will be screened back to him and the people he loves most. 'I try to follow this ethos because when I go to bed every night I want to feel I've done absolutely all I can to move forward in my life. I need that intense self-scrutiny because setting goals and chasing them is crucial.'[30] Tellingly, he doesn't say why it is crucial but the statement really needs to be reversed for its true significance to be understood. If all the things that he is, that make him less than proud, are played back to him and to those he loves, they will not love him and they will think that he is an unworthy person. He cannot sleep or rest if he is less than 100 per cent focused on being the best person he can be 24 hours a day. If he can achieve this, then he cannot be criticised or humiliated by the person who is holding the video camera. We are back in the territory of the shadow and its suppression.

While Wilkinson's lifelong devotion (subservience) to the demands of his superego has made him arguably the greatest rugby kicker of all time, it has taken a terrible toll on both his physical health and his mental sense of wellbeing. Far from pursuing the illusion of the perfect kicking practice or the perfect game, he is in desperate need of redemption; he needs forgiveness for the 'sin' of being imperfect, for being human.

We wrote, somewhat controversially, at the beginning of this chapter that while Wilkinson is undoubtedly one of the greatest kickers the game of rugby union has seen, he would not lay claim to being one of its greatest players. He can win games with his kicking but he does not possess the magic, the off-the-cuff genius of, say, a David Campese or a Barry John. Who knows, Wilkinson may well be capable of such genius but it cannot emerge from within his present psychological framework. To understand this, we need to look at the complex relationship that exists between obsessional states of mind, levels of anxiety and sporting creativity. We might think of the sporting genius as a 'free spirit', someone confident in their ability, free from doubt and dread; someone excited by opportunities and possibilities, someone undaunted by fear of failure. They are able to exist/think in the moment, unencumbered by worries about what should or shouldn't be done. Free from these negative thoughts, they are able to exploit opportunities and act quickly and incisively. This mindset implies a particular relation both to anxiety and also to the superego. If anxiety is too great, then performance is affected by the paralysing quality of fear. We have written earlier that the individual's relation to their superego is critical in how they feel about themselves. The 'free spirit' has a healthy supportive or even dismissive relationship with the superego; a relationship that facilitates exploration and curiosity and is understanding and forgiving of mistakes.

The obsessional, by contrast, is plagued by doubt and fear of failure. It is a state of mind characterised by control and accompanied by excessive levels of anxiety; especially when rituals are being threatened. However, it is the relationship with a hostile and demanding superego that militates against the possibility of sporting creativity or moments of genius. The obsessional has no such freedom or support from the superego. Their relationship is built on conformity, servitude and duty; doing the right thing, rather like a member of a religious cult. It punishes any sign of the individual's independence or creativity by heaping guilt and shame on them for their disloyalty and disobedience. But, more importantly, it is unforgiving in its attitude to mistakes or wrong options. It's a crippling mindset, one that Wilkinson battles with before every big game and has done since he played mini-rugby.

In 2006, England goalkeeper David James in an interview in the *Observer* insightfully asked, 'How normal is kicking a ball 1,000 times a day?' He went on to dissect the art of specialist kickers. 'With dead-ball specialists such as Beckham or [Frank] Lampard, the game stops when they put the ball on the floor. It's all about control. You strike the ball as you have done thousands of times in training – and it ends up in the same place. You expect it to, there is satisfaction in achieving it, but it's no surprise . . . Everyone is happy to talk about superstition in football, but superstition is easy to confuse with obsession. Magpies are one thing, but many footballers have an obsessive routine that goes way beyond normal.'[31] In March 2009, he signed a contract to play for Toulon in France. As far as we know, the video camera travelled with him.

Wilkinson's dramatic resurrection was relatively short lived. He played reasonably well in the 2007 World Cup in France. A shambolic England team somehow managed to fight their way into another final. There was to be no repeat of the 2003 heroics from either Wilkinson or the team, however. A tense but dull final was won by South Africa at a canter. On the back of some decidedly average performances, Wilkinson was dropped from the team at the end of the 2008 Six Nations championship and, although picked for the summer tour to New Zealand, had to withdraw yet again with injury, citing the need for another shoulder injury operation.

He seems to have had an epiphany of sorts during his recovery from his last injury. In his latest autobiography, *Tackling Life*, he reveals that he has a new, more joyful and relaxed attitude to life and rugby. Sadly, it seems that some of the old dynamics are still to be worked through, however. In October 2008, Wilkinson badly injured his left knee, four games into yet another comeback and was sidelined for several months. According to Wilkinson it was his most painful injury yet, but he is quick to reassure us that he will be back better than ever.

8

The End

The dying animal – potency and impotence in the ring and on the court

'What someone is, begins to be revealed when his talent abates, when he stops showing us what he can do.'

Nietzsche

The Washington Wizards went into their game with the New York Knicks at Madison Square Garden on the last Tuesday of October 2001 in an upbeat mood. Games against the Knicks were always tough and playing in New York ensured a hostile reception for visiting teams. The atmosphere was unusually tense, heightened by the fact that it was being viewed as a definitive showdown with immortality. Was Michael Jordan, aged 38 – with a damaged knee and not having trained for three days – still the greatest basketball player ever seen or was 'His Airness' about to return to earth?

Michael's shooting was awry, his passes misplaced and his lack of fitness was showing badly in the final quarter of the game. Despite this, the Wizards were still in the match as the ball was moved quickly into Jordan's hands with 20 seconds left on the clock. Everyone in the arena knew this was 'Jordan time'; throughout his career, he'd been close to infallible in such situations. A lesser mortal at 38, carrying a dodgy knee, may have had a reality check, accepted he was running out of miracles and passed to his unguarded colleague, Chris Whitney. Michael, naturally, took the shot. And missed. The Wizards lost and the game was up.

When a great athlete returns to the arena he once so comprehensively dominated, we greet it with a mixture of hopeful excitement and trepidation. The reality, however, is always the same: the struggle with sporting mortality is an unedifying and painful spectacle. As greatness fades, furies, slights and resentments stoke the fire of the competitive drive. The attempts to recapture something lost – a failure to let go and move on – leaves the god stripped not only of his inviolability but often his dignity, too. We, the fans, are momentarily confused, maybe troubled or even amused by their bumblings. And then we shift our allegiance to the next hero.

In the instant Jordan and the Wizards lost to the Nicks, an era finally came to an end that probably should have ended considerably earlier. Jordan was married, had three children, had earned around $400m and won everything there was to be won. So why did he feel the need in 2001 to risk his reputation and health by making a comeback with the Washington Wizards at the age of 38?

Love of the game? Maybe – but Jordan's relationship with his chosen sport was far more complex than that. Money? That can be ruled out, too – Jordan was worth more than some countries. Could it be that a far more likely explanation is that his psychic map told him the basketball court was the most reliable place he'd yet found where fears of humiliation could be best defended against? It seems that, for Michael, sporting relationships were always about two things: victory and humiliation of others, or defeat and personal humiliation. The basketball court had steadfastly been where he had found far more of the former than the latter. By the age of 38, having experienced the frustrations of retirement, Jordan had found his addiction to combat growing increasingly strident. The voice inside was now yelling at him that age – like any other 'weakness' – was simply a contemptible excuse, the final refuge of losers. For Michael, the winning, the glory and the success of his career had largely managed his competitive addiction but now, lacking this validation of his worth, it was screaming to be fed.

Perhaps the best way to understand the vicious circle Jordan and other champions find themselves in when denying the obvious physical signs of their body's mortality is initially to turn our attention to another sport, one that most clearly reveals the quintessence of its physical and mental effects. As the novelist and fight pundit Joyce Carol Oates says in her acclaimed book-length essay *On Boxing* (1987), 'If boxing is a sport, it is the most tragic of all sports because more than any other human activity it consumes the very excellence it displays.'

One 'heroic' heavyweight championship fight is perhaps more indelibly written on sports fans' minds than any other. For much of the Rumble in the Jungle, Muhammad Ali did not appear to be trapped and yet he remained on the ropes, allowing his opponent to pummel him. George Foreman landed 120 blows in three minutes and yet Ali remained standing, looking disdainfully at his assailant as he was being physically abused, as if to say, 'I can't be beaten because you cannot reach me and I cannot feel any pain.' He even coined the phrase 'rope-a-dope' to confirm this contempt. That night in Zaire, there was an air of invincibility, immortality and a god-like indestructibility about the world's greatest ever heavyweight who won back his crown by being beaten almost to death.

In the ring, the boxer does damage to others and to himself. And, as he refuses to heed the messages that he is slowing down, exponentially takes more of the latter than the former. But what does this willingness to be physically abused and to abuse signify? What is it a metaphor for?

In boxing, the illusion of invincibility would seem to be key. If you step into the ring with a scintilla of doubt, that doubt will invariably count you out. The capacity to sever the connection with the frightened, hurt and powerless child we all have inside us is imperative. To be able to endure pain and suffering, the vulnerable child must be silenced. As Mike Tyson put it, 'I'm scared every time I go into the ring, but it's how you handle it. What you have to do is plant your feet, bite down on your mouthpiece and say, "Let's go."'[1]

In order to explore the psychodynamic roots of this capacity to inflict and receive pain (legitimately or otherwise), we need to look into the heart of a violent self. Psychoanalyst Peter Fonagy writing about the psychodynamics of violence in its most extreme form – murder – outlines two crucial structures in the mind of the murderer. Although concerned with violence at its most extreme, his ideas are also illuminating when transferred to the boxing ring. The first of these concepts is the notion of an 'alien self', which refers to a split-off part of the personality where unprocessed infantile, aggressive and hateful impulses reside. The second relates to the dynamics of the murderer's actual fight, the unconscious objective of which is to wreak revenge on an abuser who bullied or humiliated him during his childhood. As we know, a high preponderance of the most 'successful' boxers are the products of impoverished and abusive childhoods. By projecting 'the abuser' into their opponent, it sanctions both the beating he wishes to administer at the same time as legitimising the unleashing of the fury of his alien self. By letting the alien off the leash, the vulnerable child inside the adult is felt to be protected from being hurt or humiliated again.

Fonagy's second structure most clearly shows itself in the ring and in other sporting arenas when athletes attempt not just to beat, but to annihilate others. Discussing a fight with Tyrell Biggs, Tyson bragged, 'I could have knocked him out in the third round but I wanted to do it slowly, so he would remember this night for a long time.' On another occasion, discussing another fight and commenting more generally on the pugilist's art, he confessed, 'I try to catch him right on the tip of the nose, because I try to push the bone into the brain.'[2]

Boxing legitimises violence and the ability to take punishment is what defines a great champion as much as the ability to administer it. Ali, standing over Sonny Liston, goading, humiliating, is the classic sadistic pose; Ali taking punishment on the ropes from Foreman is the classic masochistic position. Both suggest potency and victory and both, in a psychological sense, are defences against vulnerability. In a vignette with a female journalist, Tyson shows his incomprehension of any relationship based on anything but power, control and submission. 'I normally don't do interviews with women unless I fornicate with them. So you shouldn't talk any more . . . Unless you want to, you know.'[3]

The ebb and flow of the brutal collision between the abuser and the abused in its most dramatic form is what we find so compelling in the ring. But the capacity to ignore pain, particularly late in a career – not knowing when enough is enough – can cancel out any future. Although we may not be able to prove Parkinson's disease was caused by the physical abuse Ali took, I think we'd all agree it probably didn't help. The number of boxers who end up permanently disabled or, more disturbingly, disabling others both in and out of the ring is too long to be ignored.

What happens to the outward and inward aggression? In Ali's case, it perhaps led to Parkinson's; in Michael Watson's, a life sentence to a wheelchair; in Frank Bruno's, depression; in Sonny Liston's, a drug overdose or possibly a mafia killing; in Carlos Monzon's, a fatal car crash following an 11-year jail sentence for murdering his wife; in Randy Turpin's, suicide after being declared bankrupt; in Trevor Berbick's (the last man to beat Ali), being hacked to death in a Jamaican churchyard.

Mike Tyson has been the most infamous case of all. Tyson's mother, Lorna Tyson, brought Mike up alongside a string of abusive partners after his biological father, Jimmy Kirkpatrick, disappeared when Mike was two. Tyson constantly speaks of himself disparagingly, as someone abused and exploited from childhood.

According to a recent *Daily Mail* article entitled *Sympathy for the Devil,* written by Alison Boshoff and Paul Thompson (28 May 2009), Tyson's mother 'was a promiscuous alcoholic who may or may not have been a prostitute. Tyson is still not sure who his father was . . . He claims he was born addicted and, when Tyson went into rehab in 2007, he said of the cocaine and alcohol addiction: "I'll never beat that. That's going to be a 'til-the-day-I-die job."' His therapist, Marilyn Murray, meanwhile, quoted on the De Anza College Mike Tyson profile, says he 'is a classic case of a child who grew up in a destructive, dysfunctional environment'. The same Tyson profile goes on to say, 'He watched as multiple boyfriends beat up his alcoholic mother, Lorna, who died when Tyson was 16.'

As Tyson himself says 'I don't react to a tragic happening any more. I took so many bad things as a kid and some people think I don't care about anything. It's just too hard for me to get emotional. I can't cry no more.'[4]

As a young boy, Tyson was picked on and called 'fairy boy' because he spoke softly and with a lisp. He started collecting pigeons and still has 2,000 he continues to protect. Tyson recalls, 'One morning, I woke up and found my favourite pigeon, Julius, had died. I was devastated and was gonna use his crate as my stickball bat to honour him. I left the crate on my stoop and went in to get something and I returned to see the sanitation man put the crate into the crusher. I rushed him and caught him flush on the temple with a titanic right hand . . . he was out cold, convulsing on the floor like an infantile retard.'[5]

If one considers the pigeons as symbols of Mike's vulnerable self, it is perhaps understandable that this was perhaps the first moment he 'snapped', exploding in a rage. The alien self had been unleashed to protect the vulnerable self. From this moment, Mike's life spiralled into adolescent crime and violence and he was soon sent to a correction centre.

One is reminded of a story the philosopher Bertrand Russell told of witnessing a boy hitting a smaller child in a school playground and, when confronted about his behaviour, the boy's defence was, 'The bigs hit me, so I hit the babies . . . that's fair.'[6] Bertrand Russell commented to the effect that in that sentence, the child was recording the history of the world.

Another story Tyson tells again encapsulates the alien and vulnerable self perfectly. 'I paid a worker at New York's zoo to re-open it just for me and Robin [his ex-wife]. When we got to the gorilla cage, there was one big silverback gorilla there just bullying all the other gorillas. They were so powerful but their eyes were like an innocent infant. I offered the attendant $10,000 to open the cage and let me smash that silverback's snotbox! He declined.'[7]

Following his delinquent childhood and a series of violent assaults, Tyson found a potent solution to defend himself against humiliation by transferring the alien self to the boxing ring. After a meteoric rise, he confessed, 'I'm the most irresponsible person in the world. The reason I'm like that is because, at 21, you all gave me $50 [million] or $100 million, and I didn't know what to do. I'm from the ghetto. I don't know how to act. One day I'm in a dope house robbing somebody. The next thing I know, "You're the heavyweight champion of the world." Who am I? What am I? I don't even know who I am. I'm just a dumb child. I'm being abused.'[8]

Convicted of raping Desiree Washington – the ultimate act of an impotent man, Tyson served three years in prison before being released on parole. His other marriage to Robin Givens ended on Valentine's Day, with Givens again claiming Tyson 'had battered her during their brief marriage.'[9] Tyson himself once complained of an accusor, 'He called me a "rapist" and a "recluse". I'm not a recluse.'[10] He also admitted, 'I like to hurt women when I make love. I like to hear them scream with pain, to see them bleed. It gives me pleasure.'[11]

When athletes turn their violence against women, particularly those closest to them, it creates the greatest abhorrence. The inventory against boxers is a particularly long one. Typical are the 1991 divorce court documents that show Sugar Ray Leonard, ex-world champ at multiple weights (and named Fighter of the Decade for the 1980s), admitting to physically abusing his wife. Juanita Leonard's own testimony graphically paints the horror as reported by Stanley Teitelbaum in *Sports Heroes, Fallen Idols*. He would 'throw me around and harass me physically and mentally in front of the children . . . I was holding my six-month-old child and [he] spit in my face. He pushed me. He shoved me . . . I was on my way out the door. He wouldn't let me out. He took a can of kerosene and poured it on the front foyer in our house. He told me he was going to burn the house down . . . that he wasn't going to let me leave the house.'[12]

In 1997, the wife of ex-World Heavyweight Champion, Riddick Bowe, filed for divorce claiming, 'He knocked me out in front of my three-year-old . . . I was out cold for several minutes. It never fazed Riddick. He never thought anything of it.'[13] Shortly after this incident, he kidnapped Judy and the children and held her at knife point. He was initially kept in a psychiatric facility and subsequently pleaded guilty to the crime but was only sentenced to 30 days in jail and 4 years' probation. The sentence was later raised to 18 months in jail on the prosecution's appeal but, according to Stanley H. Teitelbaum in *Sports Heroes*, while the case was still at appeal, Bowe allegedly assaulted his wife twice more before the commencement of his jail term.

Violence to women is not, of course, restricted to the domestic boxing ring. In America, Jeff Benedict, the director of research at the Center for the Study of Sports in Society, found a 'significant relation between college athletes and sexual assault.' In his book *Public Heroes, Private Felons*, he suggested that sports stars violate 'behavioural boundaries' because their celebrity status creates a 'distorted self-image and sense of entitlement'.[14] In *Pros and Cons: The Criminals Who Play in the NFL*, Jeff Benedict and Don Yaeger claim that 21 per cent of professional players have been charged with serious crime. In brief, what would seem to take place is that the public hunger for heroes perpetuates a 'star' syndrome which can fuel an athlete's feelings of entitlement and distort his idea of self. This can lead to omnipotent fantasies of being above the law. The abuse of boundaries and criminal offences may well then be just a short step away.

Tyson regained the heavyweight title in 1996 but lost it the same year – his air of invincibility had disappeared with the time he had spent in jail. In his twilight, as his potency as a boxer deserted him, primitive cannibalism snapped through the veneer of his 'civilised' self. Spitting out his gumshield and biting part of Evander Holyfield's ear off (and later biting Lennox Lewis's right leg) was the final desperate act of a man at the end of a career where the flimsy rules that legitimise violence are punctured by the more desperate, primitive alien self. Tyson's only explanation was that he 'snapped'.

The victim of Tyson's desperate tactics, Evander Holyfield, would also have to face his own decline a little further down his own road and, like Tyson, would refuse to accept it. Holyfield's final battle was tucked away on the back pages of the *Daily Telegraph* sports section on 15 October 2007. At the age of 45, he had just been comprehensively beaten by the Russian, Sultan Ibragimov. Ibragimov's trainer, Roger Mayweather, summed up the boxing world's impatient mood. 'It's time to walk away. He's won the championship four times. What's left to prove? . . . He's been in so many wars, eventually something bad will happen if he continues. But there is no need.' The journalist reporting the fight, Gareth Davies, described Holyfield as a shell of the fighter who took on Mike Tyson, Lennox Lewis and Riddick Bowe. He, too, urged Holyfield to retire. The ex-world champion, with the same cussed determination that took him to the top, predictably refused to listen. Mayweather and Davies, like the rest of us, knew it was time for him to walk. Why didn't Holyfield, the man who stood to suffer most by ignoring the advice?

The truth is great athletes grow old but many old athletes fail to grow from a psychological perspective. Childhood experiences need to be integrated into the adult self for the athlete to grow. The sporting contest is a physical expression of an unconscious conflict within a person and the intensity of the feelings within and around the sporting contest is reflected in the energy and intensity in that unconscious conflict. The dread, weakness, pain and humiliation of loss (losing) has to be understood as an intrusion from the world of childhood; a sense of mature adulthood can only be achieved by recognising and understanding these experiences for what they are, and managing their potential for destructiveness appropriately.

A refusal to retire is perhaps perceived by the once-great as another victory, in the same manner that Ali and Holyfield accepted punishment victoriously. The reality for outsiders, however, is that the dying embers of a great athletic career can make painful and embarrassing viewing. For success in the ring or on the basketball court, the mind and body must be one but, when the body quits without the mind's consent, the stage is set for an acrimonious divorce. As the mantle of greatness slips uneasily from shoulders, the infantile conflicts that have driven athletes to become gods are laid bare.

The fear of retirement is not only about the loss of identity but also the fear of ever finding another arena in which the athlete will be able to defend himself so successfully against unwanted bits of himself by projecting them into others and then going to battle with them. The unfortunate final spectacle is of the once untouchable chasing shadows. Other sports might not display the same transparent physical manifestations of slowing down as boxing, but just because the athletes are not being beaten up, it doesn't mean there is any less denial of suffering.

We like to imagine our sporting idols with their greatness intact, segueing their way seamlessly to the next stage of life. We, after all, have already moved on to lionising our next hero. We expect grace and dignity in the twilight of careers that were all about singular obsession and ruthlessness. Very few manage it. And those who do, often return after a short retirement, lured by the dream of former greatness. Some, initially at least, perhaps believe they have dealt successfully with the transition by taking up roles in corporate hospitality or as coaches and media pundits. But the buzz, the rituals, the game mindset are too deeply ingrained and too huge a loss to bear. A fear of invisibility and emptiness descends outside the athletic bubble – a fear of death in life. This sporting hinterland only emphasises the fact that their heyday – with its extreme physicality and adrenalin rush – is over. While mere mortals may experience a feeling of redundancy at 65 at the end of a working life, our sporting heroes have to face it at half that age.

The truth, as we have pointed out repeatedly in this book, is that sporting success can feel the most impregnable place to defend against feelings of worthlessness, abandonment and other traumatic legacies of childhood. Thus the 'addiction' to 'success' can also be viewed as a kind of pathology as the issues are not psychologically resolved but rather repressed. When retirement does come, therefore, hopes for a graceful transition may woefully underestimate the power of that pathology, particularly as these athletes don't become champions by entertaining the more complex and subtle areas of psychological life – qualities such as circumspection, temperance, compromise, doubt, self-reflection and equanimity. The only trade they know is winning.

All sporting greatness, to a lesser or greater extent, involves the management of emotional conflict through action and this is very different from psychological engagement with emotional conflict. When an athletic career comes to an end, the athlete must go through an enormous adjustment that can be experienced akin to a harrowing bereavement. However, the unconscious conflicts that, to a large extent, have driven the athlete, remain alive and toxic. The extent to which the sportsperson is able to move away from the safety of the athletic life depends on how well he/she has been able to develop an adult identity separate from the sporting identity and how successfully he/she has managed to process the unconscious conflicts that have been at the heart of that particular athletic endeavour.

Ian Williamson's Casebook – Christopher

During our initial consultation, Christopher's parents described their 12-year-old son as depressed and potentially suicidal. The contrast with his earlier lively disposition, confidence and popularity – he had been the star of the cricket team and played rugby and football for the school – made the transformation particularly hard to take.

Six months before our consultation, Christopher had had a serious bicycle accident and shattered a leg. The bones had not knitted together properly and this necessitated a further operation to reset them. At the time, there was considerable doubt as to whether he would be able to resume his sporting passions.

The uncertainty surrounding his prognosis came as a hammer blow to Christopher. He became morose, depressed and argumentative. He isolated himself from his friends and was reluctant to go to school. When he told his parents that his life wasn't worth living, they decided they had to act.

The parents' account of Christopher's early life seemed unremarkable and devoid of any obvious upset or trauma, although I did note that there appeared to be a great deal of competition with two brothers and that this competitiveness often escalated into vicious fights. I wondered whether the intensity of their rivalry for attention and status had honed his competitive instincts as a sportsman.

When I first saw Christopher, he was indeed sullen, uncommunicative and reiterated his claim that his life wasn't worth living. However, over the course of our time together, as Christopher opened up a little more, it became clear that there was no serious suicidal intent behind his comments. What he seemed to be struggling with was the imminent, though as yet unconfirmed, loss of his sporting identity. During his convalescence, he had also lost his place within the family, and had fallen to the bottom of the pile with respect to his brothers and classmates.

He became tearful when describing how much he missed sport and how awful it was to be physically incapacitated. He also expressed a concern that he might never walk properly again. It was evident that the loss of his physicality, his preferred way of managing feelings and emotions, had left him overwhelmed with frustrations and impotence. I made the comment that it 'felt like the end of his life' even though, in reality, he was still at the beginning of it. We talked about being overwhelmed by feelings he had never had to think about before. I suggested it must feel like experiencing the death of someone close. He agreed that it did, indeed, feel like he was suffering a terrible bereavement.

I suspect that, in Christopher's case, there had been an over-reliance on his sporting identity as a way of dealing with the rawness of the feelings of rivalry between himself and his brothers. The 'winning' of the contests somehow kept at bay any feelings of smallness and loss. The accident had instantly shattered that identity and coping mechanism and had catapulted him into feelings of helplessness and despair. With time and maturity, it was possible that this over-reliance on a sporting identity would have diminished naturally as his personality changed and his sense of himself and his life broadened, but the suddenness of the rupture with no evolving sense of a new self had been traumatic and left him full of grief and despair.

Over our period together, Christopher wrestled with the difficulty of forging a new identity without sport at its centre. After his period of treatment, I didn't see Christopher again or find out whether his leg mended well enough for him to start playing again. I took it as a positive sign that his identity recovered regardless of that particular outcome.

The nature of personal identity is at the heart of the dilemma of the ageing athlete; has another sense of self been slowly incubating as the sporting flame begins to dim, or is he in denial, wedded to the sport like a Siamese twin? Those in denial can feel the end rather like Christopher – as a rupture, catapulting them into emptiness and despair.

If cross-sports comparisons have any validity, then basketball superstar Michael Jordan can legitimately claim to be one of the greatest – if not the greatest – sportsman ever to grace an arena. After an outstanding career at the University of North Carolina, Jordan joined the Chicago Bulls in 1984 where his leaping ability earned him the nicknames 'Air Jordan' and 'His Airness'. Apart from his attacking prowess, he also had a near-perfect defensive game and already seemed to be the complete player. In 1991, he won his first NBA championship with the Bulls and followed that with titles in 1992 and 1993. Perhaps finding his sport too easy, Jordan briefly quit basketball for baseball, but rejoined the Bulls in 1995 and led them to three more back-to-back championships (1996–98) before retiring again in 1999. In 2001, he returned to playing with the Washington Wizards and finally retired in 2003.

Jordan's individual accolades and accomplishments include five NBA Most Valuable Player awards, nine All-Defensive First Team honours, fourteen NBA All-Star Game appearances, three All-Star Most Valuable Player titles, ten scoring titles, and six

NBA Finals Most Valuable Player awards. He holds the NBA record for the highest career regular season scoring average with 30.1 points per game as well as averaging a record 33.4 points per game in the play-offs. His elevation above the mortals of the court was down to ruthless competitiveness, athletic courage and fearlessness.

Jordan possessed an archetypal athletic mindset unruffled by past successes or fears for the future. Add this to his natural talent, wonderful athletic ability and perfect basketball physique and you get the greatest player the sport has ever seen. Why was it then that, at the peak of his success, Jordan so suddenly and unceremoniously dumped basketball for baseball in 1993?

It would appear that his father, to whom Michael was exceptionally close, played a central part in his first divorce from the court. On 23 July 1993, James Jordan was shot dead by two youths in a highway rest area while driving home from a funeral in Lumberton, North Carolina. Initially, the family reported James missing as he hadn't been in contact for several days. It was only weeks later that James Jordan's car was located and his body found dumped in a nearby creek. Michael was understandably devastated and, shortly after the bereavement, stunned the basketball world by announcing his retirement, saying he needed to spend more time with his family and that he'd lost his appetite for basketball. 'I have nothing more to prove in basketball . . . have no more challenges that I felt I could get motivated for.' He also maintained that his decision to quit 'doesn't have anything to do with my father passing'.[15]

Jordan's suggestion that there was no more room for improvement on the basketball court, that he had come as far as he could, was clearly true. This mantra constantly to improve himself had come from his father and, if there was no room for improvement in basketball, then to honour his father's memory, he probably felt he should move on. Bob Greene in *Rebound: The Odyssey of Michael Jordan* points out that his decision to quit had, in fact, everything to do with his father and that, in reality,

Michael was overcome with grief and uncertainty following the death and badly needed a new direction. 'Having lost something that was so important to him that his pain was unfathomable, [he] had to decide what to do.'[16]

At the age of 31, he signed up with the Chicago White Sox in an attempt to become a major-league baseball player. In Greene's biography, Michael Jordan confesses 'this is something my father always wanted me to do. He started me in baseball when I was six years old. Two years ago, he told me that I should go for it. I'm serious. My father thought I could be a major-league baseball player.'[17]

In one way, therefore, the move to baseball can be seen as an attempt to remain a good son and respect his father's memory and mantra constantly to improve. Certainly, the enormity – some might say impossibility – of the challenge also gave him a physical focus for managing his grief. What is curious is whether, deep down, he truly believed that he would make it. Was it a grossly over-inflated estimation of his sporting prowess or did he know the likelihood was that he couldn't possibly succeed on the same scale as basketball?

His attempt was by no means a total failure but, despite Jordan's prodigious work ethic, it soon became clear he was not going to make the grade as a pro baseball player. The ending, when it came, was revealing. The major-league players had gone on strike over pay and had effectively shut down the professional baseball season. When the management of the Chicago White Sox approached Jordan to play in some exhibition matches, Jordan reacted angrily as he'd made it clear at the beginning of his baseball journey that he did not want his status to be exploited. He felt he had been betrayed. Within days of the confrontation, Jordan walked away from baseball and back to basketball with the Chicago Bulls. It is not clear what Jordan made of his two-year baseball odyssey; did he experience it as a failure or did he still cling to a belief that, given time, he would have made it? Was the confrontation a genuine reason for the end or merely an excuse?

Michael Jordan made a successful return to the Bulls in 1995 and, three back-to-back championships later, retired again in 1999. At the point at which Jordan was contemplating his final basketball comeback, he had therefore already had a taste of retirement and was 38 years old. After the second retirement in 1999, he had tried his hand at management as Club President of the Wizards but it predictably proved both disappointing and disillusioning. Like all great athletes, the merry-go-round of travelling, training and playing, while psychologically limited, provided a much-needed structure to life and a goal – winning. Without a contest to focus on, what was the point of the travelling and the whole circus?

Jordan's success had elevated him into that élite group of sporting superstars who achieve cult-like status. He had accumulated enough money and kudos to put him in the 'untouchable' category. He was the archetypal modern sporting superstar who surrounded himself with an army of assistants (flunkeys) united in their veneration, whose role was to iron out the kinks of everyday life but who, in reality, sycophantically colluded in the delusion that Jordan's view was the world view. This mindset may well be useful in the single-track pursuit of success but it is also a mindset that provides no warning lights. Connections with the real world have been cut at worst, and distorted at best. Sooner or later, this mindset crashes head-on with reality.

Jordan had lived his whole NBA career in this distorted world and, when the ultimate umpire, Father Time, pointed to his watch, there seems to have been a collusive blindness in the Jordan camp. No one was willing or able to tell him what he really needed to hear – that his athletic career was over.

As a child, Michael Jordan was no more than a solid young athlete with potential; certainly not a precociously gifted child like Tiger Woods. He was born into a middle-class black family in Brooklyn that moved to Wilmington, North Carolina, before he reached his first birthday. Michael was the third of five children reared by their disciplinarian, military father whose credo was to work hard and not waste talent. James Jordan pushed his children particularly hard in athletics, continually raising expectations, letting them know that more was always expected of them. Michael's parents also instilled a philosophy of being proactive rather than reactive. 'We have always tried to make things happen rather than wait around for them to happen. And we have always found that, if you work hard enough, you can make it happen the way you want'.[18]

Admirable though this credo is, it is palpably untrue. How things happen is a combination of many things, not just the individual's will and work ethic. What it does do from a psychological point of view, however, is create the idea that an individual is capable of achieving anything.

Jordan's work ethic became one of the cornerstones of his game. What lay behind this work ethic, though, was something more primal: a pathological hatred of losing. His basketball coach at Virgo Junior School, Fred Lynch, said of Jordan, 'Michael was very competitive. He hated losing, even then, and that made him work extremely hard when he played any of the sports.'[19]

One of the seminal tales told about Jordan's steely will occurred when he was 15 years old and it is often quoted as a turning point in his life. Michael had been playing well for his school and expected to get called up for the forthcoming play-offs. Instead, he was dropped and told he wasn't good enough. When the school team went to the regional championships, according to Bill Gutman in his biography *Michael Jordan*, Michael only made the bus because the student manager was sick. At the venue, he had no admission ticket and so had to carry the kit of the team's best player to gain entry. To make matters worse, during the game, he was given the role of handing out the towels. Michael was humiliated by the experience. 'I made up my mind right then and there that this would never happen to me again.'[20]

As a professional player, Jordan became renowned for his last minute heroics, especially in the big games. As he told Bob Greene, 'I'm not nervous at all in that situation, because I feel like

I'm in total control. Whatever's going to happen out there, it's not going to happen until I start it. And everyone in the building knows it. Moments like that make me happy.'[21] To be in total control and to follow his father's credo of making things happen allowed Michael to avoid the possible humiliation of ever being engulfed by failure again. When everyone was watching him expectantly, that was when he felt in total control of the world and that, he freely admitted, was when he felt at his happiest.

Of course, no one can always be in control or remain the centre of the world perpetually and this was the brutal truth awaiting Jordan as he struggled to recapture his former glory with the Wizards. What his father may have forgotten to tell Michael was that no one can control everything, especially ageing and the diminution of power. Eventually, everybody loses.

Jordan's relationship with his older brother Larry would appear to have been a key factor in his early years and to have largely contributed to his later relationships and extreme competitiveness. Larry was, by all accounts, a very good athlete but lacked the build to really excel at the highest level. However, as kids, Larry was a year older and bigger than Michael and punished him in the backyard as the two competed ferociously, one-on-one. His father more than once reminisced on just how much Michael loathed losing to Larry. Michael himself remembers the games as something far more than friendly rivalry and that, at times, the two ended up fighting.

It is worth speculating a little on the dynamics of these contests because they appear to provide a blueprint for Jordan's athletic mindset and they resurface with a vengeance during his slide from greatness with the Washington Wizards. Jordan's competitiveness, like Tyson's, was of such a magnitude that he didn't just want to beat his opponents, he wanted to dominate them – humiliate them – and was more than happy to gloat about it afterwards. At the height of his greatness, opponents regularly went sick or picked up mystery injuries rather than face an on-court beating from Jordan. They went down with what Michael called 'Jordanitis'.

If the Jordan boys were like many sibling rivals and as competitive as their father suggests, Larry may well have resented the arrival of a new son vying for Mum's attention and we can well imagine him teasing and humiliating the young Michael in those games. Quickly picking up on Michael's upset at losing, like most elder brothers he probably tormented him further, stirring up a rage of impotence until a fight broke out.

This tale of two fiercely competitive brothers may be everyday but it would appear that, in Michael's case, it forged a particularly ferocious competitive spirit and insatiable need to be the best. Every game, every opponent would be a variation of the one-on-one games with Larry. The drive to win, to dominate, to humiliate, the gloating, all probably followed from those unbrotherly early battles.

Michael Leahy in *When Nothing Else Matters,* tells a story about a reporter friend of Michael's called Lacy Banks that wonderfully illuminates the almost pathological competitiveness. Michael had known Banks since his early days as a professional basketball player and it was a relationship, according to Leahy, that was both complex and combative. Banks was nearly 20 years older than Jordan and regularly played poker and table tennis with him. During such contests, Jordan liked to remind Lacy of the time he'd taken all his money in a poker game and that he'd had to borrow money from him to get his car out of the parking lot. What Jordan wasn't so forthcoming about was the fact that, in those early days, Lacy used to thrash Jordan at table tennis. That humiliating state of affairs continued until Michael called a halt to the games and went off to practise secretly for weeks on end before challenging Lacy to a rematch. The practice paid off – Michael won.

This innocuous, seemingly unimportant vignette shows Jordan's enormous competitive drive and also highlights two other important aspects of his outlook: that all relationships are competitions and that everything eventually comes under your control if you work hard enough. Perhaps as a young boy Michael mistakenly internalised the idea that being loved by his parents was dependent on being successful and that meant being the best and winning if you were to be the favourite child. Constantly improving – his father's diktat – became a mantra and winning became his drug of choice. Improving through practice, obliterating all rivals, became his blueprint.

With all sporting icons there are incidents, moments in careers, when one glimpses the precarious edge of their reality. The psychological fault line may be at first barely visible but seen in the rear-view mirror of a sporting career, it can look like a chasm. Two such moments stand out in Jordan's fledgling sporting life.

Jordan first appeared on the sporting radar when he hit a winning 16ft shot for his college, North Carolina, in the final of the NCAA championship game against Georgetown with just 17 seconds to go. Overnight, he became a celebrity. However, six days later he was already bored and wanting some action. 'It was Sunday and I didn't have anything to do. So I came over to Carmichael Auditorium and there was a lot of good competition out there. So I decided to play. From then on, I came back every day. It was like I was addicted to the game. I tried to stay away but I couldn't.'[22]

Why was Michael bored six days after hitting the winning shot in an NCAA championship game, a shot that had instantly made him a celebrity and launched his career? What was so unbearable about the so-called boredom? And what was it exactly that he was addicted to? The answers to these questions are perhaps the key to understanding the dynamics of his comeback with the Wizards more than a decade later.

The second, perhaps more significant incident occurred at the beginning of his second professional season with the Chicago Bulls, following on from a hugely successful first year. The Bulls had got off to a flying start but, in the third game against the Golden State Warriors, Jordan suffered a serious foot injury having landed awkwardly after one of his trademark slam dunks.

The official diagnosis was that he had broken the tarsal navicular bone in his left foot, an injury that would require a minimum of six weeks' rehabilitation. The Bulls lost eight of the next nine games without him. But the loss of the game for Jordan was equally devastating. For the first time in his life, he was told he couldn't play basketball and he readily admitted, 'I've never gone through anything like this before, and I don't know really know how to deal with it.'[23]

These difficulties intensified after having the cast removed, when an X-ray showed the problem hadn't been resolved. The Bulls management understandably refused to give him clearance to play until the bone had fully healed. Jordan, however, couldn't cope with a further period of inaction and, against the orders of the medical team and without the Bulls' knowledge, started to practise. When this news filtered back, predictably there was a row. Jerry Reinsdorf, the Bulls owner, insisted, 'Michael has to understand that the risk–reward ratio is way out of whack'.[24] Michael, tellingly, saw it differently. 'For me, the choice is mental. If I had to sit out the rest of the year, I would go crazy. I feel I want to test the foot now.'[25]

Here was a young man, at the beginning of a career, willing to risk further – perhaps lasting – damage because he couldn't wait for a fracture to heal. Being deprived of the game and all the surrounding rituals was just too painful a loss to endure. His impatience and intolerance of his body's fragility and, by implication, his own fragility and weakness, would become a feature of his time with the Washington Wizards. What's more, if he couldn't practise, he couldn't improve and this is what he had to do every day of his life. The confrontation ended like all Jordan's battles with adversaries; Michael won. The Bulls management capitulated, reasoning that although they could stop him playing professionally, they could do nothing to prevent him playing pick-up games.

This insistence on playing, despite the most obvious evidence not to, was to be the central feature of his fateful two-season comeback with the Washington Wizards when Michael seemed to inhabit an illusory twilight zone of athletic life where he knew time was running out but the competitive heart yearned for another day in the sun. Jordan wouldn't be the first nor the last.

At a superficial, perhaps romantic, level one can take these vignettes as evidence of a young man simply in love with the game. But his need was far more compulsive than that. What was addictively compelling was the need to return to a particular relational dynamic with parts of himself and be top of the pile at all costs.

Sport is primarily driven, at times fanatically and heroically, by the need to gorge on the feelings engendered by winning. But in the great athletes, the need can be insatiable. Like pouring water into a bucket with a hole in it, they constantly have to keep filling up before the bucket empties. It is the hole in the psyche (the fear of emptiness and its attendant anxieties of loss and death) that the feeling of winning keeps at bay. We have all heard athletes talking about their 'devastation' at losing and others being labelled bad losers. But the question is: why does losing feel so catastrophic?

For most of us, physical deterioration, and with it the appearance of our own mortality, comes late in life if we are lucky. Our lives and sense of self aren't built around our athleticism, our speed of foot, sleight of hand or ability to jump. However, for great athletes, the spectre of death in the form of barely visible physical deterioration descends like some ghostly terminal illness not much more than a decade after leaving their teens. The loss is irrevocable and the deterioration relentless. This premature appearance of athletic mortality stands as a metaphor for all the other losses in their lives and the athletes' capacity to face such losses is rooted in their capacity to bear emotional pain; a capacity established early in life.

As underlined repeatedly throughout this book, psycho-analysis would suggest that all adult experiences ruffle the emotional backcloth of childhood. In the competitive athletic domain, a defeat resonates with the earliest internal childhood experience of loss, and particularly the experience of losing the mother – however temporarily – for any inexplicable reason (caring for a sibling rival, disappearing with the father, and so on). Athletes' lives can be seen to be devoted to 'winning' back that attention. Unless a more mature adult relationship is reached based on more than winning and losing, the rest of mankind is perceived as a dangerous adversary who has the capacity to return them to their unbearable pain. The psychoanalyst Melanie Klein (1959) explained it thus: 'We are inclined to attribute to other people – in a sense put into them – some of our own emotions and thoughts; and it is obvious that it will depend on how balanced or how persecuted we are whether this projection is of a friendly or hostile nature.'[26]

When Jordan joined the Washington Wizards they were, in football parlance, relegation material. It would prove to be a toxic and poisonous marriage. From the outset, the set-up was wrong. As a player, Jordan was peerless. Such was the force of his personality and single-mindedness that he provoked both fear and awe in equal measure. The ideal scenario, indeed the only realistic one, would have been for Jordan to put his experience at the service of an emerging and developing team; to nurture the younger players and cajole and challenge the more experienced ones, to play within himself and conserve his energies for important moments. But such a scenario would require an acceptance that he was no longer the force of old. It would require that he make a concession to ageing and engage with the experience of losing his power. This, it would appear, he couldn't do. Jordan had conceded nothing in 18 years as a player and he wasn't about to start now.

Although his coach at the Chicago Bulls, Phil Jackson, had brought a measure of team awareness to his play, in truth it was a disposable add-on. Everyone knew that when games got tight and the pressure was really on, Jordan took over. It would be

Jordan's way or no way. When he signed to play for the Wizards, it was never going to be a collective venture.

Michael Leahy followed Jordan's dying days with the Washington Wizards and described them in detail in a hugely enjoyable and insightful book with a most telling title: *When Nothing Else Matters*. He describes how Jordan's first act at the Wizards was to hire one of his old coaches at the Bulls, Doug Collins. While Jordan spoke glowingly of Collins' ability to motivate and improve younger players, it was a more salient fact that, while together at the Bulls, Jordan was the dominant figure and usually got his own way. According to Leahy, if further proof were needed that this was Jordan's show, he signed Collins on a four-year, $20 million deal without consulting the Wizards' owner Abe Collins.

Throughout the winter of 2001, Jordan trained seriously, mixing workouts with private games against a mixture of old friends and college hopefuls. Aside from the occasional back spasm and soreness, everything seemed on course for a smooth comeback. The illusion of timeless success was in place. But then disaster struck during a summer game; a stray elbow from Ron Artest broke two of Jordan's ribs. He would need a minimum of four weeks' rehabilitation – four weeks during which Jordan knew his physical condition would deteriorate. As soon as he could, Jordan frantically tried to make up for lost time. His personal trainer warned him to take it easy, as he risked tendonitis after such a lengthy lay-off. Predictably, Jordan ignored him. The strenuous workouts noticeably improved his physical condition but, as predicted, at the cost of tendonitis in his left knee. The reality of the injury was that it was painful and inhibiting but it was also a warning symbol of the frailty that comes with age. It required a compromise, a concession on his part. Jordan was clearly making demands that his body couldn't meet; he was in dire need of a reality check from someone.

Perhaps coach Collins could have stepped in to bring some perspective and direction to proceedings. He should have either put Jordan's comeback on hold or severely restricted his playing time until the tendonitis settled down. He did neither. The psychological downside of such ferocious competitiveness is that it is a state of mind that permeates every aspect of relationships and contaminates communication between individuals. Discussions are not explorations of ideas but adversarial encounters to be won or lost. Differences of opinion are not felt as food for thought but seen as attacks that have to be rebuffed at all costs. It is unlikely that Jordan would have listened even if Collins had tried to talk some sense into him. If Jordan said his knees were fine, they were fine. With hindsight, the outcome of the Wizards' campaign was entirely predictable after that fateful collusion.

The handling of the tendonitis problem, or rather the denial of it, provided the decision-making blueprint. The real force was with Jordan. Without a directing, mediating outside presence, the other Wizards players were effectively spectators in Jordan's war with mortality. On the court, they were the pawns only there to protect the king.

Although still able to produce moments of magic, age and infirmity robbed Jordan of his capacity to defy gravity with his leaps. He had lost that half yard of spring; that half yard of speed – the half yard that separates the gods from the mortals. But Jordan was in denial mode. He paid lip service to the notion that he was there to nurture and mentor the younger players; the truth was that he still considered himself to be the king and his team-mates his subjects. He decided the tactics and who played; his best interests were synonymous with the team's best interests. The result was he played longer and harder than he should, apparently oblivious to his own moments of mediocrity and how they impacted on the team.

What seems curious is why such an intelligent athlete couldn't see what was so obvious to everyone else. One way of understanding this is to consider the type of learning and thinking that Jordan and all great athletes engage in during their sporting careers. The psychoanalyst Wilfrid Bion explored a crucial and fundamental difference between learning about *things* and learning about *oneself* by our experience in the world. In his *A Theory of Thinking,* Bion puts the experience of oneself in the world at the heart of learning and psychological development, rather than the mere acquisition of knowledge.

Also of paramount importance is the nature of Jordan's relationship with the athletic contest. The term 'competitive' does scant justice to Jordan's understanding of the word. As mentioned earlier, he not only wanted to win but to crush, humiliate and gloat over his opponent. But his verbal attacks on team-mates he deemed 'losers' were also as legendary and ferocious. Leahy recounts in his book how, when playing for the Chicago Bulls, Jordan once declared that team-mate Horace Grant shouldn't be permitted to eat on the team plane as he hadn't played well enough to deserve an in-flight meal. On another occasion, when Grant complained of being too ill to take the court, Jordan disdainfully ordered him to take an aspirin and get out on court. Without a capacity to understand or learn from the meaning of the emotional experience of the contest in Bion's sense, he was in no position to gain emotional insight into the real battle being waged. If he had, he would have understood and learned that the contest was over and that he needed to make his peace with the part of himself that he was at war with.

All great athletes have at their core a delusional level of self-belief that's central to their greatness. It enables them routinely to bring off the impossible, defy the odds, and succeed where others have failed. What we as onlookers don't understand is that this is not an optional, or disposable, state of mind. It is at the heart of their being. As the athlete's powers start to fade, the delusional system is threatened. The certainty of 'I will' is corroded by the doubt – 'Can I?' – and doubt at the very highest level is sporting death.

As the losses and poor performances mounted, Jordan's post-match press conferences became ever more fractious and divisive as he struggled to keep his divinity intact. His comments urging his team-mates to 'step up' were, at one level, nothing more than thinly-veiled attacks on their ability and character but at an unconscious level he was also railing at his own inability to step up. Although this may have appeared unfair, it had purpose at least from an unconscious point of view, providing him with an opportunity to project his frustration with his own failings onto his team-mates. By doing so, he managed temporarily to protect his illusion of invincibility.

Throughout his career, Jordan's relationships with team-mates had always been strained. His bullying, confrontational style has been well documented. While he was winning games and championships, this negative was overlooked and accepted as part of the winning package. For those who had to play alongside him, this was classic Jordan – pushing, testing and sometimes humiliating. His view was that the strong would become better players; those who failed to rise to the challenge weren't worth bothering with anyway.

Tex Winter had known Jordan for 13 years as assistant coach of the Chicago Bulls. Despite this, according to Winter, he never got to grips with Jordan the man and never understood why he tormented his team-mates. 'For some reason, Michael gets a satisfaction out of humiliating people. I think it might be part of his competitive nature, I think he competes there . . . in personal relationships.'[27] The need to break others was possibly a re-enactment of a painful childhood experience and perhaps we need look no further than those one-on-one games with brother Larry. We know from our knowledge of the dynamics of abuse that the abuser has nearly always been the victim of abuse and that, by abusing another, he is able to triumph, albeit temporarily, over the helplessness and pain of being abused. There is no doubt that Jordan knew what it felt like to be cruelly toyed with and humiliated and no doubt the goading must have tormented him as much as the losing.

While humiliating others is a hugely unattractive trait, in

Jordan one can see that it perhaps contained the seeds of his greatness as a player. Far more than just an intense desire to win, it was this relentless desire to dominate not only other teams but his own team-mates that made him such a special athlete. It was the psychology of the jungle where only the strongest survive – and he was the strongest.

As the wheels of the Wizards' campaign started coming off, Jordan became more and more desperate. He could not, and would not, make a concession to his damaged knee or to age. Leahy poignantly described the 2003 Wizards game against the Miami Heat where Jordan became the dying animal. Prior to the game, Jordan was so incapacitated that he was hardly able to move and coach Collins urged him to rest. The Miami Heat team doctor, Harlan Selesnick, gave the same advice as he drained Jordan's knee of fluid. Michael ignored them both and played. On court, he was being beaten by players who, in another era, would have been swatted aside with disdain. All the while, his knee was swelling so badly that he had to drag it round the court. He eventually took himself out of the game with six minutes to go. The Wizards lost the game but something more profound and depressing had been witnessed – the passing of an era. 'His Airness' had been grounded.

Three days later, Michael had surgery on the knee to repair the damaged cartilage. The surgeon predicted he would need six weeks to recover. Within three, he was back playing. He knew, according to Leahy, that the knee needed more time to heal but it seemed as though the brush with his athletic mortality had panicked him; that, in some way, he still wasn't quite ready to die yet. He simply wasn't prepared.

The final chapter of Jordan's career is depressingly familiar. Michael's railing against the dying of the light was as pointless as King Canute commanding the tide to turn back.

The psychologically limited hinterland that encompasses the 'winning/losing' mentality, essentially a paranoid-schizoid mental state, has at its core the young child's need for dominance and control over parents, siblings and peers. The end of a great athletic career sees the curtain come down on the usefulness of the particular states of mind that have facilitated greatness. The war with the 'internalised other' fought over many long years is being terminated by Father Time and there is the potential for a new relationship with the 'other' to be forged. To do this, the athlete must acquire a different way of thinking; a different way of understanding the war with the 'other'. In Bion's sense, they have to learn about the emotional meaning of the contest. The difficulty of acquiring this understanding is why so many athletes are never able to move on and still turn up to dinner parties in their fifties in tracksuits.

The Wizards' season petered out amid poor results and internal tensions. Jordan finally accepted it was time to retire for good. And what now? In June 2006, he returned to the NBA as part-owner of the Charlotte Bobcats. Maybe he was moving on, or maybe he was still finding a way to feed the rage to win by getting others to do it for him as a collective alter ego. By having others do his winning, he was successfully still defending himself by also projecting the responsibility for failure on to others.

In December that year, he and his wife separated after 17 years of marriage. At the time, one of his friends reputedly said that the trouble with Michael, even when he plays cards, is that he doesn't just want to beat you and take your money, but your house and wife, too.

The irony is that Juanita is believed to have got in excess of a $168m settlement and the divorce is now number one on Forbes.com's list of 'The 10 Most Expensive Celebrity Divorces'. Michael, as he prepared to move out and move in with his ghosts, for once had to accept that you really can't win them all and Juanita, this time round, will get the land, the main house, all four guest houses, the tennis court, the basketball court, the river and the golf course. As we mentioned earlier, great athletes all grow old but not all old athletes grow.

In December 2008, Evander Holyfield at 46, reduced to

penury, fought 7ft, 35-year-old Nikolai Valuev (who only returned to the ring a month earlier) for the WBC heavyweight world championship. Valuev went on to win that fight in Zurich on a dubious points decision. Also in December, the physically and emotionally damaged 41-year-old ex-convict Riddick Bowe returned to the ring after three years' absence, and beat Germany's Gene Pukall in the eighth round. And there are still media rumours that 43-year-old Lennox Lewis is preparing for a return to the ring. Lennox was quoted as saying, 'There are a lot of people who would pay to see me fight again. It would be exciting for the sport and for me. If I come back, it will be to win, not play.'[28]

Coda

An Interview with Jonathan Edwards

Judgment day – resolving the pathology

Seeking just one athlete to interview for this final chapter, numerous names came up – some deserving of their enormous acclaim and others lionised without seemingly achieving very much. In the end, the one name we could both agree upon was Jonathan Edwards, whose athletic achievements are often overlooked.

Jonathan Edwards is one of the truly great unsung heroes of British sport. He is indisputably the greatest triple jumper of all time and Britain's most successful medal-winning athlete. For a while in the mid- to late 1990s he was virtually unbeatable in the triple jump. At the World Championships in Gothenburg in 1995, he broke the world record twice in the space of 20 minutes. His first jump took him over the 18m mark, becoming the first man to achieve that feat; he then jumped over 60ft (18.29m) with his second. The enormity of his achievement can be gauged by the fact that his world record still stands. Edwards won Olympic Gold at the Sydney Games and, at one point in 2002, he held all four major titles – Olympic, World, Commonwealth and European.

Paul Gogarty: Jonathan, we'd like to have your thoughts on what it was like to retire from your athletic career with two-thirds of your life ahead of you; how it felt to have achieved all you had and then so suddenly to have to let it go and move on.

Jonathan Edwards: *What was good about retiring was that it was the first chance I had to properly reflect on those achievements. I think at the time you're competing, you only ever look forward to the next training session, the next competition, the next performance, the next major championships. So I had no opportunity to appreciate what I had achieved nor the wonderful life I'd had. I'd been very fortunate to do something that I loved and to be that successful.*

I also think you need to take time to realise how much those achievements have been appreciated by other people, too. This was also really important because it was pretty much a monastic existence as an athlete – shut off in my own little world. The athlete's life is a bit of a bubble really – quite an isolated existence by choice, a small world with me at the centre of it, I guess. With retirement, I was able to establish a more normal existence and get some perspective on my sporting career.

PG: So the whole retirement experience was a positive one?

JE: *Positive, yes, but at the same time to suddenly have that thing that I was so objectively very good at taken away was hard, there's no denying that. The world becomes a lot greyer. The reality is there will* *be nothing else in my life that I point to and say, 'I am the best in the world at that. Here's the line in the book which tells you that I am the best that there's ever been; here are the medals and record book to prove it.'*

The majority of my contemporaries outside sport are entering their forties and starting to reach the peak of their careers and can look forward to another 20 years or so at the top by which time the natural cycle of life will start to slow them and they'll be ready to take their foot off the pedal. The thing with athletics is that everything is accelerated and the life span so much shorter before you're unceremoniously separated from something which is as much a part of you as a musician's musical talent.

Ian Williamson: And musicians have the advantage of being able to keep performing . . .

JE: *Yes, they can keep performing, and actors keep acting, but a sportsman can't keep doing it, certainly not at the same level anyway. Again, with athletics, it's very much a sport as opposed to a game. An ex-tennis pro can continue to get enjoyment out of tennis at some level. You see the Masters Tennis, for example, or golf is another good example. But there's such a physicality about the pursuit of absolute excellence in athletics. For me, it would be difficult to get enjoyment out of the triple jump in the same way for obvious reasons. It's not a game. With a skilled sport like football, the skills don't vanish altogether. It's just you're not quite as quick, but you've still got that lovely touch, so there's still an enjoyment level. Whereas the enjoyment of the triple jump for me is in being absolutely at my one hundred per cent best. Is there any delight in jumping 15 metres as a 45-year-old? I would have thought not.* [Laughs]

PG: It would be a bit crazy seeing you out there in the sand pit training now, wouldn't it?

JE: *True. And that brings up an important issue about identity.*

Maybe my identity was more tied up in being an athlete than I thought back then. As a Christian, my identity needed to be tied up with how God viewed me, rather than through my human achievements. Having given up my faith, however, I realise now that I probably got a lot more emotional, psychological support through being a world-class athlete than I ever appreciated. When that athletic career went, it became a very vulnerable position.

PG: How did that manifest itself – that vulnerability – then?

JE: *I think probably a lot of activity, running around, trying to find your place in the world, doing a bit too much. The most obvious thing was losing my faith, although I don't necessarily see that as a negative thing . . .*

PG: What do you put that down to?

JE: *I just think I had a freedom to question which I didn't really have time for as an athlete. It wasn't that I consciously didn't ask questions of my faith when I was competing, but much of life is on pause when you are a sportsman. You focus obsessively on one thing and everything else goes on hold. I came into my sport because of my Christian faith, so the two were interlinked . . . and then it was sort of frozen in time. You might modify things a little bit and enquire but only within certain parameters. I think to question my faith properly, to have it pulled apart, probably would have had a very detrimental effect on my athletics, so maybe subconsciously I was protecting it because that's how it worked as an athlete. Whatever the reason, I think I didn't particularly move on in various aspects of my personal development because I was so consumed by my athletics career. I inhabited a very small world, as I said. It's like life was put on hold until I retired and had the time to look at things.*

PG: You say you got into your sport through your faith. How did that happen?

JE: *Well, how I became a top-class athlete was almost a minor miracle because I didn't really focus on it when I was younger; I was good, but I wasn't great. I won the English Schools when I was 18 – 1984 – with a distance that wouldn't have worried anybody, 15 metres. For an 18-year-old, that's a very, very average distance. I went to Durham University, studied Physics and it was only when I left that I thought, 'Oh, I'll give my athletics a go'. I went up to Newcastle, applied for jobs in a local paper, was on unemployment benefit and it just started from there. When I left university, my best jump was 16m 35cm. If Lottery funding had been available back then, I certainly wouldn't have qualified as a 21-year-old. It wouldn't have been until 1989, aged 22, post the Seoul Olympics.*

IW: That was late, wasn't it?

JE: *It was very, very late. I was very much a late developer. So when people say 29 is quite late to find your peak, you know, actually that was just an eight-year process from 1987 through to 1995. I had always enjoyed my sport but athletics wasn't professional then. You couldn't really dream of making your living as an athlete, and particularly not in a field event. I just believed that this was something that God wanted me to do, as did my father who was always incredibly encouraging. Looking back now, it was a very simple, almost naïve decision. I did it because I enjoyed it but the decision to try and make a go of it post-university was very much based on my faith.*

PG: And your father was instrumental in this?

JE: *I think that he would say he always believed that I had a real ability and that I should give it a go. Did he ever know that I would achieve what I achieved? I'm not sure. I haven't asked him; I should ask him. He'll probably say yes, I think.*

PG: And that idea you touched on, that your faith provided a kind of glue to your existence as an athlete?

JE: *Very much so. Faith gave me more perspective on success or failure; it was my sport psychology in a way. It allowed me to step back a little from being all-consumed by the pursuit of being the best that I could be.*

IW: It kept you sane?

JE: *Yes, I think it probably did. Because I think deeply about things and I used to get very anxious a lot of the time about performing, so, yes, I think faith probably nursed me throughout my career very well.*

PG: And then you basically shed it. What do you think that was about at that point in time?

JE: *It was just a freedom to question. And I think that being a relatively late developer, it was the right emotional and psychological stage in my natural development to ask those questions. Having been brought up within a very strong Christian environment, I then launched into my athletics career and there wasn't the time or the freedom then to explore those ideas and it's only with retirement that that process could properly start. Maybe if I hadn't been an athlete, it would have happened at 23, 24, 25.*

PG: So you really faced two huge losses at the point of retirement, really. That must have been pretty devastating, I would have thought.

JE: *I didn't find losing my faith devastating. I analysed what I had always believed and it didn't seem to make sense in the way that it had done before and I just accepted it and moved on. Interestingly, however, there were points through my athletics career where I questioned elements of my faith which had been central to what I believed, saw that they were wrong, and changed my viewpoint. Not participating on Sunday was the obvious one, but also my understanding of the charismatic experience changed. It was a* *theological issue which changed my understanding of the biblical narrative. So it was not a huge issue for me to question things more in retirement. There was no great fall-out for me. It was like, OK, maybe I wasn't right after all, I move on and this is how I see things now.*

IW: It's interesting. It sounds like it was almost a relief to reach retirement. I was wondering whether in a sense there was an imprisoning aspect about being a top athlete – something that you were uncomfortable with?

JE: *There is a constant pressure. There was this fear-driven thing of 'Am I going to get to the same shape as I was last year or the year before? How will I perform when the Championships come round?' It's just a constant pressure.*

PG: How much of your self-worth was tied up in that?

JE: *Probably a lot actually. I was relatively insecure as a youngster, very uncertain of myself and I lacked confidence. I wouldn't even do the bible readings in my dad's church, I was so nervous of doing things in public. I would shy away from anything like that which is bizarre when I look at what I do now as a TV presenter and giving speeches. I never would have believed back then that I would be able to do such things. I think athletics and the success I had put me in a position that maybe I never would have reached otherwise and it helped me discover more of myself because I do enjoy those public things now. I certainly never saw myself as a performer as an athlete back then but I do a lot of that now.*

[JE halts proceedings to phone home to wish his son good luck in the GCSE exam he is taking that day.]

PG: What about your son and sport?

JE: *He's a very late developer – like me. If you saw my two boys now,*

15 and 13, they could be 12 and 10, easily. They're tiny. And they look very young. And Sam – he's the older one – particularly suffers from the fact that he's an August birthday . . .

IW: So he's a year behind.

JE: *Yes, and did you see that recent research? Quite disturbing findings. And I think sporting-wise, he's quite skilful but he just finds it very hard to get into teams because physically he just can't compete.*

IW: Another question I wanted to ask you, Jonathan, was about your drive. You talked about almost drifting into athletics from university but clearly there must have been a lot of drive for you to become the greatest triple-jump athlete of all time and one of the country's greatest athletes.

JE: *I think I am quite understated and so probably people don't realise the extent of the drive. For instance, Simon Barnes wrote in Sydney that I looked like a geography teacher; the most unlikely of Olympic champions. But Michael Johnson understood – when he did a retirement tribute piece to me for BBC's Sports Personality of the Year, he talked about my mildness off the track but said that I was like an animal when I competed. It was interesting that Michael saw that side of me; that this was something that just came alive in competition. In fact, if I was winning a competition, I would often get bored, slightly disinterested, and go through the motions. But if someone went past me, I would change in a heartbeat and become a completely different creature. So I guess I'd say I am very driven but it's not particularly obvious.*

PG: And where does that drive go now?

JE: *Umm . . . not really in sport . . . probably just succeeding professionally; working with the London Olympics. One of the other things that was always important throughout my career continues to* *be so – even though I've lost my faith – and that's this idea of purpose and meaning; doing something that matters. Being involved with 2012 has been, in a funny kind of way, my saviour post-athletics. The London Olympics work gives me that bit of soul and provides my life with a certain significance.*

IW: When you got silver in the '96 Olympics and were beaten into second place by an American athlete, what did that feel like, in light of what you said about your fierce competitiveness?

JE: *Well, actually, I thought I competed well. My philosophy was always to be the best I could be and, of course, once I had become the world-record holder, that would entail getting the gold medal because I knew I could jump further than anybody else. So, it wasn't that I was so focused on winning, but rather doing the best that I could. So, go back to '93, I won a bronze medal in the World Championships in Stuttgart and that was the pinnacle of my career at that stage and I was absolutely ecstatic. Atlanta '96 was kind of mixed because I nearly went out after three rounds – I had two fouls and then had one jump to get through to the last three jumps. And then in those last three rounds, I really found myself as a competitor and nearly won it. So, although I was disappointed to get silver when I was expected to win gold, I felt very proud of the way I performed.*

Basically, my life changed in '95 as I had to deal with a whole lot of things beyond simply jumping into a sandpit. All the pressure of expectation was on my shoulders from then on and it took a lot of energy to deal with. So I felt in a funny way that '96 was a bit of a transition in terms of getting used to this new status in athletics and being one of the headline attractions. So although it would have been nicer to have won and then become a double Olympic champion in 2000, it wasn't to be and I was still quite proud of the way I performed.

PG: Just going back to the question of where the drive goes post-retirement, surely it must have been frustrating experiencing the lack of prominence. You can't shed your drive the same way you did the sport and your faith, surely? So what's it like to be suddenly inhabiting a world where that competitive drive no longer has those clear parameters of winning and losing?

JE: *I think I'm learning to adjust because you have to, because otherwise I would go mad. I'm not actually that competitive away from sport. I play golf, I enjoy it. I get frustrated when I don't do well, but does winning or losing a golf competition really matter? Not really. Even down to playing a game of Scrabble or chess or whatever else I do, winning doesn't really matter that much to me. Maybe that's because I've achieved something already and there's a level of security there, but that competitiveness was always very channelled anyway.*

PG: It sounds like you were able to let it go pretty well. You let go of your faith, you let go of sporting success. Many don't steer such a straight course in terms of that transition and go off the road.

JE: *I was aware of those dangers. I read a few articles prior to retirement – one looked at professional sportsmen and women five years on from retirement. 75 per cent of them were either clinically depressed, divorced, bankrupt, committed suicide or had some kind of addiction. A staggering figure. And then there was an* Observer Sports Monthly *article looking at five sportsmen and women who had retired. One of them was Neil Webb, the former England [midfielder] who is now a postman. Obviously, there's nothing wrong with being a postman, but that must have been a hard adjustment for someone who'd played at Wembley for England. And I really think it's not so much the job – I doubt he has a problem with that – it's more about what other people think of you.*

Another key feature I guess in making a successful transition is having transferable skills. I'm fortunate in that I had a very good education and I thought there were plenty of things I could do after my athletics career: being able to speak in public, being able to have the intellectual capacity to work on the Olympic Organising Committee Board and to chair advisory groups. All these also give me an opening to be able to commentate and present on television. It all helps.

PG: How important was that education to you in terms of being able to reflect, let go of athletics and move forwards? It just seems that so many other sportsmen who follow their sport obsessively do not seem to be able to make such a successful transition.

JE: *I don't think the successful transition is necessarily a product of a formal education, although that perhaps helps. It's just an ability to be able to think things through and have good people around you. Some former athletes will do that instinctively. And there are some, despite all the help in the world, that will struggle to do that. It's simply not within their capacity.*

IW: Do you still keep fit?

JE: *I haven't done anything really for five years. I play golf, I've done a tiny bit of cycling but I've never been to the gym. Well, I think I did at the Commonwealth Games in Melbourne because I had nothing else to do. I occasionally do a few press-ups and some yoga exercises but I don't do anything that you could really call keeping fit.*

IW: The ease with which you seem to have let go would seem in stark contrast to many athletes who refuse to accept the inevitable end. Michael Jordan's last comeback was tragic, really tragic, as his injuries had overtaken him and he was struggling and hobbling and this rage came out that he was one of the all-time greats and he was reduced to this . . .

JE: *I think that, as an athlete, you have to feel you're invincible and that you can achieve anything if you set your mind to it. The reality, however, is you can't; you have limits.*

* * *

What was most interesting in our discussion with Jonathan was the sense of struggle in his emotional/psychological life as well as his physical life. While acknowledging his fiercely competitive nature, he still made time constantly to question and reflect on life. The fact that he has a healthy family life and a new career are clear symbols of his successful transition. The fact, too, that he can empathise so clearly with his sons' current struggles shows the psychological maturity of someone embracing fatherhood. He has moved on and quite clearly will never be one of those former athletes who turns up at dinner parties in their forties or fifties dressed in a tracksuit.

Sporting success often takes single-minded, self-centred obsession – honing one particular aspect while ignoring everything else. The question the approach of retirement raises is how, if the athlete hasn't developed a rounded reflective self, he or she defends anxieties when there's no more fêting and success.

We discussed the nature of retirement with Andrew Balfour, a psychologist and psychoanalyst and one of the leading thinkers in this area. Andrew is head of the clinical service at the Tavistock Centre for Couple Relationships and is a consultant clinical psychologist in the Tavistock Clinic, where he teaches and supervises professionals who work with the elderly. He has published a number of papers in this area, and has taught nationally and internationally. He commented, 'For an athlete, the experience of ordinary ageing and deterioration may feel like a magnification – an amplification – charting their slowing down in the most public way. But, on the other hand, there may be some kind of intolerable internal experience from the past that must continue to be out-run. This has a very driven quality – the need to be the "record breaker" – that must be sustained at all costs. Such athletes may have this tremendous imperative to win, but the tragedy is that their shelf life is so limited and they know it can't be sustained.'

The fact that the dying on the track is so public, and happens at an age when most people in other walks of life are still at an early career-building stage, compounds the difficulty. Sporting legends are used to affirming their worth by winning and having an audience to applaud them but now, instead, the audience watches their eclipse. Often, too, such characters find it impossible to make a concession to weakness. Such attitudes may have been hugely helpful in building successful sporting careers but are likely to make an easy transition at retirement impossible. The irony is that, in a sense, at the moment they most need this particular defence – the fêting and confirmation of their worth – no one's interested. When the pain is at its most acute, they're discarded and their obsessionally honed skill is now equally valueless.

'An important question,' according to Balfour, 'is how heavily and exclusively this outlet – winning – has been relied upon. If other aspects of self have been ignored and, indeed, the athlete's relationship with others, then it's a bit like getting a really strong tennis arm and being under-developed in other areas. As though some athletes develop certain psychic muscles, if you like, and neglect others. I imagine that this is even down to the amount of time spent outside normal adolescent life, when they are developing their abilities and practising relentlessly. There's potentially something very obsessively all-encompassing about the relationship to the sporting career – which one could imagine having a very structuring role for some people, and being very tightly bound up with their sense of themselves. In this scenario, maybe you have to keep being top dog to stave off persecuting feelings of worthlessness.'

For some athletes, there only seem to be two possible positions: you're magic or you're tragic. 'For such athletes, the reality is that their natural life span of their career is very short, and the premature loss of potency must be particularly difficult. And if you cannot tolerate the diminution of capacity, face the loss and mourn, then you have to amplify and increase your defence. For all of us, the losses that are current in our lives will reawaken – at least at an unconscious level – earlier experiences of loss. Our capacity to deal with this will depend on the legacy of such earlier experiences, and the extent to which our early life equipped us, or not, to tolerate them. Facing loss and mourning is very much about tolerating emotional pain. Making the transition into retirement, finding new things to do, is likely to depend upon the capacity to face loss and to tolerate this pain. If the person facing retirement can take pleasure from "passing on the baton" to the next generation, then they may find meaning. But this depends upon being able to feel gratitude for what one has had, and on being able to identify with the achievements of the next generation, to take pleasure in nurturing their talents. The psychoanalyst Melanie Klein has written about how the older generation may, in nurturing new talent, be able to re-live aspects of their own lives, and even possibly achieve the fulfilment of ambitions vicariously in this way.

'Developmentally, achieving such a mature, reflective state of mind is likely to be dependent upon an infantile experience of being "contained" sufficiently by our care-givers. In other words, as infants we need to encounter a mindfulness of our own emotional state in our care-givers. Researchers have found that the strength of the bond between the infant and their carers, and the security of the child growing up, is linked to parental sensitivity to, and understanding of, the infant's mental world. An interesting example of the empirical support for these ideas is a study called *Measuring the Ghost in the Nursery*. Researchers looked at the development of the security of attachment in infants by starting their research way back before the infants were even born, by focusing on pregnant mothers. What they found was that the mother's capacity to be reflective and to think about her own experiences was predictive of the as yet unborn infant's security of attachment, two years down the line. This is a powerful finding, and the really interesting thing about it is that it is the mother's capacity to reflect upon and think about her experience, rather than the simple facts of what happened in her earlier life, that is important here. In other words, a self-reflective mother who, by implication, is likely to be able to reflect upon her infant's experience, is likely to produce a child who will be more secure. And a child who is more securely attached will be better able to develop the capacity to mourn and tolerate loss and less likely just to experience loss catastrophically, in a very persecuted way, for example.'

Jonathan Edwards, unlike many athletes, would seem to have done exactly that – reflected, mourned and moved on.

ENDNOTES

Introduction

[1] Lance Armstrong, *It's Not About the Bike,* Yellow Jersey Press, 2001, p 21

[2] Tom House, *The Jock's Itch*, Chicago: Contemporary Books, 1989, p 127

[3] Adam Phillips, *Side Effects*, Hamish Hamilton, 2006, p xi

1: The Achilles Heel

[1] Ruy Castro, *Garrincha*, Yellow Jersey Press, 2004, book cover quote

[2] Paul Gascoigne with Hunter Davies, *Gazza: My Story*, Headline, 2004, p 24

[3] Ibid., p 24

[4] Adam Phillips, *Side Effects*, Hamish Hamilton, 2006, p 294

[5] Paul Gascoigne with Hunter Davies, *Gazza: My Story*, Headline, 2004, p 24

[6] Diego Armando Maradona with Daniel Arcucci and Ernesto Bialo, *El Diego,* Yellow Jersey Press, 2000, p xi

[7] Ibid., p xi

[8] Jimmy Burns, *Hand of God, the Life of Diego Maradona*, Bloomsbury, 1996, p 120

[9] *Daily Mail*, 16 February, 2000

[10] Steve Skerry, the *Guardian*, 21 February 2008

[11] *Daily Mirror*, 10 May 2008

[12] Patrick Nathanson, *Daily Telegraph*, 25 February 2008

[13] http://news.bbc.co.uk/sport2/hi/football/4466944.stm

2: The Pain Game

[1] From a podcast by Dean Karnazes, Final Sprint website (www.thefinalsprint.com), 5 February 2005

[2] Dean Karnazes, *Ultramarathon Man: Confessions of an All-Night Runner* (Jeremy P. Tarcher/Penguin, 2006), p 86

[3] Ibid., p 86

[4] Ibid., p 87

[5] Ibid., p 172

[6] Ibid., p 129

[7] Ibid., pp 64-65

[8] Ibid., p 86

[9] Ibid., p 290

[10] Ibid., p 173

[11] Ibid., p 173

[12] Ibid., p 129

[13] Ibid., p 55

[14] Ibid., p 43

[15] Ibid., p 116

[16] Ibid., p 174

[17] Leonore C. Terr, *Childhood Traumas: an Outline and Overview*, *American Journal of Psychiatry*, 1991, 148: 10-20

[18] Steve Redgrave, *A Golden Age*, BBC Worldwide Ltd, 2000, p 229

[19] Ibid., p 188

[20] Betty Joseph, *International Journal of Psychoanalysis* 63, 1982, pp 449-56

[21] Ranulph Fiennes, *Mad, Bad & Dangerous to Know*, Hodder & Stroughton, 2007, p 1

[22] Ibid., p 2

[23] Ibid., p 6

[24] Ibid., p 337

[25] Ibid., p 342

[26] Ibid., p 337

[27] Ibid., p 343

[28] Ibid., p 374

3: The Fastest on Earth?

[1] Andrew Taber, *Roid Rage, Health and Body*, 18 November 1999

[2] *Observer Sport Monthly*, 1 August 2004

[3] Carl Lewis, *Inside Track*, Fireside, Simon & Schuster, 1992, p 136

[4] Ron Rapoport, *See How She Runs*, Amistad imprint of Harper Collins, 2000, p 255

[5] Ibid., p 263

[6] Ibid., p 263

[7] Marion Jones, co-written with Kate Sekules, *Life in the Fast Lane*, Warner Books, 2004, p 173

[8] Ron Rapoport, *See How She Runs,* Amistad imprint of Harper Collins, 2000, p 7

[9] John Steiner, *The Retreat from Truth to Omnipotence in Sophocles' Oedipus at Colonus, International Review of Psycho-Analysis* 17 (2), p 231

[10] Susanna Abse, *Confer Lecture Notes*, November 2007

[11] Ron Rapoport, *See How She Runs,* Amistad imprint of Harper Collins, 2000, p 7

[12] Ibid., p 7

[13] Ibid., p 7

[14] Dr David Hewison. British Association of Psychoanalytic Psychotherapy Supervisors Annual Lecture, 10 May 2008

[15] S. Freud, *Standard Edition* Vol 7, p 254

[16] S. Freud, *Standard Edition* Vol 20, p 159

4: The Ice Maiden

[1] Juliet Mitchell, *Madmen and Medusas*, Penguin Books, 2000, p 335

[2] Stanley H. Teitelbaum, *Sports Heroes, Fallen Idols*, University of Nebraska Press, Lincoln and London, 2005, p 137

[3] Joseph Romanos, *Sporting Rivals*, Exisle Publishing, 2004, p 71

[4] Ibid., p 71

[5] S. Freud, *The Interpretation of Dreams*, SE, 4 and 5, 1900-01, pp 250-51

[6] J.F. Masson (Ed and trans), *The Complete Letters of Sigmund Freud to Wilhelm Fliess 1887-1904*, Cambridge, 1985, p 268

[7] S. Freud, *The Interpretation of Dreams*, SE, 4 and 5, 1900-01, p 250

[8] S. Freud, *Group Psychology and the Analysis of the Ego*, SE 18, 1921, p 120

[9] Ian Swift, *Sports Illustrated*, 13 January 1992

[10] Frank Coffey and Joe Layden, *Thin Ice*, Pinnacle books, Windsor Publishing, 1994, p 65

[11] Stan Gossfield, *Boston Globe*, 26 January 2005

[12] Ibid.

5: Daddy's Girl

[1-4] Victoria Lee, the *Observer*, 29 June 2003

[5] Peter Rocinsons, *Daily Mail*, 19 April 2008

[6] Eleanor Preston, the *Guardian*, 14 January 2006

[7] Pat Jordan, the *Sporting News*, 15 November 1993

[8] Dennis Campbell, the *Guardian*, 28 November 2004

[9] Quoted in Stanley H. Teitelbaum, *Sports Heroes, Fallen Idols*, University of Nebraska Press: Lincoln and London, 2005, p 224

[10] L. Jon Wertheim, *Venus Envy*, Perennial Books, Harper Collins, 2001, p 22

[11] Donald Winnicott, *Mirror-role of Mother and Family in Child Development*, published in *Playing and Reality*, London: Tavistock, 1967, pp 137-8

[12] Wayne Coffey, *New York Daily News*, 15 July 2008

[13] L. Jon Wertheim, *Venus Envy*, Perennial Books, Harper Collins, 2001, p 22

[14] Carl Jung, CW, vol 4, Routledge and Keegan Paul, 1961, p 154

[15] Linda Schierse Leonard, *The Wounded Woman*, Shambhala Publications, 1998, p 15

[16] L. Jon Wertheim, *Venus Envy,* Perennial Books, Harper Collins, 2001, p 71

[17] Ibid., p 176

[18] Ibid., p 70

[19] Ibid., p 76

[20] Ibid., p 77

[21-22] Paul Kimmage, the *Times*, 13 January 2008

[23] Wayne Coffey, *New York Daily News*, 15 July 2007

[24] L. Jon Wertheim, *Venus Envy*, Perennial Books, Harper Collins 2001, p 79

[25] Linda Schierse Leonard, *The Wounded Woman*, Shambhala Publications,1998, p 60

[26] Wayne Coffey, *New York Daily News*, 15 July 2008

[27] Andrew Longmore, *Sunday Times*, 24 Decenber 2006

6: He's Ma Boy

[1] Lance Armstrong, *It's Not About the Bike*, Yellow Jersey Press, 2001, p 220

[2] Ibid., p 17

[3] Linda Armstrong Kelly & Joni Rodgers, *No Mountain High Enough: Raising Lance & Raising Me,* Broadway Books: New York, 2005, p 87

[4] Carl Jung, *The Therapeutic Value of Abreaction*, *Collected Works*, 16, Routledge, 1928, para 266-267

[5] Daniel Coyle, *Lance Armstrong's War*, Harper, 2004, p 9

[6] Lance Armstrong, *Every Second Counts*, Yellow Jersey Press, 2003, p 4

[7] Linda Armstrong Kelly & Joni Rodgers, *No Mountain High Enough: Raising Lance & Raising Me,* Broadway Books: New York, 2005, p 114

[8] Lance Armstrong, *It's Not About the Bike*, Yellow Jersey Press, 2001, p 21

[9] Ibid., p 21

[10] Matt Rendell, *Blazing Saddles: The Cruel and Unusual History of the Tour de France*, Querus, 2007, p 288

[11] Daniel Coyle, *Lance Armstrong's War*, Harper, 2004, p 290

[12] Lance Armstrong, *It's Not About the Bike*, Yellow Jersey Press, 2001, p 24

[13] Ibid., p 140

[14] Daniel Coyle, *Lance Armstrong's War*, Harper, 2004, p 32

[15] Ibid., p 287

[16] Ibid., p 3

[17] Ibid., p 289

[18] Ibid., p 154

[19] M. Burger, *The Oedipal Experience: Effects on Development of an Absent Father*, *International Journal of Psychoanalysis*,1985, 66, pp 311-319

[20] David Walsh, *Inside the Tour de France*, Stanley Paul, 1994, p 14

[21] Lance Armstrong, *It's Not About the Bike*, Yellow Jersey Press, 2001, p 18

[22] Daniel Coyle, *Lance Armstrong's War*, Harper, 2004, p 19

[23] Lance Armstrong, *Every Second Counts*, Yellow Jersey Press, 2003, p 25

[24] Ibid., p 29

[25] *USA Today*, 29 June 2006

[26] Daniel Coyle, *Lance Armstrong's War*, Harper, 2004, p 109

[27] *The Times*, 10 September 2008

[28] Ibid.

7: Jonny Be Good

[1] *World Cup: Superstition, a Football Tradition*, noticia n° 182.033, 26 May 2006 http://www.noticias.info/Archivo/2006/200605/20060526/20060526_182033.shtm

[2] Ibid.

[3] Ibid.

[4] Ibid.

[5] Ibid.

[6] Maxine Frith in the *Independent*, 3 April 2006

[7] Paul Simpson, *The Struggle for Sanity: Football, Depression, OCD*, 4 February 2008 http://fourfourtwo.com/blogs/champions league/archive/2008/02/04/the-struggle-for-sanity-football-depression-and-ocd.aspx

[8] Simon Hattenstone, the *Guardian*, 15 November 2006

[9] Ibid.

[10] Robert Crampton, *The Times*, 5 June 2004

[11] Carl Gustav Jung, *Collected Works 16*, para 470. Routledge and Keegan Paul, 1959

[12] Carl Gustav Jung, *Collected Works 11*, para 131. Routledge and Keegan Paul, 1959

[13] Jonny Wilkinson, *Tackling Life*, Headline Books, 2008, p 309

[14] Ibid., p 162

[15] Ibid., p 148

[16] Ibid., p 196

[17] Tim Adams, the *Observer*, 1 June 2008

[18] Kevin Mitchell, the *Observer*, 25 February 2007

[19] Donald McRae, the *Guardian*, 11 December 2005

[20] Ibid.

[21] Simon Turnbull, the *Independent*, 16 December 2007

[22] Owen Slot and Matt Dickinson, *The Times*, 27 October 2006

[23] Ibid.

[24] Robert Crampton, *The Times*, 5 June 2004

[25] Iain Spragg and Adrian Clarke, *The Jonny Wilkinson Story*, Carlton Books, 2004, p 16

[26] Jonny Wilkinson, *Tackling Life*, Headline Books, 2008, p 214

[27] Lina Das, *Sunday Times*, 10 November 2002

[28] Ibid.

[29] Simon Hattenstone, the *Guardian*, 15 November 2006

[30] Donald McRae, the *Guardian*, 11 December 2005

[31] David James, the *Observer*, 22 October 2006

8: The End

[1] Quoted on www.geocities.com/mike_tysons_iron/Quotes.html

[2] Both quotes from the official Mike Tyson website: www.michaeltyson.com

[3] Ibid.

[4] Ibid.

[5] Ibid.

[6] Quoted by Tim Madigan, *Education and the Social Order,* London: Allen & Unwin, 1932

[7] Quoted from the official Mike Tyson website: http://www.michaeltyson.com

[8] Ibid.

[9] Stanley H. Teitelbaum, *Sports Heroes, Fallen Idols*, University of Nebraska Press; Lincoln and London, 2005, p 167

[10] Ibid.

[11] Greg Garrison and Randy Roberts, *Heavy Justice: The State of Indiana v Michael G. Tyson*, Reading MA: Addison-Wesley, 1994, p 163

[12] Messner and Sabo, *Sex, Violence and Power in Sports: Rethinking Masculinity,* Freedom, CA: The Crossing Press, 1994, p 53

[13] Timothy Smith, *A Dream Destroyed, New York Times*, 5 July 1998

[14] Stanley H. Teitelbaum, *Sports Heroes, Fallen Idols*, University of Nebraska Press; Lincoln and London, 2005, p 139

[15] Bill Gutman, *Michael Jordan*, Pocket Books, Simon & Schuster, 1991, p 159

[16] Bob Greene, *Rebound: The Odyssey of Michael Jordan*, Penguin Books, 1995, p 6

[17] Ibid., p 18

[18] Bill Gutman, *Michael Jordan*, Pocket Books, Simon & Schuster, 1991, p 5

[19] Ibid., p 7

[20] Ibid., p 10

[21] Bob Greene, *Rebound: The Odyssey of Michael Jordan*, Penguin Books, 1995, p 265

[22] Bill Gutman, *Michael Jordan*, Pocket Books, Simon & Schuster, 1991, p 44

[23] Ibid., p 80

[24] Ibid., p 85

[25] Ibid., p 85

[26] M. Klein, *Some Theoretical Conclusions Regarding the Emotional Life of the Infant*, In: M. Klein (Ed), *Envy, Gratitude and Other Works* 1946-63. London, Hogarth, 1975, p 252

[27] Michael Leahy, *When Nothing Else Matters*, Simon & Schuster, 2004, p 386

[28] Piers Morgan, *Mail on Sunday*, 23 November 2008

BIBLIOGRAPHY

Introduction
Lance Armstrong, *It's Not About the Bike*, Yellow Jersey Press, 2001
Tom House, *The Jock's Itch*, Chicago: Contemporary Books, 1989
Adam Phillips, *Side Effects*, Hamish Hamilton, 2006

1: The Achilles Heel
Jimmy Burns, *Hand of God, the Life of Diego Maradona*, Bloomsbury, 1996
Ruy Castro, *Garrincha*, Yellow Jersey Press, 2004
F. Scott Fitzgerald, *Notebook E*, edited by Edmund Wilson, 1945
Paul Gascoigne with Hunter Davies, *Gazza: My Story*, Headline, 2004
Diego Armando Maradona with Daniel Arcucci and Ernesto Bialo, *El Diego*, Yellow Jersey Press, 2000
Patrick Nathanson, *Daily Telegraph*, 25 February 2008
Adam Phillips, *Side Effects*, Hamish Hamilton, 2006
Steve Skerry, the *Guardian*, 21 February 2008
Stanley H. Teitelbaum, *Sports Heroes, Fallen Idols*, University of Nebraska Press: Lincoln and London, 2005

2: The Pain Game
Ranulph Fiennes, *Mad, Bad & Dangerous to Know*, Hodder &

Stoughton, 2007

Betty Joseph, *International Journal of Psychoanalysis*, 63, 1982

Podcast by Dean Karnazes, Final Sprint website (www.thefinalsprint.com), 5 February 2007

Juliet Mitchell, *Siblings, Sex and Violence*, Polity Press in association with Blackwell, 2003

Steve Redgrave, *A Golden Age*, BBC Worldwide Ltd, 2000

G. Schofield, G. Dickson. K. Mummery, H. Street, *Athletic Insight – The online journal of sports psychology*. Vol 4, issue 2, August 2002

John Stevens, *The Marathon Monks of Mount Heidi,* Shamble Press, 1988

3: The Fastest on Earth

Susanna Abse, *Confer Lecture Notes*, November 2007

Donald Carveth, *The Unconscious Need for Punishment: Expression or Evasion of the Sense of Guilt?*, *Psychoanalytic Studies 3*, 1 March 2001

S. Freud, *Standard Edition*, Vol 7

S. Freud, *Standard Edition*, Vol 20

Dr David Hewison, British Association of Psychoanalytic Psychotherapy Supervisors Annual Lecture, 10 May 2008

Marion Jones co-written with Kate Sekules, *Life in the Fast Lane,* Warner Books, 2004

Carl Lewis, *Inside Track*, Fireside: Simon & Schuster, 1992

Ron Rapoport, *See How She Runs,* Amistad imprint of Harper Collins, 2000

John Steiner, *The Retreat from Truth to Omnipotence in Sophocles' Oedipus at Colonus, International Review of Psycho-Analysis 17* (2),1990

Andrew Taber, *Roid Rage,* Health and Body, 18 November 1999

4: The Ice Maiden

Frank Coffey and Joe Layden, *Thin Ice,* Pinnacle Books, Windsor Publishing, 1994

S. Freud, *The Interpretation of Dreams,* Standard Edition, 4 and 5, 1900-1

S. Freud, *Group Psychology and the Analysis of the Ego,* Standard Edition, 18, 1921

Stan Gossfield, *Boston Globe*, 26 January 2005

Judith Hubback, *From Dawn to Dusk,* Wilmette, IL; Chiron, 2003

J. F. Masson (Ed and trans), *The Complete Letters of Sigmund Freud to Wilhelm Fliess 1887-1904*, Cambridge, 1985

Juliet Mitchell, *Madmen and Medusas,* Penguin Books, 2000

Joseph Romanos, *Sporting Rivals,* Exisle Publishing, 2004

Frank Sulloway, *Born to Rebel,* London: Little, Brown and Co, 1996

Ian Swift, *Sports Illustrated*, 13 January 1992

Stanley H. Teitelbaum, *Sports Heroes, Fallen Idols,* University of Nebraska Press: Lincoln and London, 2005

5: Daddy's Girl

Wayne Coffey, *New York Daily News*, 15 June 2008

Dennis Campbell, the *Guardian*, 28 November 2008

Andrea Jaeger, First Service, Health Communications Inc, 2004

Pat Jordan, the *Sporting News*, 15 November 1993

Carl Jung, *Collected Works, Vol 4,* Routledge and Keegan Paul, 1961

Paul Kimmage, the *Times*, 13 January 2008

Victoria Lee, the *Observer*, 29 June 2003

Linda Schierse Leonard, *The Wounded Woman*, Shambhala, 1998

Andrew Longmore, *Sunday Times*, 24 December 2006

Eleanor Preston, the *Guardian*, 14 January 2006

Reko Rennie, *Sport & Style* magazine, 7 May 2009

Peter Robertson, *Daily Mail*, 19 April 2008

Andrew Samuels (Ed), *The Father; Contemporary Jungian Perspectives,* Free Association Books, 1985

Jane Singer, *Androgyny,* New York, Anchor Books, 1977

Target and Fonagy, Judith Trowell and Alicia Etchegoyen (Eds), *The Importance of Fathers,* Routledge, 2002

Stanley H. Teitelbaum, *Sports Heroes, Fallen Idols,* University of

Nebraska Press: Lincoln and London, 2005

Judith Trowell and Alicia Etchegoyen (Eds), *The Importance of Fathers*, Routledge, 2002

L. Jon Wertheim, *Venus Envy,* Perennial Books, Harper Collins, 2001

Donald Winnicott, *Mirror-role of Mother and Family in Child Development*, published in *Playing and Reality*, London: Tavistock, 1967

6: He's Ma Boy

Lance Armstrong, *Every Second Counts,* Yellow Jersey Press, 2003

Lance Armstrong, *It's Not About the Bike,* Yellow Jersey Press, 2001

Linda Armstrong Kelly & Joni Rodgers, *No Mountain High Enough: Raising Lance & Raising Me*, Broadway Books: New York, 2005

W. R. Bion, *Second Thoughts: Selected Papers on Psychoanalysis*, Karnac Books, 1967

M. Burger, *The Oedipal Experience: Effects on Development of an Absent Father, International Journal of Psychoanalysis*,1985

Daniel Coyle, *Lance Armstrong's War,* Harper, 2004

S. Freud, *Three Essays on the Theory of Sexuality,* Standard Edition, 1905

Carl Jung, *Collected Works,* Routledge, 1928

Sir Thomas Malory, *Le Morte d'Arthur,* Penguin, 1969

Matt Rendell, *Blazing Saddles: The Cruel and Unusual history of the Tour de France*, Querus, 2007

Harold Searles, *The Pychodynamics of Vengefulness, Psychiatry 19*, 1956

J. Steiner, *Revenge and Resentment in the 'Oedipus Situation', International Journal of Psychoanalysis*, 1996

Judith Trowell and Alicia Etchegoyen, *The Importance of Fathers, A Psychoanalytic Re-evaluation,* Routledge, 2002

Chrétien de Troyes, *Lancelot, The Knight of the Cart*, translated by Burton Raffel, Columbia University Press, 1984

David Walsh, *Inside the Tour de France,* Stanley Paul,1994

Donald Winnicott, *The Child and the Family,* Tavistock Publications, 1957

7: Jonny Be Good

Tim Adams, the *Observer*, 1 June 2008

Dr Fredric Busch, *The Psychodynamic Treatment of Panic Disorder, Primary Psychiatry*, 2006

Robert Crampton, the *Times*, 3 June 2004

Lina Das, *Sunday Times*, 10 November 2002

S. Freud, *Inhibition, Symptoms and Anxiety*, Standard Edition, Vol 20

S. Freud, *Rat Man: Notes upon a Case of Obsessional Neurosis*, Standard Edition Vol 10

H. F. Ellenburger, *The Discovery of the Unconscious: The History and Evolution of Dynamic Psychiatry*, New York Books, 1970

Maxine Frith, the *Independent*, 4 April 2006

Simon Hattenstone, the *Guardian*, 15 November 2006

David James, the *Observer*, 22 October 2006

P. Janet, and F. Raymond, *Obsessions et la Psychasthenie*, Paris: F. Alcan, 1903

Carl Gustav Jung, *Collected Works*, Routledge and Keegan Paul, 1959

Donald McRae, the *Guardian*, 11 December 2005

Franco De Masi, *The Psychodynamic of Panic Attacks: A Useful Integration of Psychoanalysis and Neuroscience, International Journal of Psychoanalysis*, 2004

Kevin Mitchell, the *Observer*, 25 February 2007

Cristiano Ronaldo, *Moments*, Macmillan, 2007

Paul Simpson, *The Struggle for Sanity: Football, Depression, OCD*, 4 February 2006 http://fourfourtwo.com/blogs/championsleague/archive/2008/02/04/the-struggle-for-sanity-football-depression-and-ocd.aspx

Owen Slot and Matt Dickinson, *The Times*, 27 October 2006

Iain Spragg and Adrian Clarke, *The Jonny Wilkinson Story*, Carlton Books, 2004

Dan J. Stein MB and Michael H. Stone MD, *Essential Papers on Obsessive-Compulsive Disorder*, New York University Press, 1997

Simon Turnbull, the *Independent*, 16 December 2007

Jonny Wilkinson, *Tackling Life*, Headline Books, 2008

Jonny Wilkinson, *My World*, Headline Books, 2004

8: The End

Jeff Benedict and Don Yaegar, *Pros and Cons: The Criminals Who Play in the NFL*, Warner Books Inc, 1998

Jeff Benedict, *Public Heroes, Private Felons,* Boston: Northeastern University Press, 1997

W. R. Bion, *Second Thoughts,* London Heinemann, 1967

Peter Fonagy, *Preventing Mass Murder in Schools; Understanding Violent Children from Peaceful Families,* Conference at the Dallas Society for Psychoanalytic Psychology, 15 March 2001

Greg Garrison and Randy Roberts, *Heavy Justice: The State of Indiana v Michael G. Tyson,* Reading MA: Addison-Wesley, 1994

Bob Greene, *Rebound: The Odyssey of Michael Jordan,* Penguin Books, 1995

Bill Gutman, *Michael Jordan*, Pocket Books, Simon & Schuster, 1991

Melanie Klein (Ed), *Envy, Gratitude and Other Works 1946-1963,* London, Hogarth, 1975

Michael Leahy, *When Nothing Else Matters,* Simon & Schuster, 2004

Tim Madigan, *Education and the Social Order,* London: Allen & Unwin, 1932

Messner and Sabo. *Sex, Violence, and Power in Sports: Rethinking Masculinity,* Freedom, CA: The Crossing Press, 1994

Piers Morgan, *Mail on Sunday*, 23 November 2008

Timothy Smith, *A Dream Destroyed, New York Times*, 5 June 1998

Stanley H. Teitelbaum, *Sports Heroes, Fallen Idols*, University of Nebraska Press: Lincoln and London, 2005

Mike Tyson profile on De Anza College website:
http://faculty.deanza.fhda.edu/kavabradley/stories/storyReader$30